PAST
MISTAKES

First published in the UK in 2020 by
Icon Books Ltd, Omnibus Business Centre,
39–41 North Road, London N7 9DP
email: info@iconbooks.com
www.iconbooks.com

This edition published in the UK in 2021 by Icon Books Ltd

Sold in the UK, Europe and Asia by
Faber & Faber Ltd, Bloomsbury House,
74–77 Great Russell Street,
London WC1B 3DA or their agents

Distributed in the UK, Europe and Asia by
Grantham Book Services
Trent Road, Grantham NG31 7XQ

Distributed in the USA
by Publishers Group West,
1700 Fourth Street, Berkeley, CA 94710

Distributed in Australia and New Zealand by
Allen & Unwin Pty Ltd,
PO Box 8500, 83 Alexander Street,
Crows Nest, NSW 2065

Distributed in India by
Penguin Books India,
7th Floor, Infinity Tower – C, DLF Cyber City,
Gurgaon 122002, Haryana

Distributed in South Africa by
Jonathan Ball, Office B4, The District,
41 Sir Lowry Road, Woodstock 7925

Distributed in Canada by Publishers Group Canada,
76 Stafford Street, Unit 300
Toronto, Ontario M6J 2S1

ISBN: 978-178578-690-7

Typeset in Warnock by Marie Doherty

Printed and bound in Great Britain
by Clays Ltd, Elcograf S.p.A.

PAST MISTAKES

HOW WE MISINTERPRET HISTORY AND WHY IT MATTERS

DAVID MOUNTAIN

ICON

For Karima

ABOUT THE AUTHOR

David Mountain is a writer, speaker and editor, based in Edinburgh. After studying biology and geology at the University of Bristol he became a scientific editor at an environmental NGO, working across the savannahs of central Kenya and the gardens of suburban Java to tackle the problem of invasive species. He has since studied the politics of nationalism at the University of Edinburgh, devoting more time to exploring, and writing about, history. He is fascinated and infuriated in equal measure by history, politics and philosophy, and can't resist pointing out flaws and contradictions in how we think we understand the world.

Contents

INTRODUCTION

Blue beards and white power

Standing in the Ashmolean museum I have the sudden urge to laugh. Given that I've come to Oxford to see an exhibition of classical sculpture, this might seem odd. But the busts and statues before me aren't the dead-eyed marble creations we've come to associate with the ancient world. Rather, they're plaster reconstructions of what the artworks might have looked like when they were first created over 2,000 years ago – complete with their original, very loud, coats of paint.

The effect is startling, to say the least. Cold marble is transformed into warm skin tones. White robes become vibrant costumes. Bronze figures stare back at you with disconcertingly lifelike eyes. Particularly alarming is a sculpture of Paris, the archer and playboy prince from Greek mythology. In the marble original, carved some 2,500 years ago on the island of Aegina and now faded to a dirty white, he looks noble and deadly; in the replica, dressed in a luridly patterned outfit of yellow, blue, green and red, he looks like he's just graduated from Clown College.[1] I can't help but snigger.

Perhaps the most remarkable thing about these reconstructions, however, is that they probably would have been utterly unremarkable to inhabitants of the ancient Mediterranean. We don't know the exact tints or techniques they employed, but an increasingly sophisticated array of ultraviolet, infrared, X-ray and chemical analysis tells us for certain that classical sculptures were almost never left unadorned. In fact, just about everything the Greeks and Romans could slather in paint or bedeck in jewels, they did.[2] The 40-foot statue of Zeus in Olympia – one of the Seven Wonders of the Ancient World – was garishly clad in gold, ivory, gemstones and brightly painted wood. The Parthenon once housed a similarly gigantic and gaudy statue of the goddess Athena until it burned down sometime in the 3rd century CE. Even the Parthenon itself was brightly decorated with colourful friezes. And while there's evidence that some artists aimed for a naturalistic finish, with realistic skin and hair tones, it's clear that others opted for all-out psychedelia: archaeologists have uncovered the remnants of green horses and blue-maned lions. The limestone remains of a three-headed monster discovered at the Acropolis is known to have had black eyes, yellow skin and blue beards.

The Greeks and Romans were by no means unique in their love of colour. A wide range of ancient and historic cultures – from the Japanese to the Vikings to the Aztecs – were united by their appreciation of what archaeologists call polychromy: the use of colour in art and architecture. China's Terracotta Warriors were once brightly painted with greens, reds, violets, pinks, whites and blues. Mesoamerican cultures like the Maya decorated their sculptures, structures and even pyramids in blocks of red, blue, yellow, pink and green. The castles of medieval Europe, in contrast to the dark and dingy lairs of popular imagination, were stuffed with brightly coloured furniture and wall hangings.[3] The fantastical stone carvings in the 12th-century abbey at Cluny, in eastern France, were so garish that St Bernard of Clairvaux complained that they were distracting the monks. 'One would rather spend the whole day gawking at them … than in meditation on the word of God,' he grumbled.[4]

St Bernard may not have approved, but there was sound reasoning behind the carnivalesque colour schemes of his contemporaries and others. Bright hues helped friezes and sculptures mounted high up on temple walls to be clearly visible. Artworks often carried religious or political meaning, and distinctive colours conveyed a more intelligible message than a block of monochrome marble. What's more, in the days before the mass production of paints, colour was expensive. Pigments had to be extracted from such obscure sources as tropical plants, toxic metals and the ink sacs of cuttlefish. The bright blue details on Tutankhamun's funerary mask came from the mineral lapis lazuli, which was mined only from a remote valley in what is now Afghanistan and was more valuable than gold. The gaudier the art, therefore, the wealthier the patron.[5]

Such motivations become lost or obscured in the sterilised scholasticism of the art gallery or exhibition hall. As a result, attempts to recapture lost polychromy, as with the exhibition at the Ashmolean, can be jarring to those who have long admired the austerity of classical sculpture or the solemnity of Gothic architecture. When an ancient Egyptian statue of the falcon-headed god Horus was recreated in its original hues by the British Museum in 2011, complete with big cartoon eyes, the result bore an unsettling resemblance to *Sesame Street*'s Big Bird. When a famous statue of the Roman Emperor Augustus was reconstructed with violently crimson clothes and bright scarlet lips, one shell-shocked historian claimed to 'suffer … trauma' when he saw it.[6] Other colourful replicas have been described as 'tasteless', 'tacky' and 'childlike'. Ongoing renovations of Chartres Cathedral in France, aimed at restoring the building's original bright and colourful interior, have sparked numerous complaints and petitions accusing it of 'erasing history from the Gothic masterpiece'.[7]

Why is all this such a shock to us? If the past really was an eye-watering kaleidoscope of colour, as archaeologists are insisting, then why isn't such information more widely known? It's not as if the ancient Greeks were being coy about their love of colour. The tragedian Euripides mentioned it in a number of his works, for instance. 'Look!' cries a character in his play *Hypsipyle*, 'cast your gaze upward, and marvel at the painted sculptures in the gable!' He even has Helen of Troy, sick of her dangerously good looks, wishing she could 'shed my beauty and assume an uglier aspect, the way you could wipe colour off a statue'. The sculptor Praxiteles shared this view, acknowledging that his favourite creations were those which had been painted by the artist Nikia. There are even depictions on Greek vases of artists painting statues.[8]

The first explanation is simple enough: colour fades. Paints exposed to the elements, like those at the Acropolis, gradually bleach and peel. Artworks that end up buried underground are often better preserved, although they can rapidly deteriorate once brought to the surface. A visitor to the Acropolis in the 1880s noted that a newly-unearthed artefact would often be 'surrounded by a little deposit of green, red and black powder which had fallen from it'.[9] When the Terracotta Warrior pits were first opened in the 1970s, remaining traces of paint began flaking off the statues within minutes due to the changing humidity of the tomb.

It's the second explanation, however, that's far more interesting: classical sculpture is monochrome because we want it to be. When the remains of ancient Rome were first uncovered in the 15th century – by which time much of their original hues had vanished – it became widely accepted that they had always been white. Renaissance artists such as Michelangelo sought to recapture the majesty of classical sculpture by creating unadorned statues. 'The more painting resembles sculpture, the better I like it,' the old master opined, 'and the more sculpture resembles painting, the worse I like it.'[10] The 'noble simplicity' of pure white marble came to be revered as beautiful in its own right. 'Colour contributes to beauty, but it is not beauty,' declared the influential art historian Johann Winckelmann in 1764. 'The whiter the body is, the more beautiful it is.' Colour – especially bright colour – was dismissed as a childish plaything of 'uneducated' and 'savage' cultures.[11]

So when evidence for ancient polychromy began to creep into academic circles during the 18th and 19th centuries, archaeologists and artists, having invested heavily in the myth of classical whiteness, resisted. Facts were forced to fit theory. Remnants of paint were dismissed as dirt or soot. Greek statues with pigments still intact were attributed to other, less revered civilisations, such as the Etruscans. Many archaeologists actually scrubbed any remaining traces of colour off statues in order to 'restore' the marble's gleaming whiteness. The renowned chemist Michael Faraday subjected marble friezes from the Parthenon to abrasive grits, alkaline solutions and even nitric acid in an attempt to recover 'that state of purity and whiteness which they originally possessed'.[12] In a move subsequently lamented as a 'cock-up' by the British Museum, sections of the same friezes were attacked with metal scrapers and chisels in the 1930s by staff trying to remove 'discolouration' from the stone. The discolouration, it turned out, included remnants of the friezes' original bright paints.[13]

Even today, more than 40 years after ancient polychromy was finally accepted by the majority of archaeologists, it's a subject that can still surprise. Depending on your perspective, the image of classical sculpture slathered in bright paint can be funny, shocking or even upsetting. It will take time and effort to see past centuries of collective colour blindness and shake off the myth of a monochrome past.

The temptation is to leave the story of ancient polychromy there – as a colourful footnote in the history of humanity, but one that need hardly concern the non-specialist. However, it's here that the story really gets interesting. In September 2016, universities in the United States started receiving flyers and posters from an unknown organisation calling itself Identity Evropa. Within a month, students at more than two dozen campuses across the country were finding these posters pinned to noticeboards, taped to walls and scattered around libraries. More were discovered in 2017 in universities and around towns throughout the USA. In 2018 the leaflets were even dropped from a plane. They all included a call to action – phrases such as 'Protect Your Heritage' or 'Serve Your People' – printed in bold over the image of a scowling, white marble statue.[14]

Identity Evropa soon made its motivation known online. As the name implies, the organisation sees itself as defending the USA's 'European heritage', which it believes is being eroded by a growing 'anti-white' bias in the country. 'We are dedicated to educating the people of European heritage about the importance of a Eurocentric identity,' the group explained.[15] Don't let the pseudo-scholarly language or allusions to classical antiquity fool you: this is white nationalism in a rented tweed jacket. Identity Evropa is one of the many new or revived far-right organisations that have appeared in the USA in recent years under the broad 'alt-right' label. The group advocates the complete shut-down of immigration into the Unites States and supports 're-migration': the deportation of US citizens not of European descent. Its leaders have espoused misogynist, racist and anti-Semitic abuse.[16] And they consider classical sculpture the perfect mascot for their crusade.

Identity Evropa – which has since rebranded itself as the American Identity Movement – isn't alone among the far-right in its enthusiasm for the classics: a range of hate groups around the world have expressed their admiration for the ancient world. Nor is it the first – both Fascist Italy and Nazi Germany conveyed their particular brands of white supremacism with the help of white marble sculpture. It seems that the myth of a monochrome past has had consequences far beyond aesthetics. The snow-white marble statues of popular imagination have given rise to the impression that the ancient Mediterranean was inhabited solely by snow-white people. Artists and art historians, raving about the beauty of white marble and the savagery of colour, helped cement the belief.

The 'Ideal Beauty of the Ancients' came to be held up as a paragon of white beauty. One statue in particular, a mulleted young man known as Apollo of the Belvedere – which can be found on Identity Evropa's propaganda today – was particularly admired for its apparent aesthetic perfection. Johann Winckelmann described in positively lascivious tones the sculpture's 'blooming beauty' and 'perfect virility', concluding that it was 'a form more perfect than your eye had ever seen'.[17] When concepts of race and racism bled into science in the 18th century, anatomists began proposing the Apollo as the holotype of the white race. A number of biologists even guessed what the statue's skull would have looked like and, through degrading comparisons with the skulls of apes and 'lower races', used this fictional anatomy in an attempt to scientifically prove their racial hierarchies.[18]

These ideas later fed into the Nazi myth of Aryan supremacy. Hitler was at times personally involved in acquiring Greek and Roman sculpture for the Third Reich, repeatedly holding them up as the aesthetic standard for his subjects to match and surpass. 'Man has never been more similar in appearance and in sensibilities to the men of antiquity than he is today,' he told a crowd at a Munich art gallery in 1937.[19] Classical sculpture also played an important role in Mussolini's short-lived bid to build a second Roman Empire, and Fascist Italy was festooned with bright white marble statues of young, virile, improbably muscular young men, embodiments of 'the Italian race'.[20]

For those who still harbour an inordinate fondness for pale skin, Greek and Roman sculpture retains these racial connotations. Groups like Identity Evropa see the Apollo of the Belvedere and other works as the sole property of white Europeans and Americans, and their whitewashed view of classical history allows them to establish an exclusive line of descent from the glories of the ancient world to present-day 'people of European heritage'.

Of course, it's ironic that a group championing white, male, European identity should adopt as its mascot classical sculpture. Not only were ancient statues never intended to appear bone-white, but they weren't always intended to represent 'white' people. Analysis of trace pigments on Roman busts reveals that they once represented people with complexions ranging from rosy white to deepest brown (the Roman Empire, after all, stretched from Scotland to Syria). A painting of the emperor Septimius Severus, who came from a wealthy Berber family, depicts him with brown skin that would have excluded him from groups like Identity Evropa. Then there are the numerous Roman sculptures of African people, often carved out of dark basalt rock and with traces of mahogany paint still present.[21]

Trying to force modern conceptions of colour and race onto the ancient Greeks is an even more hopeless task. The Greeks' perception of colour was so notoriously weird to modern sensibilities that the former British Prime Minister and amateur classicist William Gladstone suggested they suffered from mass colour blindness. They had only a handful of words to describe the spectrum and seemingly no concept of blue (Homer famously described the sky as 'bronze' and the sea as 'wine-dark'). Moreover, the few words they did use were bafflingly slippery in meaning. Depending on the context, the word *khloros* could be used to describe the colour of leaves, honey, blood, sand or 'the pallor of the skin of the terrified'. Their term for white could also mean a fast-moving dog. This bizarre conception of colour extended to people, who are variously described in Greek writing as having yellow hair, green skin and black eyes. In the *Odyssey*, Homer repeatedly described the hair and beard of the hero Odysseus as 'similar in colour to the hyacinth flower'.[22]

Funnily enough, the one colour a Homeric hero would have resented being described as was white. Pale skin was associated with house-bound women and the description was considered an effeminate slur if applied to a man. Tim Whitmarsh, professor of Greek culture at the University of Cambridge, writes that ancient Greeks 'would have been staggered' to discover they were now celebrated as icons of whiteness. And yet that's exactly where they find themselves in the 21st century. All because artists and archaeologists didn't see – or didn't want to see – paint on classical sculpture.

This isn't a book about the past. Not quite. Rather, it's a book about how we mistake and misinterpret the past, and why that matters to us in the present. Like how a mistake about the colour of ancient sculptures can inadvertently fuel white nationalism, or, as we'll discover, how a travelling circus convinced Americans that their country was won with guns, or how an ancient Roman smear campaign still informs our conception of who is and isn't 'civilised'.

Humans are wonderful at making mistakes. We do it all the time, whether through honest accident, unintentional bias or wilful ignorance of what we know to be true. And history is by no means immune. Many archaeologists accepted the enigmatic crystal skulls of Central and South America as genuine artefacts until studies revealed them to be modern hoaxes. Hopeful amateur historians spent centuries trying to decipher a mysterious runic inscription in southern Sweden before it was shown to be natural cracks in the rock. When the archaeologist Karl Mauch explored the ruins of the medieval city of Great Zimbabwe in southern Africa in 1871, he refused to believe that such a sophisticated settlement could have been built by Africans and instead made the far stranger assertion that it was Phoenician or Semitic (a conclusion he reinforced by claiming wood at the site smelled like his cedar pencil and therefore must have come from Lebanon). As a result, many of our treasured beliefs about the past are simply testaments to past mistakes – a fact shoved in my face during that trip to the Ashmolean.

And as with the case of painted sculpture, it would be short-sighted to dismiss the myths, mistakes and misconceptions about the past as something solely of professional interest. Because history, perhaps more than any other discipline, is used to explain and justify the world we live in. We appeal to the past to show how progressive or retrograde we are; how peaceful, violent, connected, isolated, educated and ignorant we've become. Consequently, whenever society is debated or scrutinised, our depictions of the past – whether printed on a page or carved in stone – become lightning rods for emotion and action. When the murder of George Floyd, an unarmed black man, by US police in May 2020 sparked worldwide protests against racial inequality, attention quickly focussed on public monuments to historical figures associated with racist practices. In the USA, dozens of statues of the explorer Christopher Columbus, as well as memorials to Confederate leaders, have since been vandalised or torn down. In the UK, depictions of slave traders and imperialists have received similar treatment. Australian protesters have likewise demanded that memorials to the architects of the 'White Australia' policy, which attempted to prevent all non-European immigration into Australia, be removed from public view. These calls have in turn incited others to defend statues against what they consider to be the 'historical whitewashing' of protesters.

Regardless of where we stand on these and other debates, it's impossible to deny the role of history in shaping our perceptions of society, both past and present. And so when we get our history wrong, it can have far-reaching and unexpected consequences for how we view ourselves and make sense of our world. History, whether we like it or not, has an annoying habit of being relevant.

CHAPTER 1

The false dawn of civilisation

The history of civilisation used to be a simple thing. The curtains rose some 10,000 years ago on the grasslands and woodlands of Southwest Asia. Humans had just emerged from the grievous rigours of the Ice Age, where they eked out a meagre existence hunting wild game and gathering fruits and roots, much like their predecessors had done for millions of years. It made for a brutal, and brutally short, life. Technology was limited to wood, bone and stone. Artistic expression amounted to small pieces of jewellery and the occasional cave painting. People were almost certainly spiritual, but what religious beliefs they had were undoubtedly simplistic.

The world was changing, however, and the retreat of the ice sheets and permafrost opened up new possibilities for our distant ancestors. Somewhere in the fertile hills east of the Mediterranean, people began to realise that they could make a better living for themselves if they farmed animals rather than hunted them and harvested plants rather than foraged for them. As it happened, the ancient Near East was full of domesticable plants and animals. Cereals like wild wheat and barley, and pulses such as lentils and chickpeas grew freely on the plains. In the mountains to the north, the ancestors of cows, pigs, sheep and goats could be found. A few forward-thinking groups set down their spears, picked up their sickles, and set to work on the long process of domestication.

The effect is revolutionary – perhaps the greatest turning point in humanity's history. Agriculture ties farmers to the land, ending aeons of restless wandering. Permanent houses and settlements soon build up in fertile areas. With a steady food supply, people are living longer and healthier lives than their hunter-gatherer ancestors. Farmers are able to amass surplus food which they can store for the future, allowing agricultural communities to survive tough years that might wipe out a band of hunters. With food in reserve, they use their free time to develop new skills such as pottery, artwork, carpentry and masonry. Inventions soon come thick and fast: sophisticated tools, metalworking and the wheel, the epitome of ancient ingenuity. Agricultural surpluses also allow individuals to accumulate more resources than they could otherwise acquire by their own efforts, thus beginning the rise of political power and a religious and bureaucratic aristocracy. Villages grow into sprawling cities with elaborate palaces, tombs and temples, where a nascent priestly class presides over complex religious rites and mysteries. Commerce between cities prospers as trade routes reach further afield in search of new and exciting goods. In order to keep track of these ever-growing networks, merchants begin to use little pictures and symbols to record their transactions, paving the way for the emergence of the first writing systems sometime around 3000 BCE. Within a few thousand years, humans have transformed themselves from nomadic hunters, living in bands of no more than 40 individuals, to literate urbanites in cities teeming with tens of thousands. Civilisation has dawned.

Most of us have heard this story before, at least in outline. It's a familiar and compelling image of humanity's irreversible and inevitable progress. And, as we'll see, it's an image that's proved enormously influential – not just in history and archaeology, but philosophy and politics in general.

It's also completely wrong.

~

People have always been fascinated about their origins. Where did we come from? How did societies, cities and civilisations arise? Today we attempt to answer these questions with evidence-based history and archaeology, but this wasn't always the case: for much of humanity's history, religion and mythology provided the answers to such questions. The ancient Greeks told of how Prometheus, the Titan, incurred the wrath of the Olympian gods by imparting the secrets of fire, medicine and mathematics to the first humans. In Inca mythology, the god Viracocha willingly taught people the arts of civilisation as he wandered the Earth. For ancient Mesopotamians, meanwhile, humans were created solely to relieve the gods from the burden of physical toil.

In Christian Europe, the Bible and its old Hebrew myths were the sole authority on the matter. In the beginning, God created the heaven and the Earth, raising land out of the oceans and populating it with plants and animals. Humanity, banished from paradise, found themselves huddling together in the first cities for protection against the fearsome world beyond Eden. The discoveries of agriculture, music and metallurgy soon followed, each invented by one of three brothers. It was a simple, if simplistic, answer to questions about the origin of civilisation. And, for a few thousand years, it was as good a guess as anyone's.

So long as the biblical account held supreme authority, Christians felt no need to investigate the prehistoric past. After all, prehistory – the time before writing and recorded history – simply didn't exist, given that people in medieval Europe had a written account of history reaching all the way back to the very first day of creation. Evidence of a distant past not described in

Genesis often surfaced, but these finds were regarded as natural or fantastical curiosities. When farmers in Central Europe kept unearthing ancient potshards, they assumed that pottery must grow naturally in the soil. Teardrop-shaped hand axes were widely known as thunderstones and believed to be the result of lightning striking the earth. Stone arrowheads and other weapons, meanwhile, were variously ascribed to elves or angels and believed to have magical properties.[1]

It wasn't until the 16th century that these ideas began to be challenged. By this time, Europeans were starting to explore the Americas, and were returning home with tales of 'barbarous Nations' wielding stone tools and weapons remarkably similar to the thunderstones and elf bolts being unearthed back home. If people were using such items today, might Europeans have once done the same? Might they once have lived like Native Americans? And, if so, might the Bible be wrong?[2]

These questions fundamentally changed our understanding of the distant past. Inspired by the half-terrified accounts of the New World reaching Europe, the primaeval Earth was no longer the paradise of Genesis or the Arcadia of classical legend, but a howling wilderness of beasts and savages. As the English philosopher John Locke opined in 1689: 'in the beginning all the world was America'.[3] This new view of humanity's beginnings was most famously expressed by Locke's contemporary Thomas Hobbes, who described 'the Naturall Condition of Mankind' as 'solitary, poore, nasty, brutish, and short'. Before civilisation, insisted Hobbes, 'there is no place for Industry ... no commodious Building; no Instruments of moving, and removing such things as require much force; no Knowledge of the face of the Earth; no account of Time; no Arts; no Letters; no Society; and which is worst of all, continuall feare, and danger of violent death.'[4]

With serious doubts now hanging over the biblical account of civilisation's origins, European scholars made the first attempts to study prehistoric artefacts and monuments in a scientific manner – 'to make the Stones give Evidence for themselves', as the 17th-century antiquarian John Aubrey put it.[5] Early prehistorians like Aubrey began to carry out deliberate excavations, carefully documenting not only the artefacts they found but the locations in which they were unearthed. From these efforts emerged, slowly and fitfully, the bare bones of prehistoric archaeology. By the late 1700s it was becoming clear that ancient tools and weapons in Europe tended to be made out of one of three materials – stone, bronze or iron – and archaeologists began to order the distant past into successive ages based on these three substances. The subsequent development of typology – the study of an artefact's appearance – allowed scholars to construct relative chronologies for arrowheads, brooches and other ancient items based on the change in their designs over time.[6]

The decisive break with the version of history described by scripture came in the early 19th century, when antiquarians abandoned the biblical chronology they had relied on up until now. By this time the sheer quantity of prehistoric finds was becoming difficult to squeeze into the few thousand years of history allowed for by Genesis, which, if its dates and genealogies were to be believed, insisted that the world could be no more than 7,000 years old. (In 1650, the Archbishop of Ireland even managed to calculate the very moment of creation: the evening of Saturday 24 October, 4004 BC.[7]) This was especially problematic for stone and bronze artefacts, given that the Old Testament made no mention of either a Stone Age or a Bronze Age; Adam's descendants are said to be working with iron in little more than a century after the creation of the world. Archaeologists turned instead to the new science of geology, which had shown through the study of the unfathomably slow processes of deposition and erosion that the Earth must be much older than the Bible asserted. As the pioneering geologist James Hutton concluded in 1788: 'we find no vestige of a beginning, no prospect of an end.'[8]

The understanding that the Earth must be millions, if not billions, of years old transformed prehistory. It was no longer a few hundred or thousand years long, but hundreds of thousands of years long, stretching back into the deepest past. This was *terra incognita* for 19th-century archaeology – a vast expanse of time for which religion and mythology had no answers. And somewhere in this uncharted territory were the secrets to the origin of civilisation.

⁓

To understand 19th-century archaeology, it helps to understand the 19th-century archaeologist. He – and it was a he – was almost without exception a wealthy white Westerner. He was among the lucky few for whom the ongoing upheavals of the Industrial Revolution were a wholly positive experience; the working-class world of choking pollution, rampant poverty and appalling labour conditions was out of sight and out of mind. For him, the age of coal was an age of cheaper goods, faster transport and increasing convenience, where each generation found themselves living longer, staying healthier and working less strenuously than that last. 'Our pleasures are increased, our pains are lessened; in a thousand ways we can avoid or diminish evils which to our ancestors were great and inevitable,' proclaimed the pioneering prehistorian (and fantastically wealthy baronet) Sir John Lubbock in his 1865 book *Pre-historic Times*.

For Lubbock and his fellow prehistorians, progress was the order of the day. The dizzying pace of scientific and technological advancement convinced many of them that it was an inherent feature of the modern world. And not only in science and technology: with the superior civilisation of the West blazing the trail, all human endeavours would surely improve – art, religion, politics and morality, even human nature itself. Looking into the future, they boldly predicted the coming dawn of a technological 'utopia' as the ultimate and inevitable end-point of this progress.[9]

It was a short-sighted worldview, one that was either unable or unwilling to consider the many problems associated with industrialisation outside the upper echelons of society. It's doubtful whether such a confident outlook would ever have come from the subjects of Britain's sprawling empire (just months after Lubbock's *Pre-historic Times* was published, over 400 Jamaicans were hanged for rebelling against British rule) or indeed from the lower classes back home, for whom the miseries of industrialisation meant stagnating or even falling life expectancies.[10]

But then academia was a short-sighted world, and it embraced the Victorian worship of progress wholeheartedly. And so when scholars ventured into the world of prehistory they did so not just to understand the past, but to better comprehend 'the progressive nature of man' through the development of civilisation.[11] As the American archaeologist Alice Kehoe writes: 'prehistoric archaeology's *raison d'être* was to reveal the trends operating on human development.'[12] Typologists arranged artefacts from crude stone tools to increasingly complex iron creations as a demonstration of humanity's growing ingenuity. Geologists adapted stratigraphy – the study of rock layers – to argue that archaeological finds could be ordered into distinct bands of progressively more complex societies. 'Like the successive geological formations, the tribes of mankind may be arranged, according to their relative conditions, into successive strata,' declared the 19th-century American anthropologist Lewis Henry Morgan. 'When thus arranged, they reveal with some degree of certainty the entire range of human progress from savagery to civilisation.'[13]

The publication of Charles Darwin's *On the Origin of Species* in 1859 had a profound influence on these lines of thinking. Darwin's theory of evolution, which posited that only the organisms best adapted to their environment would survive to pass on their characteristics, encouraged prehistorians to regard humanity's 'progressive tendencies' as not merely trends but as a fundamental fact of life. If species could evolve, why not cultures? The archaeological record already seemed to show a clear progression from simple to complex, primitive to advanced; now evolution provided the mechanism to explain this process. 'From their first struggles in the battle for life,' explained the archaeologist Sir James Simpson in 1861, 'our primaeval ancestors successively passed upwards through the varying eras and stages of advancement.'[14]

Encouraged by notions of cultural evolution, prehistorians began to regard progress as a fundamental 'law of nature', as inescapable as the laws of physics. 'The inorganic has one final comprehensive law, GRAVITATION,' bellowed the Scottish geologist Robert Chambers. 'The organic ... rests in like manner on one law, and that is DEVELOPMENT.'[15] This Law of Progress was expressed through 'a natural as well as necessary sequence' of cultures, a set of developmental stages through which all human societies must pass if they are to 'progress towards a higher stage of civilisation'.[16] Wherever you dug in the world, it was argued, you would find evidence of groups evolving through the same stages of savagery and barbarism, before finally arriving at civilisation. Resting atop the pinnacle of progress were, of course, Western Europe and North America, with their cities and railways and factories.[17]

It was, as the philosopher Bertrand Russell once noted, 'a very convenient doctrine'.[18] By a remarkable coincidence, every proponent of the Law of Progress just so happened to belong to the most advanced culture on Earth. Upper-class European man John Lubbock somehow concluded that upper-class European men were the most highly evolved group of humans, above other ethnicities, genders and even economic classes. For the American Morgan, meanwhile, it was the network of railways criss-crossing North America that represented the culminating 'triumph of civilisation'.

The Law of Progress went deeper than simple self-praise, however. By positioning the West as the most advanced civilisation, the inevitable end-point of human development, it allowed Europeans and North Americans to dismiss other cultures that didn't resemble the West as 'primitive', 'inert' and cultural 'dead ends'.[19] Unfamiliar features of society were scorned purely because they were non-Western, regardless of what other qualities they might possess. The Chinese writing system for example, despite having served successive empires perfectly well for millennia, was considered uncivilised because it wasn't phonetic like European alphabets. Contemporary hunting and foraging societies bore the brunt of this denigration, being regarded as little more than living fossils of Stone Age savagery. 'However little we may be interested in the American Indians personally,' yawned Morgan, they could at least provide us with 'an exemplification of the experience of our own ancestors ... in the Lower Status of barbarism.'[20]

Needless to say, such contemptuous views of people beyond the Mediterranean proved very useful for the West's rapidly expanding colonial ventures. As interpreted by the likes of Morgan and Lubbock, prehistory proved that the West, as the most highly evolved civilisation, was morally justified in its imperial conquests of the rest of the world. There was no point mourning the deaths

of incarcerated Tasmanians under British imperialism, or the deci-
mation of Native Americans under the United States' westward
expansion: as less-highly evolved cultures, it was only natural that
they should be overpowered by European civilisation. Indeed, it
was inevitable: an inescapable outcome of the immutable Law of
Progress. It was literally written in stone: the West was destined
to dominate. These ideas were sometimes expressed in openly
racist terms, with serious attempts to correlate the evolution of
lighter skin with advances in civilisation.[21]

Not every European or American subscribed to this view.
'If you would see the most extensive acquisition of knowledge
enforced by the necessities of life, you must know what is the
life of a savage,' wrote the Scottish author John Wilson in the
19th century. 'If you have the imagination to represent to your-
selves one-twentieth part of the knowledge which a savage will
thus be driven to possess by his mere physical necessities, you
will be astonished to find how much like a learned man he is.'[22]
The pioneering prehistorian Daniel Wilson (no relation) shared
this view, arguing that there was nothing to prevent savages from
becoming civilised – nor civilised Europeans from turning savage. Such protests were in the minority, however. By calling into
question the philosophical foundations of empire, they proved far
too inconvenient to ever be popular.[23]

Consequently it was the prophets of progress, and not their
more sceptical contemporaries, who laid the foundations for our
understanding of prehistory. Their scorn for hunter-gatherers,
itself a hangover from Hobbes' primaeval nightmare, survives
today in the familiar stereotype of the knuckle-dragging, club-
wielding caveman. The unmistakable stink of white supremacism
still lingers in the iconic 'evolution of man' image, which almost
always depicts a line of dark, shambling apes evolving into

upright, light-skinned men. The singular importance of Western society emphasised farming as the dividing line between savagery and civilisation, and the ongoing Industrial Revolution shaped the notion of an equally dramatic 'agricultural revolution' as the catalyst for innovation and progress. If this is sounding familiar, there's a good reason: from these elements of Victoriana arose the classic account of civilisation's origins which opened this chapter, an account which was to define the way we looked at prehistory and the present for well over a century.

⁓

This perception of civilisation was shattered one evening in October 1994, when a German archaeologist named Klaus Schmidt climbed into a taxi in the Turkish city of Urfa. His directions were curious, to say the least. Somewhere in the dusty limestone hills beyond the city could be found a low mound with a single mulberry tree growing atop it. The locals called it 'Potbelly Hill', in Turkish: *Göbekli Tepe*. With Schmidt that evening were Michael Morsch, an archaeology student, and a local boy who knew the way to the hill.[24]

Göbekli Tepe had been investigated once before, in 1963 by an American archaeologist who dismissed it as the site of an unremarkable medieval graveyard. Coming across the archaeologist's notes, Schmidt was intrigued by its description of a hilltop littered with chipped and carved stone. It sounded remarkably like a Stone Age 'tell' – an artificial mound formed through the accumulation of man-made detritus – of which there were many in this region of southern Turkey. He decided to investigate Potbelly Hill for himself.[25]

As the road became impassable, Schmidt and his motley band – taxi driver included – set out on foot to find the hill. At first the area didn't look like a promising archaeological site: 'nowhere was the slightest archaeological trace,' he later recalled.[26] Just as things were looking hopeless, however, their guide pointed to something in the distance. Schmidt's doubts vanished in an instant. As soon as he saw the hill, he knew Göbekli Tepe wasn't a natural feature of the landscape. To his experienced eye this was indeed a tell – and, at 50 feet tall, an enormous one at that, representing centuries of prehistoric activity. 'Only man could have created something like this,' he recounted. 'It was clear right away this was a gigantic Stone Age site.'[27]

Schmidt returned to the site to begin archaeological excavations the following year, excited but uncertain as to what he might find. His team quickly realised that the 'medieval gravestones' noted in the 1963 survey were in fact prehistoric in origin. The people of Göbekli Tepe, whoever they were, were competent and confident stonemasons. On the very first day of digging, the team found a relief carving of some four-legged animal poking out of the hill, and over the following years they discovered other statues of animals, a larger-than-life carving of a human head, stone masks, and a rather arresting foot-long penis sculpture. They also uncovered the mysterious remains of large stone rings, more than a foot in diameter, whose purpose remains completely unknown.[28]

The most remarkable finds, however, were a range of enormous T-shaped pillars, the biggest standing twenty feet tall and weighing ten tons. Despite their severe geometric design, these pillars are thought to have represented people: they have stylised arms and hands and a hint of clothing, though no other traces of a body. Many of these faceless giants are intricately carved with geometric designs and a menagerie of fearsome-looking animals, including spiders, snakes, scorpions and vultures, as well as foxes, boars and cranes. There's something unsettling about the world they conjure: wolves bare their teeth in savage grins, emaciated lions display prominent ribs, and carvings of severed heads decorate a number of the pillars.[29]

Since Schmidt's initial discovery, more than a decade of digging has built up a detailed – though still incomplete – picture of what Göbekli Tepe once was. The site consisted of a number of circular enclosures sunk some ten feet into the ground and ringed by a stone wall and bench. In the centre of each enclosure stood two T-shaped pillars, with a further ten or twelve smaller pillars placed at intervals in the surrounding wall. If the enclosures were once roofed, as some archaeologists suspect, entering one of these subterranean spaces would have been a foreboding experience. The site was exclusively religious; the usual traces of daily life, such as fire pits and rubbish heaps, are conspicuously absent. Moreover, the recent discovery of human skull fragments, with traces of red ochre and ritualistic carving still present on them, suggests that some sort of skull cult may have practised there. Curiously, the enclosures were deliberately filled in with rubble after a relatively short period of use, and new enclosures were built on top of them. Over the seven centuries that Göbekli Tepe was in use, the constructions became smaller and less impressive until the entire site was eventually abandoned.[30]

It was undoubtedly a remarkable archaeological discovery. But something troubled Schmidt and his team. According to the accepted development of complex societies, Göbekli Tepe had to have been the product of a farming community. There's simply no way that hunter-gatherers could have found the time to develop the skills needed to construct such a monumental site. And yet the hilltop positively glittered with flint arrowheads. What need would farmers have had for bows and arrows? More puzzling still were the many pieces of animal bone discovered at the site. After examining some 15,000 samples, it was found that every single one of them belonged to wild animals such as gazelle, wild boar and aurochs, the ancestor of today's cattle. Not one bone fragment belonged to a domesticated animal, implying that the builders of Göbekli Tepe weren't farmers, but hunters.[31]

It was only when they dated the stone tools at the site that they could explain the arrowheads and missing farm animals: Göbekli Tepe was built between the 10th and 9th millennia BCE, some 11,500 years ago, before farming had even been invented. That's 6,000 years older than Stonehenge, and a full 7,000 years before the construction of the Great Pyramid at Giza. Göbekli Tepe is more distant in time from both those ancient monuments than they are from us today. This carefully crafted and richly artistic religious complex was indeed built by hunter-gatherers. According to the standard account of the origin of civilisation, it shouldn't exist.[32]

While researching this chapter I failed to meet a single archaeologist who wasn't stunned by Göbekli Tepe and its implications for our understanding of the past. 'It turns everything upside down,' says Trevor Watkins, an expert in Near Eastern prehistory who's visited the site many times. 'This was pre-domestication, pre-farming, and yet there were people building these huge stone monuments.' Not only does it show that Stone Age hunter-gatherers had complex belief systems, but that they had the time to hone the skills necessary to carve and erect ten-ton monoliths. 'It would have been a colossal amount of labour to quarry, carve and move these huge stones,' Watkins explains to me. 'And then remember that Göbekli Tepe sits atop a bare limestone ridge. You can't live there. There's no water, no soil. So whatever effort you need to build this monument, double it, because you have to factor in the logistics of keeping its builders supplied with food and water.'

All this would have required detailed planning and extensive cooperation between hundreds of individuals from numerous nomadic bands throughout the region, something few believed was happening on such a scale at this time. 'This is a level of social organisation that no one had expected from "primitive" hunter-gatherers,' adds Watkins. Artistically, too, the site shows a level of planning rarely attributed to the inhabitants of prehistory. The carvings are raised reliefs, rather than simple scratches in the rock, meaning that their creators knew what they were going to make before they started. In addition, different enclosures around the site appear to have different themes, with one filled with depictions of boars, another snakes, and another foxes.[33]

All this cooperation and creativity was driven by an urge that can only be called religious. Attempts to interpret the beliefs that once gave this place meaning are fraught with danger, given the amount still unknown about the site (more than 90 per cent of it remains unexcavated), but the site's size and detailed iconography indicate that the religious convictions of the people who built and used Göbekli Tepe were unexpectedly complex. The fact that the enclosures would have required hundreds of people to build them, yet could only house a few dozen inside, suggests that only a select few were initiated into whatever rites took place among the stone pillars and animal carvings. If true, this would be yet another surprise: religious elites weren't supposed to have existed until the establishment of sizeable farming settlements, thousands of years after Göbekli Tepe. As the prehistoric archaeologist Ian Hodder commented in the wake of Schmidt's discovery: 'all our theories were wrong.'[34]

The finds at Potbelly Hill were certainly unexpected, but they weren't entirely unprecedented. In fact, cracks had been appearing in the classic account of civilisation's origins ever since it was first formulated in the 19th century. The first shock came in 1879, when an eight-year-old girl named Maria de Sautuola discovered Ice Age cave paintings in Altamira, Spain. These remarkable works of art directly contradicted the supposedly artless savagery that was thought to have existed during the Ice Age. Many archaeologists simply refused to believe their eyes and rejected the authenticity of these artworks, arguing that they were 'stylistically too advanced to have been produced at an early stage of human development'. The influential French archaeologist Gabriel de Mortillet alleged that the Altamira cave paintings in Spain had been painted by priests in a plot to discredit the scientific study of progress in prehistory.[35]

The next big surprise came in the 1950s with the excavation of Tell es-Sultan, better known by its biblical name of Jericho. Led by the archaeologist Kathleen Kenyon, these digs uncovered a Stone Age farming settlement, complete with a 28-foot-tall stone tower and a 13-foot-high stone wall, but no evidence of any pottery. This was another unexpected discovery, as it was thought that, in the development of civilisation, large stone constructions could only come after pottery. Then in the 1980s excavations at the Turkish site of Nevali Çori uncovered another pre-pottery town that had not only free-standing stone buildings but a variety of remarkable stone sculptures, including the remains of a totem pole, a statue of a bird-human chimera, a fragment of a stone bowl depicting two people dancing with a turtle as well as smaller versions of the T-shaped pillars that would later be found at Göbekli Tepe. Until this point, Stone Age sculpture was thought to consist solely of figurines of clay, bone or stone, small enough to hold in the palm of your hand. It was finds such as these that led Schmidt – who worked at Nevali Çori in the 1980s – to question the description of Göbekli Tepe as nothing more than a medieval graveyard.[36]

By now it's clear that the old account of the origin of civilisation, in which complex society sprang from the development of farming, is seriously flawed. For a start, the lives of pre-agriculture hunters and foragers may not have been as brutal as once thought. 'We used to think that hunter-gatherers led miserable, malnourished lives, trying each day just to survive,' explains Ulf-Dietrich Schoop, an archaeologist at the University of Edinburgh. 'But nothing about Göbekli Tepe had anything to do with survival.' On the contrary, it and other sites in Southwest Asia show that their builders had plenty of time to develop complex beliefs, hone inessential skills like masonry and establish far-reaching social networks that would have served no purpose for gathering food. These finds force us to abandon the notion that hunter-gatherers must have lived simplistic and unchanging lives, cramped by the basic needs of securing food and staying alive.

The study of ancient trade networks supports this view. In Ice Age Europe, inessential items such as mammoth ivory, marine shells and amber were often traded across distances of up to 60 miles. As far back as 120,000 years ago, humans in Africa were trading the highly prized rock obsidian over distances of more than 180 miles. Similar trade networks would later spring up in Southwest Asia around the time of Göbekli Tepe, where archaeologists have found sea shells and baskets from the Red Sea in central Turkey, over 500 miles away.[37]

This archaeological evidence is backed up by anthropological research which shows that many present-day hunter-gatherers spend as little as twenty hours a week searching for food, and have more leisure time to enjoy than the average 21st-century

European. This isn't to say our prehistoric ancestors lived in some state of pristine innocence and perfect health, as New Age beliefs and fads like the paleo diet would suggest. Nevertheless, to dismiss all hunter-gatherer lifestyles as nasty, brutish and short is nothing short of caricature. The stereotype of the club-wielding caveman is especially overdue a makeover. For one thing, no archaeologist has ever found a prehistoric club – the notion that they must have carried them comes from the wild man of medieval mythology. For another, very few of them are thought to have lived in caves, and even then only as a temporary measure. Our prehistoric ancestors generally preferred to live in their own huts and houses, which had the distinct advantage over caves of not being inhabited by bears and hyenas. Archaeologists often dig in caves, however, because their sheltered environments preserve remains and artefacts much better than the exposed outdoors.[38]

The importance of farming as the catalyst for civilisation has also come under serious scrutiny. Clearly, given the sophistication of hunter-gatherer lifestyles on display at Göbekli Tepe, farming was by no means a prerequisite for complex social and religious structures, as was once maintained. But what about its much-vaunted health benefits? Recent archaeological work has now cast serious doubt even on this. By studying the skeletons of prehistoric farmers and hunter-gatherers, it's possible to build up a picture of the lifestyles these people once lived – the activities they took part in, the injuries they sustained, the food they ate. These investigations show that, in many cases, the adoption of farming actually made our ancestors *less* healthy.

Nineteenth-century archaeologists – who, in case you were wondering, had little hands-on experience of subsistence agriculture – simply assumed that the advent of agriculture must have had a 'healthful and invigorating influence' on a par with the changes wrought by industrialisation.[39] Had they attempted to recreate Stone Age agriculture for themselves they might have reached a different conclusion, one that any farmer today will tell you: farming is hard work. At many sites around the world, the uptake of agriculture in prehistory corresponds with a significant rise in joint pain and back problems, indicating that farmers endured a more physically demanding life than their foraging predecessors. Land needed to be cleared, seeds planted and grain harvested and processed. Permanent homes and granaries needed to be built. All of this took a heavy toll on our ancestors.

Moreover, farmers had to make do with a severely restricted diet compared to their hunter-gatherer neighbours. Early agriculture offered slim pickings: only a small number of crops had been cultivated and the few domesticated animals were typically smaller than their wild relatives. The drop in meat consumption made it harder to get enough vitamins, iron and zinc, and the corresponding rise in carbohydrates in the agricultural diet led to an increase in tooth decay. This unvaried, low-protein diet of early farmers has been linked to a sharp global rise in anaemia following the adoption of agriculture. Coupled with the strenuous working life, malnourishment stunted the growth of farming populations by as much as two inches.[40]

Other aspects of health also took a step backwards. Hunter-gatherers in the eastern Mediterranean typically lived in groups of less than a hundred and would often move between a number of temporary seasonal camps. Farming villages, in contrast, could have hundreds or even thousands of people living together permanently in close quarters, where they were at increased risk of contracting infectious disease such as smallpox, measles and rubella. Not only that, but living in close proximity to farm animals – along with new pests such as rats and mice

– introduced humans to previously unknown diseases like bird flu and bubonic plague. (Humans repaid the favour by transmitting tuberculosis to cattle around the same time.) Moreover, previously pristine water sources around these settlements would have become clogged with dirt, increasing the number of parasites infecting our ancestors.[41]

Not only was farming a harder, sicklier way of life compared to hunting and gathering, it was a riskier one too. For sedentary farmers tied to the land, a bad winter or dry summer could spell disaster, whereas mobile hunter-gatherers in the same situation could simply up sticks and move to a more promising area. Food surpluses could be acquired, but stores of grain are also vulnerable to theft or damage. By studying pauses in enamel growth on ancient teeth, archaeologists know that early farmers suffered from periodic food shortages significantly more frequently than hunter-gatherers did. Women seemed to have borne the brunt of these lifestyle changes, taking on a greater share of food cultivation than female hunter-gatherers. Women in agricultural societies were also having children younger and more often. This made pregnancy and birth much more dangerous, to the point where female life expectancy actually drops with the adoption of farming. On average, women in early farming settlements in Southwest Asia were dying a full seven years younger than men.[42]

In short, farming is no longer regarded as an obvious improvement on hunting and foraging, and certainly not 'the brilliant success ... in helping men to survive' that the influential archaeologist Vere Gordon Childe claimed it to be in 1944.[43] Which begs the question: if it entailed so much toil and trouble, why did anyone bother with it? 'Why farm?' cried the palaeobotanist Jack Harlan in 1992. 'Why give up the twenty-hour work week and the fun of hunting in order to toil in the sun? Why work harder, for

food less nutritious and a supply more capricious? Why invite
famine, plague, pestilence and crowded living conditions?'[44] The
short answer is that no one knows. A number of archaeologists
argue that hunter-gatherers could only have submitted to the
burden of agriculture as 'a last resort' due to unavoidable environmental pressures. But just what these pressures may have been is
also obscure. Overpopulation, climate change and the extinction
of big game have all been suggested, but none have proven con-
clusive, and it's likely that different factors pushed people towards
agriculture at different times and in different locations.[45]

What is clear, however, is that farming didn't represent a
clear progression in the history of humanity. Had extraterrestrials
visited Earth 10,000 years ago it's unlikely they would have singled
out farming communities as being in any way more advanced
than their hunter-gatherer neighbours. The hunters themselves
certainly didn't think so: rather than eagerly adopting agricultural
lifestyles as the obvious 'next step in the scale of human progression', archaeologists have found evidence of hunter-gatherers
living side-by-side with agricultural communities for thousands
of years without feeling the need to adopt their way of life. And
where it did occur, the shift from hunting and gathering to farming was not so much a revolution as it was a slow, gradual process,
lasting millennia. For thousands of years following the beginnings
of domestication, many early farming communities still relied on
hunting and foraging to secure up to half of all their food. For a
long time in Southwest Asia, groups would harvest both domesticated crops and their wild-growing relatives.[46]

Nor was there anything inevitable or irreversible about the
switch to farming, as the Law of Progress insists. Given that the
transition was slow and tentative, it's possible that people would
have alternated between farming and hunting lifestyles according

to changing environmental conditions. Stone Age Britons actually abandoned cereal farming sometime around 5,300 years ago and returned to foraging for their plant-based food. A number of indigenous groups on the American Great Plains likewise stopped farming in the 18th century and took up hunting. 'For us, it is natural to look back at the beginnings of farming and see how mixed farming supported great population growth and the rapid expansion of farming populations in all directions,' explains Watkins. In reality, however, these advances 'were long un-directed processes made up of many small steps along meandering pathways; the ultimate arrival at effective mixed farming economies was neither planned nor foreseen'.[47]

This wanton disregard for the Law of Progress holds true beyond farming. Few, if any, hunting and foraging groups seem to have followed the script for cultural development that was later written for them by 19th-century archaeologists like Lubbock and Morgan. Interestingly, a number of hunter-gatherer societies in historic times shifted between more and less complex societies on an annual basis. Until the mid-19th century in north-west Canada, for instance, coastal groups came together every winter into rigid hierarchical societies, complete with hereditary nobles, before disbanding into more egalitarian bands for the summer fishing season. According to a strict interpretation of cultural evolution, this shouldn't happen at all, let alone every year. And while this type of flexibility in hunter-gatherer lifestyles makes any analogy between historic and prehistoric groups tentative at best, archaeological evidence does suggest that a similar social fluidity was at work in the distant past. The discovery of individuals buried with a wealth of Ice Age treasures, such as ivory bracelets and seashell necklaces, indicates that some groups had adopted forms of political or religious power well over 25,000 years ago. In the

Near East, meanwhile, a number of hunter-gatherer groups were experimenting with sedentary lifestyles thousands of years before the development of agriculture.[48] 'In our rush to get to the origin of civilisation we tend to dismiss hunter-gatherers,' Schoop tells me. This is a mistake, he argues: not only does it disregard some 95 per cent of human history, it overlooks the variety and ingenuity of hunter-gatherer societies. 'Hunters and foragers never put all their eggs in one basket. They have a plan B and a plan C and D and E.' The result was – and still is for remaining societies – a remarkable diversity of lifestyles, beliefs and practices, of which farming was but one route taken by some groups.

As a result, many archaeologists have abandoned the old 'unilinear' system of cultural evolution, whereby human societies could only develop in one predetermined direction, for a multilinear understanding which acknowledges that different cultures might develop in different directions. For people living in the Amazon rainforest, the Central Asian steppe or the frozen shores of the Arctic Circle, it makes no sense to 'progress' to the next stage in civilisation by adopting agriculture, when farming is an untenable lifestyle in these environments. This doesn't mean that they're 'stranded' at a lower stage of civilisation, as was once thought; just as farming was an adaptation to the fertile country of Southwest Asia, so are canoe fishing, nomadic pastoralism and seal hunting adaptations to these different environments. There's never been one destination for human civilisation, nor indeed one form of human civilisation.[49]

~

The history of civilisation is no longer a simple thing. It is, quite frankly, a confusing jumble of trial and error, experimentation and adaptation. The once-clear image of humanity's irreversible and inevitable progress seems to grow blurrier with each new discovery, and we find ourselves having to squint pretty hard to discern any unifying narrative in the accounts they tell. This isn't to undermine the significance of agriculture in the course of human history: it's still true that farming was eventually able to support much larger populations than hunting and foraging ever could, and that it eventually became the basis of large, literate civilisations, beginning with Sumer and Egypt around 3000 BCE and China some 2,000 years later. And it's still true that these developments have changed the world in countless ways. But they represent just one line of development among the many that our ancestors trialled. As a result, few archaeologists or historians accept the Law of Progress today, and are wary of anyone who does. 'Discussions of progress ... are now red flags for any historian,' writes Ada Palmer, a professor of European history at the University of Chicago.[50]

This might seem like an overreaction. The history of civilisation may be complicated, but is it really necessary to go so far as to deny the inevitability of progress? Humanity has, after all, progressed. Most of us live longer than our Stone Age ancestors. Far fewer of our children die. Many of us have survived diseases and injuries that were once death sentences. Our tools are of such staggering complexity that most of us struggle to understand how they work at even a basic level. We can communicate instantaneously with people on the other side of the world and be there in person within little more than a day. We may genuinely admire the ingenuity and artistry of ancient hunter-gatherers, but how many of us would trade places with one?

It's true that there has been an overall trend towards greater complexity over time, even when we account for the many stalls and reverses throughout history. But a trend is not a law, and we have no grounds for assuming that it must always continue. 'The belief in historical destiny is sheer superstition,' thundered the 20th-century philosopher Karl Popper. 'There can be no prediction of the course of human history by scientific or any other rational methods.'[51] For Popper, the history of humanity was a unique event, and laws could only be derived from repeatable events. You can keep dropping apples from a tree until you're satisfied that there must exist a law of gravity, but you can't replay human history to see if it follows the same path of development. Consequently, we can never know what 'ought' to happen based on what has taken place in the past. 'The most careful observation of *one* caterpillar will not help us to predict its transformation into a butterfly,' wrote Popper.[52]

It's telling that the confident predictions of 19th-century archaeologists have so far proved to be spectacularly wrong. For Lubbock, the unceasing progress of the prehistoric record clearly foretold of a future nirvana. 'Utopia, which we had long looked upon as synonymous with an evident impossibility ... turns out on the contrary to be the necessary consequence of natural laws,' he wrote in the conclusion to *Pre-historic Times*. And yet the 20th century wasn't the progressive paradise he anticipated, but a century of world war, genocide and countless other conflicts. 'Men wiser and more learned than I have discerned in history a plot, a rhythm, a predetermined pattern,' noted the historian Herbert Fisher in 1937. 'I can see only one emergency following upon another.' He concluded: 'progress is not a law of nature. The ground gained by one generation may be lost by the next.'[53]

Fisher was by no means alone in his glum assessment: shocked by the apparent resurgence of savagery and barbarism in the 20th century, most scholars began to look at the Law of Progress with increasing discomfort. If Europeans and Americans could appeal to progress in order to sanction land grabs, incarceration and killing – what novelist Anthony Trollope called 'civilisation gone mad' – could they really denounce similar justifications by their enemies?[54] Had the crimes of Stalinism and Maoism not sprung from the Marxist belief that proletarian revolution was unavoidable? Were the horrors of Nazism not inspired by the conviction that Aryan supremacy was the inevitable 'fulfilment of world history'?[55] Even the Third Reich's notorious concentration camps were adapted from the detention centres used by colonial forces to corral 'lower races'.[56]

Many went further and argued that the idea of historical inevitability contradicted the very concept of morality. If all history is unfolding according to some immutable law, it was asked, then people must be powerless to change its course. So why bother with notions of morality or personal responsibility at all? As the philosopher Isaiah Berlin pointed out, it makes no sense to praise or blame someone for their actions if they're merely obeying the law of history; you might as well praise or blame them for obeying the law of gravity.[57]

Many of us today would agree with these criticisms, even if we don't share Fisher's war-weary pessimism. And yet the belief in inevitable progress still continues to influence our understanding of the world more than we might care to admit. How often do we hear of a politician's 'unstoppable rise' or 'inevitable fall'? Or of the steady 'march of history'? How often do we describe especially violent or cruel acts as 'medieval' and express our shock that such things could happen in the 21st century, as if violence and cruelty were stages of human development we've since outgrown? We talk of 'forward-thinkers' and people 'ahead of their time', assuming that human thought can only develop in one predetermined direction. History books relate such events as 'Britain's last execution', with the clear implication that we could never revert to such practices having abandoned them once before. These examples are just a smattering; the idea of historical inevitability is still so widely held that we'll continue to encounter it throughout this book. Indeed, so widespread is this urge to find meaning and patterns in events that psychologists suspect it's an inherent feature of human thought.[58]

It can be comforting to think that there's a plan for this world. Those early religious attempts to explain the origin of civilisation all found that reassurance in their divinely ordained accounts of the past. But this is the empty comfort of resignation, of surrendering ourselves to forces beyond our control. The Law of Progress, despite trying to distinguish itself from these earlier worldviews, is but the latest in a long line of superstitions attempting to find some comfort in the chaos of history.

Prehistoric archaeology, once held up in support of this fatalistic ideology, now teaches us a very different lesson. The origin of civilisation is in fact the origins of civilisations: a tangled genealogy of divergent lifestyles, beliefs and practices, none of which gives the impression of following some predetermined path. None of this is to deny that progress can happen. It does – but we have to make it happen. The advances in the quality of life since prehistory aren't the result of some ethereal law but of the insatiable human desire to improve our condition. Canoes, snowshoes, mathematics, medicine, writing, metalworking, money: whatever innovations we choose to measure progress with, all were deliberate efforts by our ancestors to make their world safer, easier or simply more convenient. 'Progress rests with us,' concluded Popper. 'We may become the makers of our fate when we have ceased to pose as its prophets.'[59]

Prehistoric archaeology has one other lesson to teach us: never take the past for granted. It's unpredictable, exciting, and shows absolutely no respect for your pet theories – and it's all the more fun for it. As Klaus Schmidt once said, when you appreciate history for the glorious mess it is, it becomes a much more 'colourful and dynamic' place.[60] Another Göbekli Tepe might be unearthed tomorrow, with equally revolutionary implications for our understanding of the past and the present. Potbelly Hill itself might still have some surprises in store as archaeologists scrape away the dust and debris from the remaining nine-tenths of the site. We have, quite literally, only just scratched the surface.

CHAPTER 2

Pythagoras and the cult of personality

It's easy to feel small when looking at the past. The annals of history seem to be full of pathological overachievers, supremely gifted people we can't help but pale in comparison to. How could any inventor hope to live up to the prodigious output of Nikola Tesla, the Serbian-American electrical engineer whose 300 patents revolutionised our understanding of electromagnetism? How could today's composers outshine the Russian maestro Igor Stravinsky, whose music for the ballet *The Rite of Spring* was so revolutionary that it sparked a riot at its premiere? And how could any tactician outmanoeuvre George Washington, whose military victories secured the United States' independence?

For the aspiring scholars among us, sooner or later we realise we're living in the shadow of the ancient Greek philosopher Pythagoras. Renaissance, medieval and Roman accounts of his life reveal a truly incredible man. Born sometime in the middle of the 6th century BCE on the Greek island of Samos, just off the coast of what is now Turkey, Pythagoras would grow up to become not just a mathematical genius, but an all-round scientific and philosophical powerhouse. His 80-odd written works laid the foundations of Western medicine, acoustics and astronomy, among other disciplines, and pioneered radical ethical positions such as vegetarianism, animal welfare and reincarnation. He was, in the words of his 3rd-century biographer Porphyry, 'remarkably gifted in every way'.[1]

Today, he is best remembered for discovering the theorem which bears his name: that the square of the hypotenuse of a right-angled triangle is equal to the sum of the squares of the other two sides. Or, more concisely: $a^2 + b^2 = c^2$. But his impact on mathematics has extended far beyond this achievement. He's credited with the discovery of prime numbers, irrational numbers and the concept of odd and even, with inventing the abacus, and even with coining the very word 'mathematics'. He was also the first to apply mathematical principles to the world around him and the first to suggest that numbers and geometry underlie the workings of the universe. Walking past a blacksmith's one day, Pythagoras noticed that heavier hammers made lower sounds when they struck metal. By weighing the hammers he determined the mathematical ratios between the notes of the musical scale and thus the principles of musical harmony. His mathematical enquiries also enabled him to introduce the first standard set of weights, measurements and coins to the Greek world, transforming commerce in the ancient Mediterranean.

His stature outside the field of mathematics is no less gigantic. In astronomy, he's credited with being the first person to systematically study the motion of the planets and the first to realise that the Earth was round, as well as the small matter of discovering the planet Venus. The astronomers Nicolaus Copernicus, Johannes Kepler and Galileo Galilei, who together established much of modern astronomy and physics, all suggested that it had been Pythagoras and his followers who developed a heliocentric model of the universe nearly two millennia before Renaissance Europeans. Copernicus even called his sun-centred system 'Pythagorean astronomy'.

Pythagoras' genius extended into the realm of philosophy too – indeed, the term 'philosophy' is said to be another of the man's coinages. He travelled far and wide in his quest for knowledge, discussing ethics with the oracle at Delphi, symbolism with the high priests of Egypt and the science of dreams with the ancient Hebrews, synthesising what he learned into a new, enlightened understanding of the world. Sometime in around 530 BCE he left his native Samos to establish a philosophical community in the town of Croton, at the southern end of the Italian peninsula, which was then part of the Greek-speaking world.[2] Here, Pythagoras encouraged his fellow Greeks to abandon luxuries and live a simple life dedicated to scientific enquiry and philosophical introspection. Challenging the depressing Greek view of the afterlife, in which our souls are forever stranded in the bleak underworld of Hades, Pythagoras is regarded as being the first European philosopher to have taught reincarnation, insisting that our souls are set free when we die and take up shelter in a new living being. Since our dearly departed might reappear as an animal, Pythagoras also urged his followers to treat fellow creatures humanely and adopt vegetarianism. Writing in the 1st century BCE, the Roman statesman and scholar Cicero effused that the 'supreme wisdom' of Pythagoras' teachings 'brought harmony to the world'.[3]

In short, Pythagoras is credited with being nothing less than the fountainhead of much of Western knowledge, from scientific rationalism to esoteric mysticism. Amazed how one person could have accomplished so much, historians have repeatedly set out to discover more about the sage from Samos. But here begins the problem with Pythagoras: the more you look, the less you find.

∼

It's the first rule any historical detective learns: if you want the truth, find the earliest sources. History is like the world's longest-running game of Chinese whispers, and the further your information is from the original source, the less reliable it's likely to be. Details are lost, accounts are confused, stories scrambled. Cicero was writing about Pythagoras more than four centuries after the philosopher had died; his biographer Porphyry more than eight centuries after – so while they have plenty to say about him, we can only put so much trust in what they tell us. If we want to uncover the truth of Pythagoras' remarkable genius, we need to find the earlier Greek sources.

The older the source, however, the less remarkable Pythagoras' genius becomes. Writing in the mid-4th century BCE, less than two centuries after Pythagoras' death, Aristotle portrays him as little more than the founder of a clunky mathematical philosophy, and makes no mention of his supposed mastery of medical knowledge or his trove of astronomical discoveries. Writing a generation earlier, Aristotle's teacher Plato was apparently unaware even of Pythagoras' mathematical achievements, describing him simply as a mysterious religious guru.[4]

By the time we arrive at contemporary and near-contemporary accounts from the 5th and 6th centuries, the few surviving descriptions of the 'wisest of men' come as something of a nasty shock. Gone is Pythagoras the mathematical genius, the scientific pioneer and the universally revered sage. In his place is Pythagoras the megalomaniac, the swindler and the reviled crackpot. His philosophical community in southern Italy is described as a reclusive cult, where brainwashed followers worship their leader with unnerving devotion. Pythagoras himself is widely accused by his contemporaries of being nothing more than a pompous charlatan, a tinpot philosopher who uses pseudo-theological fireworks to dazzle the simple and con his way to fame and power. The philosopher Heraclitus brands him 'the inventor of deceit' and 'the

Prince of Cheats', who dealt in 'quackery' and 'knavery'. The ora-tor Isocrates lampoons him as a fame-hungry fraud who peddled attention-seeking philosophical beliefs purely to gain notoriety. About the nicest thing anyone has to say about Pythagoras is that he was 'not the feeblest thinker among the Greeks', as the histor-ian Herodotus begrudgingly acknowledged.[5]

Perhaps most surprising, however, is what these earliest sources don't say. None of them makes any mention of Pythagoras' work in mathematics, harmonics, astrology, or any other scholarly venture. No writer recounts his globetrotting quest for knowledge, nor provides any evidence to suggest he advocated vegetarianism or promoted any moral philosophy. None of his contempor-aries reference any of the 80 works that he supposedly wrote, and – together with the fact that not one scrap of one scroll of Pythagoras' writings has survived – most scholars today suggest that the 'prodigious genius' never even put pen to paper.[6]

In fact, the majority of historians now question whether Pythagoras made any contribution to science or philosophy at all. We can be certain he didn't discover harmonic ratios in a blacksmith's, because the account of how he did so is physically impossible: the sound a hammer makes when it strikes an object isn't directly proportional to its weight, as the story supposes. (Another tale describing his discovery of harmonic ratios, in which he plucked strings tautened with various weights, is also a physical impossibility.) We can also be certain that Pythagoras didn't introduce standardised weights and coinage to the Greek world, as they first appeared in Asia Minor, at the opposite end of the Mediterranean to his adopted home of Croton. Other achievements attributed to him can be quickly disproved as well. The planet Venus was well-known to the ancient Hindus a thou-sand years before Pythagoras supposedly 'discovered' it. Prime numbers had been common knowledge for Egyptian scholars since the 2nd millennium BCE, around the same time that the Babylonians began investigating irrational numbers. And the historian Herodotus (he of the backhanded compliment) credits the invention of the abacus to the Egyptians, not Pythagoras.[7]

Lastly, there's absolutely no evidence that Pythagoras came up with any theorem involving triangles. For one thing, it's a full 400 years after his death before anyone associates him with 'his' theorem. For another, that relationship between the sides of a right-angled triangle was widely known among carpenters and craftsmen for well over a millennium before Pythagoras, which they used (and still use) as a practical way to achieve right angles. Its use wasn't just limited to practical know-how, however: a 3,700-year-old Babylonian clay tablet, acquired by Yale University in 1912, depicts a mathematical exercise involving a variation on Pythagoras' theorem 1,100 years before Pythagoras was born.[8]

So how did a widely-ridiculed cult leader with no apparent interest in geometry become immortalised as a founding father of mathematics? To understand Pythagoras' remarkable trans-formation we need to take a closer look at the community he established in the town of Croton. Pythagoras may not have had any mathematical know-how, but – like any cult leader worth his salt – he did have a body of loyal followers, eager to heap praise on their wise and benevolent master.

⁓

The first Pythagoreans, as his followers came to be known, were simply those citizens of Croton who came to listen to the stranger from Samos as he preached in and around their town. Within a few years, however, they had organised themselves into a secretive communal society which became something like a cross between the Freemasons and the Manson Family. The cult quickly grew in size and influence, and for a few generations it appears to have been a particularly painful thorn in the side of the Greek establishment in what is now southern Italy. When the commune in Croton collapsed, perhaps due to a violent uprising by locals or persecution by the authorities, Pythagoreans dispersed across the Mediterranean, where they would continue to have intermittent influence on philosophical debates for centuries.

The Pythagoreans were, to put it mildly, an odd bunch. To their fellow Greeks, they seem to have occupied a similar place in popular culture as hippies did in 1960s America: long-haired counterculture rebels with a dangerous disdain for traditional society. The barefoot vegetarian Pythagorean was for a while a stock character in Athenian comedies, and Pythagoras himself, as we've seen, was the subject of less than reverential attention beyond the confines of his commune.[9]

The Pythagoreans' unusual social practices did little to challenge such stereotypes. Simply joining the secretive society was an ordeal in itself. Just as potential employers today will dredge your social media accounts for a sniff of unsavoury activity, hopeful initiates had to undergo extensive background checks whereby their hobbies, interests and personal relationships were all subject to intense scrutiny. If they were accepted, they then had to forswear all private property and agree to share their possessions with the other members of the commune. According to some accounts, there then began a five-year initiation process in which the neophytes had to silently listen to Pythagoras lecture from behind a curtain. If they made it the full five years – and if they hadn't been kicked out for breaking any rules – they were then, finally, welcomed as a fully-fledged member of the community and permitted to gaze upon their master.[10]

Things didn't get much easier once they were allowed into the inner circle, however. Members of the community were told to avoid all 'venereal pleasures' until they turned twenty, and even then they 'should rarely engage in them'. Marriage was encouraged, but sex must only be for the purpose of having children; should any couple catch themselves enjoying the act, their offspring would turn out 'miserable' and would 'resemble cattle'. Needless to say, participation in religious orgies – a notable feature of some other Mediterranean cults at the time – was strictly off limits.[11]

The lives of Pythagoras' followers were limited by a bewildering number of taboos outside the bedroom too. Pythagoreans must never urinate in the direction of the sun, never clean their teeth with laurel twigs, and avoid any place 'where an ass has crouched down'.[12] Bathing was essential to achieve spiritual purity, but public baths were to be avoided at all costs (this one was actually sound medical advice: public baths in the ancient Mediterranean were essentially standing pools of warm water and bodily fluids, and bathers were almost certainly more likely to catch a disease than be cured of one).[13] In the kitchen, Pythagoreans were forbidden from eating any animal that lays eggs, from picking up crumbs, or from drinking alcohol, as drunkenness was thought to lead to insanity. Particularly sinful was the consumption of beans: for reasons lost to time (suggestions range from their resemblance to testicles to a particular aversion to flatulence), Pythagoras considered beans 'a vexatious food' and insisted his followers avoid them at all costs. These dietary commandments might sound bizarre, but they were taken no less seriously than Muslim avoidance of pork or Jewish rules around kosher food today. The Pythagorean philosopher Empedocles once lamented that he had become 'an exile and a wanderer from the gods' because he gave in to temptation and ate some beans.[14]

There was more to the Pythagorean philosophy than just self-denial, however. Surviving fragments from the writings of Pythagoras' disciples, while providing no hard evidence that their leader was a mathematician, do reveal that numbers and shapes played a central role in Pythagorean thought – albeit in a totally unscientific way. The Pythagoreans were numerologists, firm believers in the mystical power of numbers. In the Pythagorean school, as in many numerological systems today, each number and shape had distinct characteristics: a little like the star signs of astrology. They considered the number ten to be sacred and seemed to be deeply superstitious about the number seven. Squares were preferred over oblongs and odd numbers over even (with the exceptions of seven and ten). And while there's no evidence to link Pythagoras with his eponymous theorem, triangles do seem to have held a special place in Pythagorean cosmology as symbols of harmony and cosmic order.[15]

For a number of Pythagoreans, the mystical belief that 'number rules the universe' proved fertile ground for genuine advances in mathematics. The philosopher Hippasus, working decades after Pythagoras' death, was probably the first to prove the existence of irrational numbers, which the Babylonians had first begun to investigate over a thousand years earlier. And it was his fellow Pythagoreans Philolaus and Archytas who first explored the mathematical ratios between musical notes. Archytas was also the first known mathematician to solve the problem of how to double a cube, producing a geometrical solution so complex that mathematicians today still praise it as 'a tour de force'.[16]

Astronomy was another popular intellectual pursuit for the Pythagoreans. Some members of the community, such as Philolaus, were the first scholars in recorded history to reject the notion that the Earth was the centre of the universe. And although they never developed a heliocentric model of the universe as suggested by Copernicus in the 1500s, they came enticingly close, arguing that the Sun, Moon and planets all revolved around a 'central fire'.[17] Other attempts to explain the solar system were wider of the mark. Philolaus also argued that the moon was inhabited by beautiful aliens, fifteen times larger than the inhabitants of Earth. Others believed that the Milky Way was the final destination of our souls once they broke free of their earthly bonds. Some Pythagoreans, convinced that there must be ten heavenly bodies – ten being the perfect number – yet troubled that they could only count nine (Earth, Moon, Sun, five planets and a fixed dome of stars), simply invented a new planet, the 'anti-Earth', to balance the cosmos.[18]

There wasn't really a coherent school of Pythagorean thought, especially following the break-up of the Croton commune. Some of his disciples studied mathematics, others debated metaphysics. Some believed there was a single god, others three, and others still placed their faith in the traditional Greek pantheon of Olympians. What unified them was their unwavering devotion to their leader, something which Pythagoras himself may have encouraged. A number of the anecdotes we have about him, such as his Wizard of Oz-style refusal to let the uninitiated gaze upon him, or his followers' reluctance to utter his name (referring to him instead as *tou andros*, 'the man'), hint at a god delusion.

If Pythagoras did indeed suffer from such a conceit, his followers were willing enablers, crediting him with miraculous feats and accomplishments. He could predict the future, they said, and could appear in two places at once. He could stare at the sun without blinking. On one occasion he made a bear promise not to harm any living thing; on another he persuaded a bull to stop eating beans. Intellectually he was unsurpassed, and the Pythagoreans became notorious for believing that any utterance attributed to their master was absolute fact. The obscure word 'ipsedixitism' – meaning the dogmatic assertion of an argument – comes from the Latin translation of their expression 'he said it himself'.

Following Pythagoras' death sometime around 495 BCE, the miraculous nature of his feats only increased in magnitude. He could rise from the dead and visit other worlds. He had a thigh made of solid gold – a sure sign of divinity for the ancient Greeks. Some openly claimed that he was a descendant of Zeus or an incarnation of Apollo. In the early 1st millennium CE a number of Greeks deliberately deified him in an attempt to provide a pagan alternative to the Jewish martyr Jesus, whose own followers were emptying Greek and Roman temples at an alarming rate. (Ironically, much of the mythology accumulating around Jesus at this time was itself taken from pagan religion; the earliest depictions of Christ are suspiciously similar to contemporary portrayals of the god Apollo.)

The stage was thus set for Pythagoras' metamorphosis from crackpot to genius. In order to bolster the reputation of their leader, it became common practice among the Pythagoreans to credit any discoveries they made – such as irrational numbers or harmonic ratios – to Pythagoras himself, even when such discoveries took place decades or centuries after his death. This habit was reinforced by a long tradition of forging philosophical and scientific books in Pythagoras' name, which allowed his followers to assert that he really was every inch the polymath they claimed him to be. By the Middle Ages there were hundreds of Pythagorean forgeries circulating through Europe, covering every subject from statesmanship to magical plants to – of course – the geometry of triangles. A thousand years of hero worship had paid off, and Pythagoras assumed his unrightful place as the founding father of Western philosophy and science.

Magic numbers, evil beans, gigantic moon aliens – is this really the same ancient Greece that gave us logic, democracy and brightly-coloured statues? Where are all the po-faced philosophers, the valiant statesmen and the indomitable athletes that the classical world is famous for?

They existed, certainly, but they were part of a much larger and more varied landscape than the ancient Greece of popular imagination. When someone talks about the history of ancient Greece they almost always mean the history of ancient Athens, the city-state in the south-east of the Greek peninsula – which is a little like trying to tell the history of England without leaving the confines of Oxford.

Even this analogy, however, makes the mistake of treating ancient Greece like a modern-day country. Ancient Greece was never a single political unit. It was more akin to the Arab world today: a loose affiliation of states, stretching from the cliffs of Iberia in the west to the far shores of the Black Sea in the east, which shared a common linguistic, religious and cultural heritage. Athens and its surrounding territory was only one of hundreds of Greek city-states throughout this vast and varied region. There was the tiny island town of Delos, just two square miles in size, and there was the Sicilian metropolis of Syracuse, whose territory covered over a million acres. There was the ancient city of Argos, with the goddess Hera as its patron, and there was the upstart colony of Corcyra, which worshipped the hunting goddess Artemis. Some states were ruled by kings, others by dictators, and others still by popular government.[19]

The geography of the Mediterranean – scattered islands, rugged terrain – made it unwieldy to unite and maintain a large territory. This was made more difficult by the Greek city-state itself, which, by dividing territory into small autonomous chunks, fomented deep and bitter rivalries. Any remaining hopes of Greek unity were repeatedly dashed by the feeble sense of political loyalty displayed by many soldiers and politicians. Even when the Greeks managed to temporarily unite to fend off an invading Persian Empire in the early 5th century BCE, an achievement typically held up as 'Greece's finest hour', personal pride often trumped political allegiance. Consider the case of Hippias, a one-time ruler of Athens who, when deposed, felt no qualms about siding with the invading Persians and fighting against Athenian forces at the battle of Marathon. The Spartan king Demaratus, ousted in a political coup, also chose to side with the Persians. Even the Athenian general Themistocles, whose tactical gymnastics helped win the war, eventually jumped ship and joined his former Persian enemies. As the historian Robert Littman writes: 'betrayal and treason were national pastimes of the Greeks.'[20]

Consequently, the ancient Greeks spent far more time and effort murdering each other than they did repelling foreign invaders. It made the Mediterranean a dangerous place to be. Throughout the entirety of the 5th and 4th centuries BCE, Athens never managed to go a full decade without declaring war on some enemy, Greek or non-Greek, and was at war more often than it was at peace. A number of these conflicts were brutal, even by ancient standards. In 416 BCE, as the Peloponnesian War pitted Greek against Greek, Athenian forces laid siege to the peaceful island of Melos because it refused to pay an unmediated tribute, eventually killing every man and enslaving every woman and child they could find. Three years later a mercenary force on Athens' payroll, frustrated at having arrived too late to join a campaign to Sicily, slaughtered the defenceless inhabitants of the town of Mycalessus, including the children they found in the town's school, as they made their way back home. During that same war an army from Sparta – Athens' military-obsessed rival-turned-enemy – stormed the city of Iasus, murdering and enslaving the inhabitants in retaliation for their continued support of Athens.[21]

If traitors and massacres aren't the first things that come to mind when you picture ancient Greece, there's a good reason for that. Ancient Athens – and, by extension, the wider Greek world – has been the benefactor of more positive press coverage in the West than just about any other society in history. Beginning in the Italian city-states of the 15th century, the European redis-covery of classical art and philosophy sparked an obsession with all things old and Greek that would consume the continent's lit-erati. Architects bedecked cities with neoclassical designs. Artists depicted their patrons in Greek robes. Philhellenic philologists attempted to Hellenise the English language, inserting unneces-sary H's into 'ache' and 'author', 'Anthony' and the River 'Thames', in the mistaken belief that they were originally Greek words.

Ancient Greece proved so popular partly because it could be different things to different people. For Europe's intelligentsia it was a philosophical nirvana, a golden age of truth and beauty free from the distractions and mundanities of modernity. For artists it became an aesthetic ideal, a world of beautiful maidens and muscle-bound athletes. For the emerging middle classes – una-ware of the many older attempts at democratic government in ancient Sumerian city-states – it became an inspiration and model for democratic reform.

In each case the successes of Greek life were emphasised and its failures downplayed or ignored, leading to a highly romanticised understanding of ancient Greece as the 'cradle of civilisation'.[22] Many came to believe that its art and scholarship were not only great, but the greatest that humanity could produce,

unsurpassable by modern efforts. Pythagoras and the Greek philosophers were 'the first mighty conquerors of ignorance in our
world', thundered the English statesman William Temple in 1690,
'and made greater progress in the several empires of science than
any of their successors have since been able to reach'.[23]

It's undeniable that ancient Greece was a remarkable civilisation. It's also true that Europe and the wider world can trace,
however indirectly, many aspects of their politics, art, culture,
philosophy and science back to the ancient Greeks. A number of
modern academic disciplines, such as psychology and zoology,
date to the philosopher Aristotle's pioneering systematisation of
ancient knowledge. The tragedies, comedies and satires of Western
theatre are still rooted in the conventions that were developed by
Greek playwrights some 2,500 years ago. (In perhaps the greatest
compliment that can be paid to a satirist, in the late 1960s the military junta in Greece banned a number of Aristophanes' political
satires for being subversive, more than two millennia after they
were first penned.[24]) This very book owes an enormous debt to
that same civilisation: around one-third of the English language's
half a million words can be traced back to Greek.

However, this familiar (and, for many Europeans, self-
congratulatory) tale is only one side of the story. It's not just noble,
upstanding words like 'democracy' and 'diplomacy' that we inherited from the ancient Greeks, but more questionable ones like
'tyranny' and 'oligarchy', 'slander' and 'scandal', 'catastrophe' and
'cataclysm'. To tell the story of 'the Greek miracle', as so many have
done, requires that a lot of less than noble and upstanding features
of ancient Greek life be left unsaid. It's not only the warmongering
and treachery of the Greek world that fails to make the cut. Gone is
the gruesome tradition of stoning people suspected of desecrating
holy shrines, or the widespread political practice of assassination.

Gone too is the Athenian habit of publicly torturing slaves with whips, racks and fire.[25] Even the most well-known and widely-praised aspects of ancient Greece, its democracy and philosophy, turn out to be a little more complicated than the plaudits would suggest.

First introduced in 507 BCE, Athenian *demokratia* – literally 'people power' – was a curious creation. On the one hand, it cemented and celebrated the misogynistic, xenophobic and elitist character of ancient Athenian society. On the other hand, it went further than any previous attempt at self-government in granting citizens an equal vote in the running of their city. There were three branches to this democratic government. The first was the Council of 500, which met daily to deal with the state's finances and military matters, and to draft motions to be voted on. Voting took place at the Assembly, the second branch of government, which was summoned by the Council at least 40 times a year. There was no such thing as a ballot box, by the way. Members of the Assembly voted with a simple show of hands, and – rather than count them all – the result was simply guessed. (If you think that's bad, the Spartans cast their votes by shouting.) The third branch was the law courts, where enormous juries of citizens – numbers ranged from 201 to a whopping 2,501 jurors – voted on the complaints and accusations brought before them, including those pertaining to the actions of the Council and Assembly. Athenian democracy, working with a pool of just 20,000 citizens (roughly equivalent to the population of Newquay), was able to be far more direct than its modern descendants. Participation in the Council of 500 was chosen not by election but by annual lot, with each and every citizen liable to be chosen to serve all but the most senior military and financial positions. Jurors were likewise selected from the citizens by lot. The Assembly, meanwhile, was open to any citizen who wanted to take part. To ensure that personal wealth wasn't a limiting factor in political participation, the Athenians introduced a salary for those on jury duty or in public office.[26]

It's easy to see why the system, which persisted for 185 years, has been described as 'the Greeks' greatest gift to the world'.[27] There was, however, a catch. While Athenian citizens were accorded remarkable rights and important duties, only a small fraction of the Athenian population qualified. One of the most significant barriers to citizenship was ethnicity. Ancient Greek society was deeply xenophobic, and although they lacked our modern conceptions of race it was common for them to describe non-Greeks as inherently inferior in ways that would unhesitatingly be condemned as racist today. Under Athens's rigid class system, the city's 40,000 or so foreign residents were denied citizenship no matter how long they had lived in Athens. Even someone as respected as Aristotle, who spent more than twenty years of his life in the city after moving there from his native Macedonia, was never made a citizen. Foreigners were thus prevented from holding public office, voting in the Assembly or owning property, and had to pay a tax which citizens were spared. A murderer would even receive a lighter punishment for killing a foreign resident than a citizen. In the mid-5th century BCE, as more immigrants moved to Athens, citizenship rules were tightened even further so that only someone whose parents were themselves both Athenians could be a citizen. This effectively ruled out mixed marriages for all self-respecting Athenian families.[28]

Even more despised than foreigners were the 150,000 or so slaves who lived in Athens during the 5th and 4th centuries BCE. Although slaves could hold fairly senior positions in society – working as bank managers, tax collectors and naval captains – Athenian law allowed them to be bought, sold and beaten by

their masters. Perversely, legal testimonies from slaves were valid
only if they had been extracted by torture. In Sparta, where citizens could kill a slave without any legal consequence, state-owned
slaves were liable to be executed without warning by the Spartan
secret service, the *krypteia*, who hunted out the sturdiest and
most rebellious among them in a bid to prevent uprisings.[29]

In spite of these prejudices, it was possible on very rare occasions for immigrants and even slaves in Athens to be granted
citizenship in recognition of exceptional service to the state.
The one group of people in Athens who could never achieve
citizenship were the 150,000 women who called the city home.
All women – foreign, native, young, old, rich, poor – were automatically excluded from all political rights, including the right to
vote, own or inherit property, or bring a case to court without a
male guardian. This reflected a deeply engrained sexism in ancient
Greek society that preferred wives and daughters to be quiet, submissive and housebound – something which generations of male
classicists, in their paeans to 'the glory of ancient Greece', have
all too often condoned.[30]

Once all these restrictions are factored in, historians estimate
that only about one tenth of the Athenian population were fully
enfranchised citizens, a proportion so small that it can be difficult
to distinguish Athenian democracy from some oligarchic forms
of government at work in the ancient Greek world. Yet even this
was too inclusive for many aristocratic Athenians, who deeply
resented the intrusion of the hoi polloi into state affairs (the very
word *demokratia* might originally have been coined by Athenian
aristocrats to mean something like 'mob rule'). Twice they staged
coups against the democratic government in Athens, installing
short-lived but brutal oligarchic regimes in its place. In the second of these takeovers, in 404–3 BCE, citizenship was restricted

to just 3,000 inhabitants, and any remaining citizens who challenged the government were liable to lose their political rights.
The resulting eight-month reign of terror led to the murders of
more than 2,500 Athenians, including 1,500 citizens.[31]

Civil strife and upheaval like this were fairly commonplace
in Greek city-states as democrats, oligarchs and military strongmen wrestled for power. The colony of Byzantium, today Istanbul,
lurched between democracy and oligarchy six times in the second
half of the 5th century BCE alone.[32] A civil war between democrats
and oligarchs in the city of Corcyra descended into a bloodbath of
such brutality that even fellow Greeks were shocked. 'Death raged
in every shape,' recounted the historian Thucydides; 'there was no
length to which violence did not go.'[33] Ambitious individuals were
often able to exploit the chaos and install themselves as tyrants,
singlehandedly ruling states with varying degrees of despotism.

Perhaps surprisingly, given ancient Greece's democratic legacy, the overwhelming majority of Greek philosophers sided with
the oligarchs and against the democrats in these struggles. As long
ago as the early 5th century BCE, when democratic institutions
were in their infancy, the philosopher Heraclitus spent his time
railing against the masses and their political ambitions. When
the citizens in his hometown of Ephesus expelled the oligarch
Hermodorus, Heraclitus likened them to asses and dogs, meddling in matters they didn't understand. 'The Ephesians would do
well to hang themselves, every last one of them,' he fumed.[34] A
century later, the Pythagorean Archytas agreed that aristocracy
was a more just form of government than democracy. The masses
'must be sufficiently restrained', he wrote, 'for the common people
are bold and rash'.[35]

Similar concerns about 'the poor and the bad' were widely held
among the educated elite of Athens. None expressed them more

forcefully than Plato, one of the giants of philosophy. A wealthy aristocrat, Plato made no effort to hide his contempt for those 'inferior in virtue and breeding', or for the democratic 'madness' which put them in power.[36] The 'excellent' alternative political system he envisaged in his *Republic* is, to most minds at least, an authoritarian, totalitarian, communist nightmare, in which every possible trace of individuality and humanity is replaced with slavish devotion to the state. 'There is common property of wives, of children, and of all chattels,' he explained. 'Everything possible has been done to eradicate from our life everywhere and in every way all that is private and individual.' To avoid unwanted personal attachments, babies are taken from their parents at birth, and no one is permitted to know their children or parents. Energetic music, the works of Homer and 'loud laughter' are all forbidden as dangerous distractions. Governing this 'ideal state' are, conveniently enough, the philosophers, who alone Plato considers wise enough to rule.[37] (Ironic, then, that Plato appears to have been an awful political mentor: at least *nine* of his pupils and associates rejected his doctrine of the noble philosopher-king and instead became tyrants of various city-states, and a number of them would even murder each other while vying for tyrannical power.[38])

Open contempt for democracy and the masses isn't the only surprise in ancient Greek society. For a place celebrated as the 'birthplace of rational thinking', ancient Greece could be surprisingly irrational. Belief in magic, the supernatural and mysterious phenomena was widespread across the Mediterranean. Preachers and diviners could make a decent living predicting futures and interpreting dreams. Mystery cults attracted thousands of members with their curious and often secretive rituals. Writing in the 4th century BCE, the philosopher Theophrastus ridiculed his fellow Athenians for their many superstitious practices, such as

avoiding graves, sprinkling themselves with holy water and asso-
ciating weasels with bad luck. Seen in context, the bizarre beliefs
and taboos of the Pythagoreans no longer seem so out of place.[39]

Nor were the Pythagoreans the only cult whose leader may
have nursed delusions of divinity. The classical world was positively
swarming with self-declared prophets and messiahs. There was
Epimenides, who was alleged to be nearly 157 years old when he
died. There was Aristeas, who claimed to use Apollo's powers to
travel through time. Abaris of Scythia insisted he could live without
food (a trick still attempted by mystics today); Amphion of Thebes
could move rocks with his mind; the Pythagorean Empedocles is
alleged to have hurled himself into the crater of Mount Etna in a bid
to prove his divinity. Perhaps the most audacious ancient prophet
was Alexander of Abonoteichus, who achieved fame and fortune
for his ability to summon the snake god Glycon – which was, in
fact, a sock puppet he created out of linen and horsehair. This was
enough to convince his thousands of followers, who declared him
a reincarnation of Pythagoras and claimed that he too had a thigh
made of solid gold.[40] (Not everyone was fooled though: the Greek
writer Lucian, the man who exposed Alexander of Abonoteichus'
fraud, memorably described the prophet's followers as 'drivelling
idiots ... bereft of their brains and sense'.[41])

Occasionally people didn't even need to pose as mystics to
become the subject of mythologising. Alexander the Great was
proclaimed to be the son of Zeus so many times during his lifetime that he seems eventually to have believed it himself. Plato
may have established a cult for his teacher Socrates after the latter was found guilty of impiety and 'corrupting the youth', and
forced (by democratic vote) to commit suicide. Following Plato's
own death, his followers echoed the Pythagoreans before them by
calling their leader 'divine'. The writer Diogenes Laërtius claimed

Plato was descended from Poseidon and hinted that he was conceived with the help of divine intervention, Nazareth-style.[42]

~

The ancient Greeks weren't the first to worship people as heroes, and they certainly weren't the last. Many of humanity's oldest surviving stories centre on the adventures of a hero. As early as 1700 BCE the Babylonians were reading *The Epic of Gilgamesh*, in which the titular character overcomes a deadly ocean, a land of permanent darkness and giant talking scorpions in his quest for the plant of eternal youth. Two centuries before this, the Egyptians were recounting *The Tale of Sinuhe*, which follows the exploits of a royal courtier as he ventures across the desert, explores a foreign land and battles an axe-wielding warrior. In ancient China, the real-life exploits of the 3rd-century general Guan Yu were extolled and embellished to the point where he's now worshipped as a deity by millions of Buddhists and Taoists.

Hero worship seems to be an innate part of the human psyche. We still see it at work today in the toxic fandom of social media, where devoted fans send death threats to anyone who besmirches their celebrity idols, or in the die-hard supporters of demagogues like Nicolás Maduro and Narendra Modi, who refuse to accept any criticism of their idols as anything but conspiracy-mongering. More than anywhere else, however, we see it in our retellings of the past. All around the world, history is taught through the great deeds of great individuals, whether it's kings and queens, saints and martyrs or founding fathers and national heroes.

No one articulated this view of the past with more certainty than the Scottish historian Thomas Carlyle. In a series of six public lectures delivered in May 1840, Carlyle expounded what's come to be known as the 'Great Man' theory of history: that the engine of historical change isn't environment, society, ideology or chance, but the sheer willpower of a few remarkable men determined to change the world. As Carlyle famously declared: 'the history of the world is but the biography of great men.'[43]

These great men can take many forms. Carlyle's examples include preachers like Muhammad and Luther, poets such as Dante and Shakespeare, and military leaders like Cromwell and Napoleon. What unites them isn't their calling but their conviction, a 'savage sincerity' with which they pursue their goals. Blessed with God-given vision and confidence, they rise above the concerns that ensnare lesser men with a purpose Carlyle described, not unsympathetically, as 'despotic'. As for the unheroic 'dull millions' – in which camp most historians are included – our only duties are to worship these great men and record their achievements for posterity.[44]

To a modern reader, Carlyle's 1840 lectures feel strange. His weakness for exclamations, excessive capitalisations and other am-dram histrionics quickly grows exhausting, and his repeated invocation of God and 'destiny' (another form of historical inevitability) seems out of place in a historical study. 'The Great Man,' insists Carlyle in a typically perfumed passage, is 'a messenger ... sent from the Infinite Unknown with tidings to us.' More serious is his reluctance, even refusal, to offer evidence to support his mystical worldview; Carlyle simply takes it as given that a few are born heroes, and the many will worship them. 'We all love great men,' he asserts; 'does not every true man feel that he is himself made higher by doing reverence to what is really above him?' In the words of the historian Jane Ridley, Carlyle's theory is little more than 'romantic claptrap'.[45]

Influential claptrap nonetheless. Hero worship was already a prominent theme in the study of history; Carlyle's lectures lent it a veneer of academic rigour and respectability, turning it into something like a religious conviction for the upper and middle classes of Victorian society. Biographies of politicians and soldiers, both long-dead and recently deceased, enjoyed enormous popularity, and for some years in the late 19th century a new biography was hitting the shelves at the rate of one a day.[46] The historian Thomas Macaulay, who once called his contemporary Carlyle 'an empty-headed bombastic dunce', complained that the cloisters of Oxford University were 'reeking with Carlylism'.[47]

That influence continues today, no matter how often historians condemn Carlyle's Great Man theory for its snobbish dismissal of the 'idle multitude', its inherent sexism (women are, once again, excluded by default), its celebration of political and military strongmen, or its anti-democratic insistence that the 'few Wise take charge of the many Foolish'. Even in the 21st century, which keeps telling itself that the Great Man theory is 'dead', one in every five history books sold is a biography, and 70 per cent of those are biographies of men.[48] Painfully complex and convoluted events like the Second World War are all too often reduced to a battle of wills between a handful of famous figures.

And just like Pythagoras, many of these famous figures continue to take undue credit for other people's achievements. Consider the oft-repeated claims that King Henry VIII wrote the song 'Greensleeves' (he didn't), or that the light bulb was invented by Thomas Edison (it wasn't), or the belief that Christopher Columbus discovered America, a heroic myth so deeply rooted it will take its own chapter to properly dismantle. Or consider the phenomenon of 'quote magnetism', whereby sayings become misattributed to famous figures such as Mark Twain, Oscar Wilde and Winston Churchill. As Mark Twain once wrote (and he actually did write this one): 'any invented quotation, played with confidence, stands a good chance to deceive.'[49]

Taken individually, each of these mistakes might not seem like too much of a problem. Over time, however, facts begin to warp under the combined weight of such misattributions and exaggerations. Take the three historical figures mentioned at the start of this chapter: in each case the real person has been obscured by decades or centuries of hero worship. While Nikola Tesla certainly did file some 300 patents, his scientific contributions in the fields of electronics and electromagnetism tended to be improvements to existing ideas and machines rather than revolutionary new concepts, for which he's increasingly misremembered. He wasn't the first to build a rotary magnetic field, as is often claimed – the physicist Galileo Ferraris beat him to it by two years. Nor did he invent alternating current, another popular accolade granted to him: that had been around for a quarter of century before he was even born. Even the famous photograph of Tesla calmly taking notes in his lightning-filled laboratory isn't real, but a double exposure created for publicity purposes.[50]

Igor Stravinsky is widely regarded as a bold and original composer, and his jarring music for *The Rite of Spring* was, in the words of one music historian, 'earth-shattering'. But there was no riot at the premiere. Some in attendance did laugh and joke during the performance, and others told them to be quiet, but there's no evidence the disagreements became physical, let alone riotous. Records show that the ballet dancers took five curtain calls that night, which seems unlikely if the performance had descended into the anarchy of popular legend.[51]

And what of George Washington? Accounts following his death praised him as an unrivalled 'military genius' in terms frequently bordering on deification. 'He was bolder than Alexander ...

wiser than Caesar,' gushed the historian Albert Bushnell Hart; 'more sagacious than Napoleon, and more successful than Scipio.'[52] In reality, Washington was ill-experienced to lead America's Continental Army and lost far more battles than he won. It was his resilience and cool head, rather than any innate military genius, that helped secure the United States' independence.

None of this is to deny the genuine achievements of these people. Tesla is still a remarkable scientist, Stravinsky an innovative composer and Washington an accomplished leader. Even Pythagoras, despite the threadbare contemporary accounts we have of him, was clearly charismatic enough to achieve widespread fame in his own lifetime. Nor is this to reject the possibility that individuals can, and do, change the course of history. Most historians today are happy to compromise, arguing that history is neither the sole product of a few great individuals, nor the inevitable consequence of an impersonal force like progress, but a combination of large-scale, long-term processes – economic, demographic, climatic – and the ability of groups and individuals to address, adapt and respond to these processes.

Not only is this approach a better representation of reality, it's a more appealing way of looking at the past. Pythagoras the unrivalled genius is not only a lie but a bore: an unrelatable and unbelievable overachiever. Pythagoras the crackpot cult leader, on the other hand, cuts a far less heroic but much more intriguing figure. What inspired him to develop his doctrine? Did he believe his own hype? And why did he hate beans? The same can be said for history in general. A past full of heroic men gets a little repetitive after the umpteenth unconquered general, visionary artist or valiant statesman. It's the real history of real people – heroes and villains, men and women, failures and successes – that's not only more accurate but far more interesting.

CHAPTER 3

Barbarians, Vandals
and other victims of slander

On a cold, windswept morning in the year 468 CE, at one of the farthest edges of the Roman Empire, a bishop named Hydatius sits down to write an account of the impending apocalypse. In crude and tortuous Latin he sets out to compile 'all the calamities of this wretched age', from the famine and pestilence stalking the Earth to the comets and eclipses haunting the skies. He records strange tales of cockerels crowing at sunset, of blood welling up from the ground and of flocks of sheep mysteriously bursting into flames. In Hydatius' own province of Gallaecia, in north-west Spain, bright green lentils have been seen raining from the sky. And now there appears the surest sign yet of God's wrath: the barbarians.[1]

'The barbarians run wild through Hispania,' writes Hydatius. With grim relentlessness he recounts atrocity after atrocity taking place at the hands of these bloodthirsty savages. 'They find crowds of people of every kind and immediately slaughter them. They plunder the cities. They abduct the young women. They break into the holy churches, tear down and destroy the altars and carry off every holy object. They set fire to any remaining buildings and lay waste to the fields.' The pages of Hydatius' account become monotonous with similar accounts. The bishop must have looked to the end of days – just fourteen years away, according to his calculations – with a sense of relief.[2]

Such pessimism was rife among the Empire's literati during the 4th and 5th centuries, as previously stable frontiers across the Roman world crumbled under the attacks of the 'savage and uncontrollable' barbarians. In Gaul – an area roughly equivalent in size to present-day France – the poet Rutilius numbly observed how neither town nor fortress was 'able to overcome the traps and arms of barbarian fury'. On the eastern frontier, the historian Ammianus reported that 'the realm of savagery was spreading far and wide'. Even in Italy, the very heart of the Empire, the scholar Procopius described how the barbarians 'destroyed all the cities which they captured … and killed anyone who got in their way, both young and old alike, sparing neither women nor children'. There was a growing sense that the once-unassailable Empire was rapidly unravelling. 'As the host of enemies grew stronger,' panicked one military chronicler, 'the power of the Romans was weakened to its very foundations.' Many agreed with Hydatius when he wrote that Rome was 'trapped in desperate straits' and 'about to collapse'.[3]

The situation throughout the Empire had become so hopeless that many also found themselves agreeing with Hydatius in regarding the barbarian invasions as portents of the Second Coming. Some theologians described the barbaric strangers as 'the Scourge of God'; others even identified them as the horsemen of the apocalypse or Apollyon, the Angel of Death. Whatever the interpretation, it was widely agreed that the end was nigh. On the distant island of Britain, which had been abandoned by the Romans and was now besieged by the Saxons, the monk Gildas described a country 'rushing headlong down to hell'.[4] From his bishopric in North Africa, St Augustine, looking out upon a world 'rotting and disintegrating' around him, encouraged his followers to reject the 'earthly city' of Rome in favour of the heavenly City of

God. His pupil Prosper – who had witnessed barbarian invasions first-hand as a young man – summed up the situation with a nihilism typical of the time: 'with sword, plague, starvation, chains, cold and heat – in a thousand ways – a single death snatches off wretched humankind.'[5]

The destruction of Rome at the hands of the barbarians remains one of the most iconic stories in world history. In the space of a single century – from the first breach of the imperial frontiers in 376 CE to the deposition of the last Western Roman Emperor in 476 – a civilisation that had dominated the Mediterranean world for over 600 years was wiped out across much of Europe and North Africa. As various barbarian hordes swept across the Empire, looting and destroying everything in their path, the lights of science, reason and culture went out across Europe. By the time the dust had settled, the survivors found themselves at the grey dawn of the Dark Ages: a thousand-year reign of superstition and ignorance that would only be broken with the rediscovery of Europe's classical heritage during the Renaissance.

It's easy to see why the story has survived so well. The fall of Rome has all the pathos of the Greek tragedies the Romans loved so much: there's the hubris of the decadent Empire, convinced of its own immortality; there's the plight of the innocent citizens, trapped in machinations beyond their control; and then there are the barbarians, surely some of history's greatest villains.

Indeed, the drama has had such staying power that our understanding of the barbarians has hardly shifted in the 1,500 years since Hydatius penned his account of the Empire's final days. Just consider the opprobrium that still drips from the word 'barbarian' or the negative connotations still attached to the various barbarian tribes. The Goths lent their name to anything dark, macabre or violent. The Huns, before being associated with German soldiers during the First World War, were used to refer to any senseless destroyers of beauty. The wanton destruction of the Vandals, meanwhile, was so notorious that the crime of vandalism was named in their honour. Barbarity itself has become a byword for savage cruelty, reserved only for the most brutal or grisly of crimes. In the same week that I wrote this sentence, the following 'barbaric' events were all reported in the news: illegal organ-harvesting in China; reports of female genital mutilation in Scotland; accounts of animal abuse in Yucatan; a terrorist attack which killed 46 police officers in India; a violent sexual assault in Nigeria; the vivisection of dogs in the USA, and the mutilation of an alpaca in Oxfordshire. That's one hell of a legacy for the barbarians.

But is it justified? Were the barbarians really as barbaric as we've been led to believe? Were the Goths gothic and the Vandals vandals? It's only in the past few decades that archaeologists and historians have come to grasp the surprising truth about these people and to challenge the stereotypes heaped upon them. Far from being the villains of the story, the barbarians are in fact the victims of one of biggest smear campaigns in history.

~

Anyone trying to uncover a more nuanced portrait of the barbarians immediately comes up against a number of hurdles. The first is the very concept of 'the barbarians' as a group of people. The classic presentation of Late Antiquity as a monumental show-down between civilisation and barbarism is misleading, as it suggests that non-Roman forces formed some sort of coalition or shared a single identity. In reality, 'barbarian' was an umbrella term used by the Romans to denote anyone who didn't belong to their empire. By the 4th century the word covered a wide range

of very different and often completely unrelated groups. From
northern Europe came Germanic nations such as the Goths,
Vandals, Franks and Saxons. The Eurasian steppe was home to
the nomadic Huns, Avars and Alans. Scattered across the continent were also the Celts, a group that had once dominated Europe
but now found themselves being pushed increasingly to its edges.
Then there were the more obscure tribes – peoples like the Zumi,
the Roxolani and the Hamaxoikoi – who have been largely lost to
history. At no point did these highly diverse groups express any
pan-barbarian identity or solidarity, and they just as often fought
each other as they did Rome.[6]

Adding to the confusion is the fact that these various cultures have bequeathed very few physical remains to posterity. The
Romans, with their penchant for coins, pottery and massive stone
monuments, left an archaeological footprint across almost every
square inch of Europe; the barbarians, with their small wooden
homes and simpler economies, have in many places vanished
without a trace. Archaeologists often have nothing more than
their burial sites to go on, but even these don't necessarily reveal
much about barbarian life. Until recently it was widely assumed,
for instance, that any burial goods found alongside the deceased
were placed in the grave so that they could be used in the afterlife.
That might have been true for the ancient Egyptians, but there's
no evidence European barbarians ever held such beliefs. Likewise,
archaeologists used to believe that the Scandinavian tradition of
placing their dead aboard boats before pushing them out to sea
was to allow the departed to reach Valhalla, until it was realised
that many women – who were barred from the boys-only celestial
banquet hall – also received these prestigious boat burials.[7]

The third and perhaps most daunting obstacle, however, is
the one-sided nature of the information that has come down to us

about the barbarians. It's often said that history is written by the victors. In many instances this is true, and historians can spend lifetimes picking the grains of truth out from the reams of propaganda that make up the bulk of many historic sources. But this rule only works, of course, if the victors can write – and the barbarians had never so much as held a stylus when they first crossed the frontiers of the Roman Empire. Some barbarian groups, like the Huns and Picts, apparently never wrote a single word before fading from the scene.[8] As a result, we're left in the curious situation whereby the history of the end of the classical world has been written by its losers.

And the Romans were incredibly sore losers. A civilisation which had sustained itself on centuries of military victories did not accept defeat gracefully. Consequently, the majority of our sources of information about the barbarians are mired in an anti-barbarian bias that borders on hatred. By the 5th century, when it was clear that the Empire was in serious jeopardy, Roman animosity to these 'abominable people' had reached fever pitch.[9] The barbarians, they tell us, were stupid and stubborn, cruel and savage; greedy, gluttonous drunks with fierce manners and ferocious tempers. They were so treacherous and untrustworthy that it was 'more painful to be their friends … than their enemies'.[10] Physical descriptions of them verged on the inhuman. They were filthy and gave off an unbearable stench – the Avars of the Eurasian steppe were 'unkempt', 'dirty' and 'unsightly'; the Cantabrians of Spain bathed in their own urine, and the Slavs of Eastern Europe were 'at all times covered in filth'. They were enormous, hairy brutes, 'so monstrously ugly and misshapen that one might take them for two-legged beasts'.[11]

The savagery of these classical authors is a little astonishing, even today. But it wasn't just writers: hatred towards barbarian peoples was a borderline obsession for many Romans, working its way into many aspects of Roman life. The murder and subjugation of barbarian people was a favourite theme of imperial artwork, appearing on columns, arches, reliefs, statues and frescoes. The victory column of the emperor Marcus Aurelius – who's today celebrated as a noble-minded philosopher-king – celebrates the beheading of barbarian warriors, the enslavement of their wives and children and the destruction of their homes. The gravestone of a Roman soldier discovered near the English town of Cirencester shows the deceased trampling a barbarian to death under his horse. Even Roman currency gave vent to this vitriol: one of the most common copper coins in the Empire during the 3rd century depicts a Roman soldier impaling a barbarian. The accompanying inscription reads: 'the return of the good times'.[12]

Attempting to navigate past the prejudice and propaganda isn't easy. Classical works cast such a long shadow in academia that, until recently, historians still studied the collapse of the Roman Empire through the apocalyptic lens of Hydatius and his fellow Christian doomsayers. Edward Gibbon, who spent seventeen years writing his 4,000-page *History of the Decline and Fall of the Roman Empire*, described the barbarians as 'voracious and turbulent' and 'impatient to ravish the fruits of industry', and summarised Rome's collapse as 'the triumph of barbarism and superstition'.[13] Even today, when historians have long since abandoned notions of divine wrath, there's still a tendency to describe the barbarian incursions as 'waves', 'floods', 'deluges' and 'advancing tides', as if they represented an irrepressible force of nature that the Romans were hopeless to defend against.

However, different interpretations are now making themselves heard. With the advent of postcolonial studies in recent decades, and with a renewed scrutiny of the historical evidence, there have been clear signs of change in how many historians look at both the Roman Empire and its barbarian foes. 'A postcolonial approach allows us to critique previous approaches to interpreting the past,' explains Nicky Garland, an archaeologist and specialist on Roman Britain. 'Too often western historians and archaeologists have interpreted "other" groups in a colonial way – as less civilised, as the conquered, or as inferior. We need to better understand the context in which our current interpretations were created and spread.'

So how trustworthy are the Roman descriptions of the barbarians? Let's start with the things the Romans got right: it seems that plenty of barbarians really were big and hairy. Classical authors regularly wrote about the 'huge bodies' of the Germanic warriors they encountered, and – allowing for a little poetic licence on the Romans' part – archaeological evidence does seem to back them up, suggesting that the average Germanic barbarian was at least an inch or two taller than their Roman counterpart. We can also be fairly confident about the barbarians' famed hairiness, thanks to the sheer number of imperial chroniclers who wrote about it. The Romans – always a conservative bunch when it came to hairstyles (they didn't even have a word for moustache) – were fascinated and a little scared by the variety of coiffures sported by the various barbarians they encountered. When the Avars first arrived in Constantinople from Central Asia, an eyewitness reported that 'the whole city ran to watch them' and catch a glimpse of their long, braided hair. When a particularly hirsute band of Germanic barbarians settled in northern Italy, clean-shaven Romans simply called them the Long Beards; over time they became the Lombards, and their new home in Italy became Lombardy.[14]

As for the notorious barbarian 'stench', however, there's good reason to think this was a bit of imperial slander. For one thing, the Roman word for soap, *sapo*, made its way into Latin via the Germanic languages of the northern barbarians. The Vandals' love of hygiene was actually a source of ridicule in the ancient world, and Romans would mock their decadent habit of 'indulging in baths ... every day'.[15] In all likelihood, the seething metropolis of Rome – with its near-total lack of rubbish collection or sewer system capable of handling human waste – was a far more unhygienic place than any barbarian settlement.[16]

Other evidence also suggests that the life of a typical barbarian wasn't one of unremitting violence or savagery. We now know that music, singing and poetry were often important aspects of barbarian culture, and that barbarians expected their leaders to demonstrate musical as well as military skill. They were also keen artists and master metalworkers, and their gold jewellery was highly prized even among the Romans. When the imperial statesman Cassiodorus received a sword from the Gothic king Theodoric he marvelled at its construction, remarking that it could have been the work of Vulcan, the Roman god of the forge, himself. It's also known that barbarian societies were far from lawless. Surviving examples of barbarian legal codes are not only surprisingly detailed – a Frankish code of law from the early 6th century has twenty clauses covering different kinds of pig theft – but emphasised punishment through fines and compensation rather than violence. Back in the 1st century CE, when the Roman establishment felt more confident in their superiority over the barbarians, even they were willing to admit that their neighbours were 'kind and hospitable' and 'in no respect base or evil-doers'.[17]

Another misconception that needs dispelling is the notion of the barbarians as mysterious strangers streaming over the imperial borders. With the notable exceptions of the Huns and Avars, who caused so much excitement upon their arrival in Constantinople, many of the barbarian groups who overran imperial frontiers in the 4th and 5th centuries were already well known to the Romans. As the historian Walter Goffart writes: 'the barbarian invasions definitely did not happen to an unsuspecting empire, as though mysterious beings had landed from outer space. On the contrary, Rome had always had warlike tribesmen at its gates and had centuries of experience in dealing with them.'[18] In the late 2nd century BCE the Roman Republic fought a gruelling twelve-year war against the Germanic tribes of the Cimbri and Teutones. In 9 CE the Empire lost three entire legions – about 12,000 men – to an ambush attack by the Germanic Cherusci tribe, delivering the Romans one of their greatest ever military defeats. In the 250s, when the Empire was suffering from a barrage of internal crises, it faced attacks by sea from the Goths and by land from the Franks.

Romans and barbarians didn't just meet on the battlefield, however. There were extensive commercial links between the two, with the Romans trading pottery, glass, wine, crockery and occasionally weapons with various barbarian nations in exchange for cattle, fish, salt, slaves and amber. The fact that the word for wine in almost every European language, including English, can be traced back to the Latin *vinum* reveals the extent of the Roman wine trade. It has even been suggested that Norse legends of mysterious metalworking dwarves are a distant memory of the Romans and their high-quality swords which they once traded with Germanic tribes.[19]

With trade came integration. The Empire was home to barbarian slaves, merchants, soldiers, politicians and even imperial advisers. Perhaps surprisingly, the Roman army became especially dependent on barbarian troops to sustain its numbers, to the point where 'the barbarians' was slang for the army in parts of the Roman world. Even the Huns, the arch-barbarians of antiquity, were recruited into the imperial army on occasion, where they are reported to have fought with great loyalty. A significant number of barbarian soldiers rose through the ranks to become generals, and one – Claudius Silvanus – even proclaimed himself emperor in 355 CE (although he was murdered just 28 days later).[20]

Centuries of contact, trade and intermarriage between these two worlds blurred the lines between Roman and barbarian. Barbarians could become Roman – and Romans could turn barbarian. Barbarian fashion became all the rage in the later Empire, with young Roman men imitating their uncivilised neighbours by growing their hair and beards long and adopting barbarian-style clothes. Imperial authorities grew so concerned about this 'senseless fashion' that in 399 they made it a crime to wear trousers – considered a sure sign of barbarism – anywhere in the city of Rome. A further law from 416 expressly forbade any Roman man from growing his hair long or sporting clothes made from animal skins.[21] Barbarians may not have been popular, but they were an inseparable part of the late Roman world.

~

Admittedly, the rehabilitation of the barbarians can only go so far. As much as they may have appreciated poetry and beauty regimes, it remains a fact that between 376 and 476 CE the barbarians subjected the Roman Empire to repeated military invasions. The first decade of the 5th century was a particularly bloody period, with violent barbarian incursions in Italy, Gaul, Spain, Britain and Central Europe, which ended with the Empire forever relinquishing control of Britain and parts of the Iberian Peninsula it had held for centuries. It would be irresponsible to dismiss the many accounts of barbarian violence from the 4th and 5th century as simply products of anti-barbarian prejudice.[22]

Could the barbarians be barbaric? Absolutely. Warfare formed an integral part of many barbarian nations' identities, and barbarian warriors did indeed kill, pillage and rape while on campaign. The Gauls had an unpleasant habit of nailing the decapitated heads of their enemies to trees and doors. The Franks threw women and children into the River Po during one 6th-century battle. But were the barbarians particularly violent or immoral by the standards of Late Antiquity? No, and certainly not when compared to the Romans themselves. We like to think of the Roman world as an oasis of civilisation and reason in a desert of barbarism – an image they themselves tirelessly promoted – but Rome had its own undeniable flair for barbarity. This was, after all, a civilisation that decapitated ostriches for sport and crucified dogs for religion. (The moral nadir arguably came during the reign of the deranged emperor Commodus, who, believing himself to be the reincarnation of Hercules, forced amputees into the Colosseum, armed them with sponges and proceeded to club them to death.) The Roman world excelled in the quantity as well as the quality of its violence. An estimated 3 million gladiators were slaughtered in its amphitheatres and a further 3 million on its battlefields. A contemporary of Julius Caesar suggested that the general be tried for war crimes following his conquest of Gaul, in which an estimated 700,000 lost their lives.[23] As the historian Michael Grant writes: 'extremely few epochs of human history ... have achieved cruelty on a scale as numerically lavish as ancient Rome.'[24]

Violence formed the backbone of the Roman world. The Empire and its much-lauded 'Pax Romana', lest we forget, was forged through military conquest and maintained only with the presence of an enormous army.[25] The Romans were well aware of this and made no effort to hide the brutality of their wars or their disregard for their enemies. The 3rd-century emperor Probus boasted that he had slaughtered 400,000 Germanic barbarians in his campaign of 278 CE. His predecessor Trajan destroyed the barbarian kingdom of Dacia, in present-day Romania, simply because he wanted to be treated to a triumphal military procession through Rome. Roman panegyrics revelled in the death of the 'despicable' barbarians: an account of the Roman war against the Bructeri tribe gleefully relates how so many captured soldiers were sent to the amphitheatres that the lions grew too tired to kill them all. A similar report, of the battle of Fiesole in 406, recounts how the victorious Romans enslaved so many barbarians that 'whole herds of men were sold ... as if they were the cheapest of cattle'.[26] As the Caledonian chief Calgacus remarked of the Empire: 'to robbery, murder and outrage they give the lying name of government, and where they make a wasteland they call it peace.'[27]

Evocations of the Roman world as a haven of reason and rationality are also overly generous, ignoring as they do the deeply religious and superstitious character of most Romans. Roman farmers believed they could avert a hailstorm by holding a mirror up to the sky and showing a threatening cloud its own reflection. The pagan priests of Rome were made to promise, on pain of death, never to reveal the name of the city's guardian god for fear that the deity might be tempted to join Rome's enemies if they could call its name. Before a battle, military commanders would consult a roost of sacred chickens that were brought along especially: if the chickens ate the food given to them, all was well; but if they refused, flapped their wings or flew away, engaging in hostilities was considered an inauspicious move. (The word 'inauspicious' actually comes from the Latin word for bird-watching, *auspicia*.)[28]

Classical condemnations of the barbarians lose much of their moral punch when we remember the brutality and ignorance of the Roman world. Barbarian soldiers were forcing people into slavery? So were Roman troops, who supplied the Empire with so many slaves that the Latin equivalent of the expression 'cheap as chips' was the far more sinister 'Sardinians for sale'.[29] The barbarians were torturing Romans citizens? So were the imperial authorities, who regularly resorted to torture in order to punish or extract confessions, and did so to a greater extent than their barbarian foes. Roman law even allowed children to be tortured if they were thought to have committed treason against the emperor.[30] Hypocritical classical writers praised the Roman forces when they employed surprise attacks and cut off enemy supplies, yet lambasted it as 'deceitful' when barbarian armies used the exact same tactics against the Romans. They applauded slaughter and destruction as victory when committed by the Romans but decried it as barbaric when committed against the Empire. Accounts of Roman 'conquests' from the 1st and 2nd centuries use almost identical language to later reports of barbarian 'atrocities' from the 4th and 5th centuries – the only difference being, of course, that the Romans have since become the victims rather than the perpetrators.

The Vandals and their barbarian brethren are by no means the only victims of slander in history. Romans may have directed much of their animosity abroad, but they were more than willing to sling mud at each other, even their emperors. The emperor Caligula was subject to a particularly muscular smear campaign following his assassination in 41 CE, which saw his name struck from monuments, his head removed from statues (not as violent as you might think: Roman statues were designed to have detachable heads) and his memory besmirched with rumours of unhinged debauchery that survive to this day. Caligula was certainly a terrible ruler, but there's no evidence that he made his horse a consul or that he enjoyed sexual relations with his sister Drusilla, as is still widely believed.[31]

The reputation of Emperor Nero has fared little better. If there's one thing we know about Nero, it's that he fiddled while Rome burned. Except he didn't. For one thing, fiddles didn't exist in ancient Rome and wouldn't be invented for another millennium. For another, it's recorded that Nero personally took charge of the firefighting as soon as news of the blaze reached him. Even the writer Tacitus, who hated the emperor with a passion, felt compelled to praise his actions, noting how he opened up the imperial gardens to house the homeless and insisted his bodyguards took part in relief work rather than stay to protect him. Following Nero's death, however, rumours quickly spread among his many enemies that the egomaniacal emperor had deliberately started the fire in order to clear space for a bigger palace, or that he had wasted time during the firefighting to deliver a dramatic oration about the fall of Troy. These rumours would find an eager audience among early Christian writers, who – despising Nero for his brutal suppression of Christianity – ensured their survival down the centuries.[32]

The dark art of spin has continued unabated ever since, with the result that many of the ideas we hold about historical figures are the products of prejudice and propaganda rather than honest works of history. Smear campaigns have sometimes been so successful that they have come to completely define their victims. Perhaps the most widely known 'fact' about Catherine the Great, for instance, is that the empress of Russia died while trying to have sex with a horse. The story is completely untrue – she died of natural causes and with no horse in sight – and appears to have been fabricated by political rivals purely to soil her reputation.[33] Today it's still common to describe short, domineering men as suffering from 'Napoleon syndrome', even though Napoleon himself measured about five foot five: average height for the time. The legend of his diminutive stature appears to date from 1803, when the British cartoonist James Gillray drew a portrait of 'Little Boney' throwing a temper tantrum. Other satirists quickly picked up the trope, and the French emperor has been shrinking in the popular imagination ever since.[34] (The legend of Hitler's undescended testicle, in contrast, was long thought to be pure fiction until the rediscovery of the Fuhrer's long-lost medical records in 2015, which showed that the rumour – although indeed fabricated purely to mock Hitler – happened to be absolutely on the ball.)[35]

In fact, the urge to vilify is so widespread and deeply ingrained that we often don't notice its handiwork. You could probably construct a reasonably accurate history of English foreign relations solely from the insults that litter the language, whether it's the many slurs against the French and Dutch (both long-time political rivals) or the seemingly inexhaustible capacity of the Scots and Welsh – both traditionally seen as junior partners in Great Britain – to function as the butt of jokes. Even today the English will speak of drunkenness as 'Dutch courage' and truancy as 'French leave' (which, if you're French, is called 'English leave'). The long-standing anti-Irish sentiment in England, meanwhile, is betrayed by the word 'hooligan', which derives from the Irish surname Houlihan – replacing the earlier, equally xenophobic term 'street Arab'.[36]

Then there are words which, like 'vandal', have been shunted by long-standing animosity and suspicion from neutral descriptors to terms of abuse. When I described the barbarians as one of history's greatest villains earlier in this chapter, I was actually indulging in a spot of class prejudice: the word 'villain' originally denoted a peasant in medieval England, but centuries of snobbery has loaded it with unpleasant, even evil, connotations (a similar process appears to be happening to the word 'peasant' today). Likewise, if you accuse someone of being boorish or churlish, you're actually accusing them of acting like boors and churls, two other medieval terms for agricultural workers that have similarly suffered at the hands of the upper classes. Etymology also hints at society's deeply entrenched sexism: terms implying sexual brazenness, such as 'wench' and 'hussy', originally meant nothing more than a female servant and housewife, respectively. Spinsters, meanwhile, were simply women who spun wool for a living before the word came to refer to unnerving unmarried women.

As unkind as these various insults are, however, they pale in comparison with the monumental smear campaign against the barbarians. Even the very name 'barbarian' has an unsavoury origin: the word began life as little more than a xenophobic slur used by the ancient Greeks. The very first barbarians were simply any people who didn't speak the various Ancient Greek dialects, such as Attic, Doric and Ionic. Just as we might dismiss an incomprehensible language today by saying 'it's all Greek to me', so the ancient Greeks mocked other tongues with the meaningless sounds *bar bar*. And so speakers of 'barbar' – whether it was the Egyptians, Persians or Scythians – became barbarians.[37] (The exact same mechanism gave rise to the term 'Hottentot', an old and now pejorative label given by Dutch settlers to the Khoikhoi people of southern Africa, which mocked the stuttering quality of their language.)

It wasn't long before the word 'barbarian' soured into something much more degrading. It became a term of abuse, designating not just someone who spoke a foreign language but a lower class of human altogether. The philosopher Aristotle famously declared the barbarian to be 'a slave by nature', since they lacked the ability to think rationally like the Greeks.[38] As with so much of the Greek world, this concept of the barbarian was adopted by the Romans, who liberally slapped the label on any foreigners they could find – including, ironically, the Greeks. The natural inferiority of the barbarian provided the Romans with a convenient justification for their burgeoning imperialism, which they presented not as an act of aggression or greed but as a paternalistic 'civilising' mission. 'The Romans took over many nations that were naturally savage,' wrote the 1st-century geographer Strabo, 'and not only brought them into communication with other peoples, but also taught them how to live under government.'[39]

With the European rediscovery of classical writers like Strabo in the 15th century, European scholars and explorers quickly assumed the mantle of civilisation for themselves, which they contrasted with the supposed backward and inferior natures of the various non-Europeans they encountered. The natives of the Americas were 'barbarians' whose language was nothing more than 'outrageous gibberish'; the inhabitants of Southeast Asia were 'lawless' and 'inhumane'.[40] The 'barbarism and savagery' of the native North Africans is still reflected in the name Berber, which evolved from the barbarian label.[41] 'The Greek and Roman division of the world into civilised and barbarian has been extremely influential on later European and western worldviews from the early Renaissance onwards,' Amar Acheraïou, a postcolonial scholar based in Montreal, tells me.

And just as it had served Roman imperialists, the need to 'humanise barbarism' provided one of the greatest theoretical justifications for Europe's rapidly expanding colonial ventures.[42]

'The division between civilisation and barbarism formed the backbone of colonial expansion,' explains Acheraïou. 'These imperial conquests needed a moral validation, and the classical idea of the barbarian provided that. It was very common for politicians from the 15th to the 20th centuries to describe colonial subjects as barbarians in order to justify imperialism and the European civilizing mission.'

In the 16th century, a Spanish theologian named Juan Ginés de Sepúlveda revived Aristotle's 'natural slave' theory to justify the genocide of indigenous Americans at the hands of Spanish conquistadors. As he explained to King Charles I of Spain, the indigenous inhabitants of the New World were irrational brutes; it was 'in their own interests to be placed under the authority of civilised and virtuous princes or nations, so that they may learn ... better morals, worthier customs and a more civilised way of life'.[43] In 19th-century Russia, imperial expansion and aggressive cultural assimilation of the 'savage' Kazakhs, Tatars and Caucasian Muslims was justified as a 'civilising mission' against 'Asian barbarism'.[44] At the turn of the 20th century, the imperialist Cecil Rhodes – who was fascinated by the Roman Empire – used a similar tactic to justify British expansion in southern Africa. 'The natives are children,' he told the House of Assembly in Cape Town. 'They are just emerging from barbarism ... To us annexation was an obligation, whereas to the natives it will be a positive relief, for they will be freed from the cauldron of barbarian atrocities.'[45] The logic remains unchanged from Strabo's 2,000-year-old apology for Roman imperialism.

The language of European imperialism may have receded, but the concept of the barbarian remains firmly entrenched in our minds. As those headlines at the beginning of the chapter demonstrated, the modern world has no shortage of barbarians willing

to commit barbaric acts. More troubling, barbarian ghosts continue to haunt our views of strangers, foreigners and those from
different cultures. Following the 9/11 attacks on the World Trade
Centre in New York, for instance, Muslims around the world were
repeatedly stereotyped as 'uncivilised' and 'barbaric' – typically
in contrast to Western, Christian civilisation – regardless of how
vocally individual Muslims and Islamic groups renounced terrorism. Tellingly, foreign terrorists were more likely to be described
in the media as barbaric than domestic ones.[46] This prejudice
has seeped into Western views of majority Muslim countries and
their inhabitants. 'We need only look at the way many people in
Europe and the US react to refugees to realise that the ancient
fears of the barbarians are still rife among us,' remarks Acheraïou.
Refugees trying to enter the USA, for example, have been explicitly compared to the barbarians who entered and overran the
Roman Empire, with the clear implication that the West is heading for a similar fate to Rome. British historian Niall Ferguson has
likewise compared 21st-century Europe, 'decadent in its shopping
malls and sports stadiums' and awash with 'outsiders who have
coveted its wealth without renouncing their ancestral faith', to
the licentious late Roman Empire, warning starkly: 'this is exactly
how civilisations fall.'[47]

~

Is it really, though? Equipped with more nuanced interpretations
of the barbarians, other historians have been able to gain a new
perspective on the barbarian 'destruction' of the Roman Empire.
For starters, it needs to be stressed that half the Empire never even
fell to the barbarians. Back in 286 CE the emperor Diocletian,
believing the Empire too big to govern from a single capital, split
it into distinct administrative units. What would become the

Eastern Roman or Byzantine Empire, centred around the 'New Rome' of Constantinople, withstood the barbarian invasions of the 4th and 5th centuries and continued to function for a further *millennium* after the Western Empire fell, finally succumbing to the Ottomans only in 1453.

Even in the Western Empire, where various barbarian armies did successfully overthrow Roman rule, the situation was far more complex than most classical writers would have you believe. Take the Gothic crossing of the imperial frontier in 376 CE. This event, culminating in a decisive Gothic victory over the Romans at the battle of Adrianople (today in the European chunk of Turkey) two years later, is widely considered to mark the beginning of the end for the Roman Empire. What's sometimes omitted from the story, however, is that the Goths entered the Empire in 376 not as invaders but refugees. They had been forced from their homeland around the Black Sea by the Huns, who – for reasons historians still don't fully understand – left Central Asia in the late 4th century to embark upon a period of aggressive expansion westward into Europe. Nor was there anything surreptitious about the Goths' crossing of the frontier: hearing of their plight, the Roman Emperor Valens invited the Goths to settle on Roman land, even promising them food supplies.

The goodwill quickly evaporated, however. Barbarians who had been denied entry into the Empire forced their way in anyway, and when supplies emptied they took to raiding in order to secure food. The situation was exacerbated by the Roman officials tasked with overseeing the settlement, who treated the refugees with little more than contempt. When food supplies ran low, the Romans reportedly offered dog meat to the barbarian families on the condition that they sold their children into Roman slavery (the going rate was one dog per child). There were reports of Roman commanders forcing refugees to work as agricultural labourers or sex slaves. With tensions flaring and the Goths looking increasingly hostile, Emperor Valens, perhaps regretting his previous hospitality, decided to nip the matter in the bud by defeating the Goths in battle. On 8 August 378, outside the town of Adrianople, his army assembled. The Emperor had requested more troops to bulk up his forces, but for reasons lost to history decided to engage the Goths before they arrived. It proved a fatal error: by the end of the day, two-thirds of the Roman forces had either fled or been killed by the Goths. Valens himself was killed as he tried to flee. Roman mismanagement and contempt had managed to turn a migrant crisis into a full-blown military disaster, all within the space of two years.[48]

In a way, the Gothic victory at Adrianople was a fluke. If Valens had waited for his reinforcements things might have turned out very differently. Talk of waves and floods and deluges of barbarians gives the impression that the Empire was submerged under endless attacks by hordes of barbarian warriors pouring continually over the frontier. In reality, however, barbarian armies rarely topped 25,000 men – a figure dwarfed by the more than half a million troops in the Roman army at the time. And compared to the frighteningly efficient Roman legions the barbarians weren't even particularly outstanding warriors: with the exception of Adrianople, barbarian forces failed to win a single major battle against Roman forces during the entire period of their 'invasion'. Perhaps aware of their military disadvantages, barbarian leaders often favoured diplomatic rather than violent solutions to their disputes with Rome.[49]

In light of such information, few, if any, historians now lay the blame for the fall of Rome solely at the feet of the barbarians. After all, barbarian invasions in earlier centuries hadn't pushed the

Empire into terminal decline; so what made the 4th and 5th centuries different? The answer appears to lie with Rome itself. By the late 4th century the Roman Empire was long past its prime, creaking and groaning under centuries of economic mismanagement and increasing political instability. The majority of its inhabitants, far from indulging in the bacchanalian splurges the last days of Rome are famous for, were suffering from shrinking freedoms and crushing levels of taxation required to feed Rome's enormous military machine.[50] Especially damaging was the problem of imperial usurpation, which had become so endemic – and the conflicts it sparked so destructive and destabilising – that it presented a greater threat to the Empire's political stability in its final century than even the barbarian incursions.[51] The relative danger of these two hazards can be gauged by the fact that Valens was one of just three Roman Emperors to be killed by barbarians (and one of those was by accident), whereas somewhere in the region of 25 met their end at the hands of usurpers.[52] By the 5th century a Western Roman Emperor could enjoy an average life expectancy of just seven years once they donned the imperial purple toga, with death invariably the result of unnatural causes.

For many imperial subjects, life in the unstable late Empire had become so oppressive that the prospect of barbarian rule was regarded not with horror but with a sense of relief, with more than a few going so far as to openly welcome barbarian victories against Rome. 'Everyone was calling on the barbarians and imploring their aid,' recalled the Greek historian Zosimus.[53] The Roman city of Nicopolis willingly handed themselves over to the Goths and 'to freedom', considering it 'cowardice' to stay in the despotic Empire.[54] Writing in the 440s, the priest Salvian described how peasants in Gaul were fleeing their hated landlords and tax collectors by joining the barbarians, preferring 'to live as freemen under

an outward form of captivity than as captives under an appearance of liberty'.[55] There are also numerous accounts of Roman
conspirators serving as local guides for invading barbarian armies,
and even of whole companies of Roman soldiers deserting to join
their former enemies. A 4th-century merchant called Antonius
was so disgusted by Roman corruption that he defected to the
Persian Empire, complete with sensitive military information, and
became one of the Persian king's foremost advisers. Similar defec-
tions allowed both the Bulgars and the Avars to learn the secrets
of building Roman siege engines.[56]

Pro-barbarian sympathies played a key role in the most iconic
event in the demise of the Roman Empire: the Goths' sack of
Rome in 410. If the battle of Adrianople had come as a shock, then
the sack of Rome – the first time in 800 years that the Eternal City
had fallen to outside forces – shook the Empire to its core. Such an
event was widely considered impossible; only a few years earlier
an imperial spin doctor named Claudian had boldly declared that
'there will never be an end to the power of Rome.'[57]

And yet the writing was on the wall, had the Romans cared to
look. Just two years earlier the Romans had launched a savage and
unprovoked pogrom against Germanic inhabitants in the Italian
peninsula, which saw Roman soldiers brutally murder the wives
and children of Germanic troops serving in the Roman army.
When news of the atrocity reached the husbands, some 30,000
of them led a mass desertion of the Roman army and joined the
Goths, who were invading Italy at the time and making their way
towards Rome. Not content with having shot themselves in only
one foot, the Romans then refused the Gothic leader Alaric's offer
to 'make peace on reasonable terms', as he put it, even when the
barbarians agreed to drop their earlier demand that Rome cede
its Adriatic provinces. On top of this, as the Gothic army reached

the gates of Rome, the city's slaves escaped their bondage to join the barbarians and turn on their own city.[58] The city's downfall was almost entirely of its own making.

Fifteen hundred years of retelling has inflated the 410 sack of Rome into an event of earth-shattering proportions, but beyond the symbolism it was of practically no military or political significance. By 410 Rome wasn't even the capital of the Roman Empire; that privilege had been moved to Milan in 286 and then Ravenna in 402, and both cities had increasingly been seen as the junior partner to Constantinople in the east. Throughout the century leading up to the sack of Rome, emperors rarely bothered to even visit the city.[59] What's more, the sack itself was a fairly restrained affair by ancient standards. It only lasted three days, for one thing (compare that to the six-month destruction of Carthage at the hands of the Romans). Moreover, the soldiers who entered the city, far from acting with 'licentious fury', as Gibbon wrote, were on strict orders from their Christian commander Alaric not to touch the basilicas of St Peter and St Paul nor to harm the many Romans who had sought shelter in them. As a result, few people were killed and relatively few buildings were destroyed – Alaric, after listening to the pleas of the clergy, spared Rome the customary fire that typically accompanied ancient sackings. Consequently, the sack of Rome quickly faded from memory once the initial shock had passed. Within a few years the citizens of Rome were carrying on with their lives as if 'nothing had happened', as one contemporary account reported.[60]

The reserve shown by the barbarian forces during the sack of Rome suggests that we should take the apocalyptic writings of Hydatius and others with a hefty pinch of salt. Far from seeking to destroy the Roman world, many barbarian rulers worked hard to uphold it in the lands they took control of: maintaining the imperial administration, promoting religious tolerance and preserving Roman law. The more ambitious ones among them even attempted to restore the Empire's lost grandeur, preserving ancient monuments and building new ones. Theodoric, a Goth who ruled the Italian peninsula and the Balkans from 493 to 526, was an enthusiastic patron of the arts and oversaw the largest programme of construction the peninsula had seen in more than a century.[61] The Vandal king Thrasamund, a lover of poetry who spent his spare time debating theology with the African bishop St Fulgentius, commissioned the construction of an enormous bath house complex in North Africa – perhaps sparking the Vandals' reputation for indulgent baths.[62] It's clear that these kings saw themselves as the heirs, not the vanquishers, of the Roman Empire. King Theodoric's ancestor, the Gothic leader Ataulf, made a point of dressing in Roman clothes. Theodoric himself implored his subjects to 'cast off barbarism' and adopt 'the morals of toga'.[63] The sole surviving portrait of the king would be – were it not for the bowl cut and moustache – difficult to distinguish from earlier depictions of Roman Emperors.

As a result, it would have been tricky for many 5th-century Romans to tell the difference between life under the last Western Roman Emperors and under the barbarian kings who initially succeeded them. Historians have traditionally attached great significance to the year 476, when the last Western Roman Emperor was deposed and the Roman Empire vanished from maps of Europe. However, after centuries of internecine usurpations and crumbling imperial authority, the office of Emperor meant so little that the event attracted little notice at the time (the emperor in question, Romulus Augustulus, was a teenage stooge who had held the throne for less than a year). As the historian Edward James concludes: 'it was in fact perfectly easy for most people in the former Western Empire not to notice that anything had changed in 476.'[64]

~

Of course, the Roman world did fade from Europe over time. A continent fractured into competing barbarian kingdoms simply lacked the central organisation, resources or manpower to maintain the levels of industry and wealth that the Romans had achieved. Despite the best efforts of leaders like Theodoric and Thrasamund, the centuries following the establishment of barbarian kingdoms saw industry shrivel and trade routes run dry across much of Europe and North Africa. Homemade crockery replaced professional, mass-produced homeware. Timber and thatch replaced stones and tiles. Coinage disappeared and barter once again became the main form of exchange. Large-scale agricultural production diminished and the population declined dramatically across Europe.[65]

As significant as the decline was, it remains difficult to say whether the barbarians ought to be blamed for the collapse of the Roman Empire, seeing as the Empire didn't so much collapse as gradually subside. As the archaeologist Bryan Ward-Perkins puts it: 'there was no single moment, not even a single century of collapse.'[66] Arguably the curtain finally closed on the classical world in 751, when the Lombards captured Ravenna; or in 1204, when the Franks briefly took Constantinople; or even in 1282, when the Welsh kingdom of Gwynedd was conquered by the English army of Edward I – making it the last portion of the old Roman Empire to fall to barbarians.

Certainly, the world didn't come crashing to a close in the year 482, as Hydatius solemnly predicted. And yet the apocalyptic interpretation of the 5th century has stayed with us ever since.

Moreover, the Roman division of the world into civilisation and barbarism has fundamentally shaped the way people interpret their own times, from the Age of Exploration to the Scramble for Africa, right down to the present day. We still look at the world – and at each other – through the lens of civilisation and barbarity handed down to us by the Romans.

The story of Rome usually ends here, with the barbarians triumphant and Europe sinking into the Dark Ages. But that was just in the West. It was a different story altogether in the East. There, with the Byzantine Empire set to continue for another thousand years after the fall of the Western Roman Emperors, Greek scholars worked hard to preserve the classical knowledge that was slowly fading from Europe. They were joined in their task by a barbarian people, the Arabs, and together they sparked an academic renaissance that would one day light up the whole world. And it's there we turn to next.

CHAPTER 4

Light in the Dark Ages

'In this disastrous epoch we will see the human spirit descend rapidly from the height to which it had been raised, and ignorance follow after it: ferocity in one place, refined cruelty in another, and corruption and perfidy everywhere. Superstitious impostures are the only characteristic of men, intolerance their only morality.'[1] So wrote the French philosopher Marie-Jean-Antoine-Nicolas de Caritat, better known to the world as the Marquis de Condorcet. The subject of his scorn? The Dark Ages, of course.

Condorcet was by no means alone in his contempt for the centuries which followed the fall of the Western Roman Empire. Many of his contemporaries in Enlightenment Europe shared his hatred for this 'miserable age'. For the mathematician Jean le Rond d'Alembert, it was nothing but a 'long interval of ignorance', in which the world forgot the cultural and philosophical heights of the classical era. For Voltaire, it was the 'infancy of mankind', a time when all art was either crude or non-existent. 'Men sang, but knew nothing of music,' he lamented. 'They versified, but knew nothing of poetry. Speaking and writing existed, but eloquence was unknown.'[2]

Nor was there anything particularly new about the Marquis' dislike of the post-Roman world. The concept of the Dark Ages can be traced back to the 14th-century Italian poet Petrarch, who devoted much of his literary talent to contrasting the 'pure radiance' of ancient Rome with the 'darkness' of his own time. The past millennium had been nothing but a 'lamentable story', he mourned, in which the bright day of the Roman Republic had descended into a 'night of chaos' populated only by 'sterile-minded and wretched men' – Petrarch himself excepted, of course.[3]

It proved to be one of the most influential ideas in history. Even today, some seven centuries after Petrarch first penned his diatribes against the age of darkness, it's still widely accepted that the demise of the Roman Empire plunged the world into a thousand years of ignorance, fear and superstition, broken only when men like Petrarch began to rediscover the forgotten knowledge of the classical world.

There's certainly no denying that life could be especially grim in the centuries that followed the break-up of the Western Roman Empire. Even once the anti-barbarian bias is swept away it's clear that the collapse of the imperial economy led to food shortages and dramatic drops in population across Europe. Abandoned villas, overgrown farms and ghost towns littered the continent. For a time it may even have been literally dark: there are numerous reports from the year 536 CE of what sounds like a nuclear winter – perhaps the result of a volcanic eruption or meteorite strike – when, for eighteen months, the sun shone across much of the northern hemisphere with a feeble bluish light that soured the wine and killed the crops.

It's also true that classical learning in the West suffered following the decline of Rome. As the Roman network of roads and bridges fell into disrepair, scholars found themselves cut off from one another and Europe's various barbarian kingdoms struggled to uphold the levels of classical education they had inherited. Household names like Plato and Aristotle slowly sank into obscurity as classical texts were lost or no longer copied as often as they once were. In the remote former province of Britannia, adrift in the North Sea, literacy all but vanished for well over a century. What's more, the schools that did survive were now firmly in the hands of the Christian clergy, many of whom were openly hostile to the pagan knowledge of their classical ancestors. 'What has Athens got to do with Jerusalem?' asked Tertullian, an early Christian theologian.[4] St Cyprian, a 3rd-century bishop of Carthage, was so ashamed of his former life as a teacher of rhetoric that he vowed to never again quote a pagan poet or orator. The resulting dearth of written material led the 16th-century historian Caesar Baronius to coin the term 'Dark Age' to reflect the ensuing centuries' 'want of writers'.[5]

There are limits to this interpretation of the early medieval world, however. If we focus solely on the struggles of Europe, we find ourselves at a loss to explain how this 'age of ignorance' could also have witnessed the preservation of classical knowledge, the establishment of universities or the invention of algebra. Where did such intelligence and ingenuity come from? To answer this apparent conundrum we need to turn our attention east, to the civilisations of Byzantium and Islam, where the notion that the world was enveloped in 'a period of barbaric darkness' quickly becomes untenable.[6] Step out of the shadow of the Western Roman Empire and the Dark Ages were very bright indeed.

Our journey east begins in the Roman Empire – but not the Empire of Rome, Gaul and Britannia. We're in the Eastern Roman Empire, a vast administrative unit wrapped around the eastern half of the Mediterranean, from Greece and the Balkan peninsula through Asia Minor, the Levant and Egypt. This unit emerged from the political reforms of Emperor Diocletian, who managed

to restore stability to the turbulent Empire in 286 CE by introducing Eastern and Western co-emperors – with Diocletian himself
shunning Rome to establish a base in the city of Nicomedia,
in what is now Turkey. Thanks to his effective management,
Diocletian holds the distinction of being the only Roman Emperor
to retire: he spent the last eleven years of his life pootling around
his palace on the Adriatic coast, shunning politics and tending to
his cabbage patch.

A further sign of the growing importance of the East came in
the year 324, when Emperor Constantine moved the capital of the
Eastern Empire from Nicomedia to Byzantium, an old Greek trading town on the Bosporus Strait. Its strategically important location
at the crossroads between Europe and Asia and the Mediterranean
and Black Seas likely convinced the emperor to make the move.
Soon renamed Constantinople, the city of Constantine, this capital
was to be the 'new Rome', complete with a senate, hippodrome,
forum, bath house and sprawling imperial palace. Constantine
embellished the city with so many monuments from around the
Eastern Empire – from Greek columns to Egyptian obelisks –
that he was accused of stripping other cities bare. As the first
Christian emperor, he also continued the construction of grand
new churches which he had begun in Rome with the basilicas of
St Paul and St Peter. These were to be Christianity's first works of
monumental architecture, quite unlike the small meeting houses
Christians had so far been accustomed to.

Within a few years Constantinople had quadrupled in size,
and would soon eclipse Rome in wealth and political importance.
This reflected an overall shift in the Roman world: while the West
wallowed in palace coups and military uprisings, the East was
increasingly acknowledged as more populous, prosperous and
easily defensible. Its farms were more productive, its tax bases

richer. Its peasants enjoyed greater economic liberty than their Western counterparts, whose shrinking freedoms were paving the way for the medieval system of serfdom. These widening divisions were formally recognised in 395 CE when the Roman Empire was officially split into Eastern and Western halves.

The Eastern Roman Empire, you may have noticed, received barely a mention in the previous chapter. Partly this was because the myths surrounding the fall of the Roman Empire are themselves focussed on Western Europe. Equally importantly, however, is the fact that the eastern half of the Empire suffered relatively little during the barbarian incursions of the 5th century. Pretty much every possible reason has been offered to explain the East's remarkable resilience, from military genius to blind luck. The geography of the Empire was certainly a factor, with the thin ribbon of the Bosporus – despite being less than half a mile wide in places – effectively cutting off the East's wealthy Asian and African territories from barbarian incursions. As a result, most barbarian forces headed west. Only the Eastern Empire's Balkan territories saw serious conflict, and even then Constantinople could dip into its considerable reserves and buy off the invaders – an option unavailable to the cash-strapped West. It also helped that Constantinople itself was virtually impregnable: surrounded on three sides by the sea, its landward face was protected by enormous three-tier walls so strong it would take more than a thousand years before they were finally breached. Lastly, it should be noted that the East made life considerably easier for itself by refusing to get too involved in the West's fights. Constantinople showed no desire to prop up the financial liability that was the Western Empire, and when barbarian forces eventually took control of the West it was more or less content to sit back and let the new owners deal with the region's problems.

And so, through various means, the Eastern Roman Empire emerged from the tumultuous 5th century largely unscathed. Indeed, archaeological evidence suggests that it actually experienced increasing prosperity during the 5th and 6th centuries. It enjoyed relative political stability and could boast of a bureaucracy that was – contrary to popular belief – both flexible and efficient. Its vast trade network, stretching from Britain to China, channelled huge sums of money into Constantinople, making the capital fabulously rich. People spoke of a city paved in gold, its fountains flowing with wine and honey, and they weren't too far wrong. Its streets and squares were lined with classical statues, its imperial palace glittered with pearls and rubies. Gardens and green spaces, a particular love of the Constantinopolitans, dotted the city. On the occasion of a royal baptism its inhabitants awoke to find the city centre draped in silks and gold. At the centre of the metropolis stood – and still stands – the gargantuan Hagia Sophia, the Church of Holy Wisdom, which would be the largest cathedral in the world for almost a thousand years. 'If we measure golden ages in terms of material remains,' notes the archaeologist Bryan Ward-Perkins, 'the 5th and 6th centuries were certainly golden for most of the eastern Mediterranean, in many areas leaving archaeological traces that are more numerous and more impressive than those of the earlier Roman Empire.'[7] As the population in the West plummeted, numbers rose in the East; as old towns in Europe emptied, new settlements were built in Asia. It would be six centuries before European standards of living would catch up to those of the Eastern Roman Empire.

Of course, with the West now in barbarian hands, it no longer makes sense to keep speaking of an *Eastern* Roman Empire. From this point on historians generally refer to the civilisation in the eastern Mediterranean as the Late Roman or Byzantine Empire, or simply as Byzantium, after the old Greek town at its heart.

Not that we need trouble ourselves with names too much. Partly because debating exactly when the Roman world became Byzantine has the distinct whiff of esoteric hair-splitting. More importantly, however, such an exercise would have struck a 6th-century Byzantine as bizarre. To them, their empire *was* the Roman Empire, just as they *were* Romans; the notion that they had just witnessed the fall of the classical world would have made little sense to them. Certainly, they saw no reason to stop referring to themselves as *Romaioi* and their high-ranking officials as *Kaisar*, or Caesar. And although Constantinople had done little to resist barbarian dominance in the West, it still regarded the old territories of the Western Roman Empire as its own. Odoacer, the barbarian king who deposed the last Western Roman Emperor, was made to pay lip service to the Eastern emperor Zeno, who treated him as a sort of imperial deputy. The 6th-century Byzantine emperor Justinian, modelling himself on earlier emperors like Augustus and Diocletian, even attempted to resurrect the Western Roman Empire through a series of military campaigns, briefly reclaiming large tracts of the Mediterranean for Byzantium.

The Byzantines – or Romans, if you prefer – were deeply proud of their classical heritage. They preserved and rebuilt old Greek temples, publicly honoured ancient Athenians such as Pericles, and revived archaic Greek names like Theseus and Achilles. Nowhere did they express this pride more clearly, however, than in their learning. Byzantine scholars considered themselves the guardians of classical Greek culture and wisdom, and worked hard to preserve and copy a wealth of ancient Greek texts that were being lost in the upheavals beyond the borders of the Empire. Thanks to their efforts, almost every single piece of ancient Greek writing that has subsequently been read and studied – from Plato to Plutarch to Aristotle to Aristophanes – can be traced back to a Byzantine copy. Without the Byzantines, much of the Greek knowledge which fuelled the European Renaissance, influenced the Enlightenment or continues to inform our current understanding of the classical past would simply not exist.

This love of the classics was widely shared throughout the middle and upper classes of Byzantine society. The Byzantines valued education for its own sake, considering it 'essential to find time to cultivate the garden of learning', as one emperor phrased it. Continuing a practice begun in the old Roman Empire, both girls and boys could go to school, where they would learn ancient Greek literature and rhetoric. Young men could continue their education at Constantinople's state-funded university, inaugurated in 425 CE, to study subjects ranging from philosophy and astronomy to medicine and music. Wealthy women, prevented from attending the university, often chose to hire private tutors instead. As a result, the upper echelon of the Byzantine world had a distinctly bookish character to it. Its inhabitants were keen readers and prodigious letter writers, their correspondence thick with obscure classical references. Riddles and mathematical puzzles were favourite after-dinner games. Where we might go to the cinema for entertainment, they filled theatres to listen to rhetorical performances from the 5th and 4th centuries BCE. Popular speeches included such edge-of-seat stuff as *On the Navy* and *Demosthenes swears that he did not take the bribe of 50 talents*. Even the Byzantines' enemies couldn't help but remark on their scholarly nature, describing them as 'a nation of theologians, physicians, astronomers, diplomats, arithmeticians, secretaries, and masters in every discipline'.[8]

If anything, their devotion to their classical heritage could be a little slavish at times. Byzantine scholars spoke a dialect known as Medieval Greek, but chose to write in an imitation of the extinct ancient Attic dialect of Greek; the result was a painfully grandiose, uncomfortably bloated and impenetrably dense writing style, riddled with grammatical errors. Even the Byzantines themselves complained that it could be 'quite unintelligible'.[9] By way of comparison, imagine if this book were written in Middle English out of an admiration for Chaucer – which ne wolde for the esieste redinge make. More seriously, a widespread feeling of inferiority compared to the ancient Greeks could actually hinder academic progress. 'The great men of the past,' opined the scholar Theodore Metochites in the early 14th century, 'have said everything so perfectly that they have left nothing for us to say.'[10] And so, as vital as their preservation of the Greek texts was, Byzantine scholars did little more than preserve. Great minds confined themselves to writing commentaries on ancient works rather than building on them. This isn't to say they were mindless in their scholarship, as is often insinuated – on the contrary, they constantly reflected on what they were transmitting – but that they saw their job as one of interpretation rather than advancement.

This scholasticism was initially supported by the Church, which for over two centuries following the foundation of Constantinople tolerated a relatively open intellectual climate in which people could freely discuss and criticise theological and philosophical issues. The majority of Byzantines saw no reason why their Christian faith should prevent them from studying classical writing or admiring pagan art. After all, many of the classical statues festooning Constantinople were of pagan gods and goddesses. A number of church frescoes even depicted ancient philosophers like Aristotle, Plato and Plutarch alongside biblical figures. Bigots and zealots existed, of course, but they were more than matched by sceptics and freethinkers; pomposity and verbosity in Byzantine scholarship were balanced by notes of humour and self-deprecation. When a group of monks known as the Hesychasts claimed that humanity could only get close to God by staring for long periods of time at their navel, they were roundly lampooned by more sceptical Christians, who invented the term 'navel-gazing' to ridicule their self-centred introspection.[11]

Sadly, Byzantium's early years of tolerance and debate weren't to last. The demise of its early scholasticism can be traced back to Emperor Justinian's attempts to reclaim the Western Roman Empire in the mid-6th century. Plotted on a map, Justinian's conquests look very impressive: within the space of two decades the Byzantine Empire captured the Vandals' North African territories and the Gothic kingdom of Italy as well as parts of the Balkans and Spain, and a Roman Empire once again dominated the Mediterranean. But the wars were far from a triumph. In Italy, the undermanned forces became bogged down in a gruelling and destructive nineteen-year conflict which, ironically, destroyed much of the peninsula's classical heritage which the Goths had studiously preserved. 'Some new and different trouble happened with each fresh day,' wrote the contemporary historian Procopius in his scathing account of the wars, 'for even Providence had turned against the Romans.'[12] Adding to the crisis, a four-year outbreak of the bubonic plague – the first time the disease had reached the Mediterranean – decimated the Empire, nearly killing Justinian himself. Most worryingly for Constantinople, the emperor's efforts had almost bankrupted Byzantium. Decades of war had produced few lasting gains, and the territories the Byzantines were able to hold on to proved to be a financial drain. Inevitable military cuts sparked mutinies across the Mediterranean. Justinian's attempt to revive the Western Roman Empire had only confirmed that it was beyond saving.

In the decades that followed Justinian's turbulent reign the prosperity and political stability of Byzantium quickly began to deteriorate, and for a while it looked like the Eastern Roman Empire would meet the same internecine end as the West had 150 years earlier. Moreover, Justinian's obsession with the western Mediterranean had come at the neglect of the Empire's eastern border with the powerful Sassanian Empire: the latest incarnation of the long-lived Persian civilisation and perennial adversary of the Byzantines. Sensing an opportunity, in 540 the Sassanians broke the optimistically titled 'Treaty of Perpetual Peace' that had been signed by the two empires just eight years earlier and captured the Byzantine city of Antioch. It was to be the start of 80 years of on-and-off war between the two powers. Faced with such uncertainty, Byzantines clung tighter to Christianity for protection, and the earlier climate of open debate hardened into something much more inflexible and resistant to pagan ideas.

It took the capable Byzantine emperor Heraclius to restore order and resist the advancing Persian troops. Scraping together what resources he could, in the 620s Heraclius launched a victorious offensive against the Sassanians – at one point even successfully taking on three Persian armies at once – and recovered the lost Byzantine territory. By 628 both empires, exhausted by war and plague, agreed to re-establish their borders to where they had been before conflict. Decades of war had achieved nothing for either side.

With the hostilities over, it looked for a while as if the Byzantine Empire might have the chance to recover its earlier prosperity. But just five years after the peace treaty with Persia was signed, urgent news reached Constantinople from the south.

The Arabs, a group of distant desert tribesmen, were racing up out of the Arabian peninsula, conquering armies and capturing territory with frightening ease. They were on a divine mission, they claimed, to strip away the decadence of Abrahamic faith and return it to its true roots.

Islam had arrived.

~

To understand where these Arabian warriors came from, we need to step back a few decades. It's the year 610 CE, and a 40-year-old merchant named Muhammad has recently taken to preaching in the bustling Arabian town of Mecca. With overland trade routes between Byzantium and the Indian Ocean booming, Mecca has grown rich as an economic, cultural and religious centre for the many traders travelling through the Arabian peninsula. With this prosperity, however, has come a widening divide between rich and poor. Loathing the inequality and injustice he sees in the streets of Mecca, Muhammad often escapes the town and retreats to a cave on the slopes of Mount Hira. There he sits, thinks and meditates.

It is while in this cave, Muhammad claims, that he is first visited by the angel Gabriel. Descending from heaven one warm August night, Gabriel grabs Muhammad and commands him to deliver the word of God to the people of Mecca. Judgement Day is fast approaching, the angel warns, and eternal punishment awaits those who refuse to take heed. Muhammad obeys. Ever since that night, he can be found proselytising in and around Mecca, railing against the greed and corruption of the town and its elites, urging his listeners to abandon the pursuit of wealth and give to the needy instead. Most Meccans ignore or make fun of their local 'madman'. And yet, whether through the simplicity of his message or the sincerity of his oratory, a small but growing number of townsfolk, particularly from Mecca's poorer quarters, are taking heed of what he says.[13]

Reconstructing the very first days of Islam like this is fraught with danger. We can be fairly certain that Muhammad existed (which is more than we can say for Jesus, Buddha or Moses), but beyond that things quickly become hazy. The religious sources are obscure, allusive and biased, and were first written some four or five generations after the events they describe. The archaeological evidence is sparse to non-existent, and much of the Arabian peninsula is yet to be properly studied by archaeologists (thanks in no small part to discouragement by the Saudi Arabian authorities). As a result, we can't be sure whether it was the widening inequality caused by an economic boom that inspired Muhammad, or in fact an economic slump that spurred him to act. Nor do we know whether it was his egalitarianism that made his message so attractive to his fellow Meccans, or whether Muhammad won adherents with some sort of anti-colonial message against Sassanian and Persian encroachment. We don't even know if Muhammad's Mecca is the same Mecca of today. Koranic references to grapevines and olive farms – in a town too dry for agriculture – make scholars suspect that something may be amiss. 'Despite a great deal of information supplied by later Muslim literary sources,' concluded Francis Peters, an expert on Islamic history, in 1991, 'we know pitifully little for sure about the political or economic history of Muhammad's native city of Mecca or of the religious culture from which he came.'[14]

What just about everyone can agree on, however, is that in the year 622 Muhammad and his followers left Mecca for the town of Yathrib, some 200 miles to the north. Over the previous twelve years the merchant's preaching had become increasingly unpopular with the Meccan elite, especially since he had taken to condemning their polytheistic practices as idolatry and to exalting Allah, the high god of their pantheon, far above all other deities. Moreover, the growing identity and strength of his movement threatened the complex and conflagratory network of clan loyalties which governed Arabian politics. He had grown from joke to nuisance to real problem, and Meccan leaders were becoming increasingly hostile to the Prophet and his converts. When death threats began to reach the faithful, they agreed that it was time to leave.

The move to Yathrib marks a fundamental shift in the history of Islam, a fact recognised by its designation as year one in the Muslim calendar. In Yathrib – better known today as Medina, the City of the Prophet – Muhammad's support for monotheism became absolute; earlier tolerance or even endorsement of polytheism was abandoned. Back in Mecca the Prophet's preaching often had a mystical, poetic quality (indeed, he had been dismissed as an 'insane poet' by some of his fellow Meccans); in Medina, his instruction was dry, legalistic and inflexible. Overall, there's a hardening of Islamic doctrine, evidenced in part by an increasing hostility to those of other faiths.[15]

Crucially, Muhammad's residence in Medina marks the beginning of Islam as a political, cultural and military force. The terms *Islam* and *Muslim* – both derived from the Arabic word for submission – begin to be used. Laws are written and customs established. Raids are launched on Meccan trade caravans, sparking a series of skirmishes and battles between Islamic forces and the old tribal aristocracy. Muhammad's troops quickly gain the upper hand on the battlefield, often against surprising odds, culminating in their victorious return to Mecca in 630 as the undisputed rulers of the town. In just two decades Islam had become the most powerful force in Arabia.

The new religion's first triumph was quickly followed by its first real crisis. In 632, two years after the conquest of Mecca, Muhammad unexpectedly died without appointing a successor. Disagreements over who should replace him quickly split the community, and still form the fundamental schism between Sunni and Shia Muslims to this day. Many tribes broke away from Islam upon hearing news of Muhammad's death; their allegiance had been to the man, not his message. Adding to the chaos, copycat prophets began springing up across the peninsula, claiming they had been chosen by Allah to continue Muhammad's work. Seeing the Prophet's achievements unravel before their eyes, a number of his close companions chose to elect Muhammad's father-in-law and chief advisor, a man named Abu Bakr, to serve as his representative (or *khalifa*) and reinstate authority. As Islam's first caliph, Abu Bakr decreed that the new faith must have both religious and political unity. Secessionists, dissenters, rival prophets: all were apostates and enemies in the eyes of the nascent Islamic Caliphate. An aggressive military campaign quickly forced most of them to repent and submit, and soon the entire Arabian peninsula was under firm Islamic control.

In many ways Abu Bakr's war against the apostates acted as a catalyst for the emerging Islamic Empire. Not only did it hone the fighting skills of Islam's new recruits, but it gave a theological justification for their fighting. Successive caliphs, keen to expand their territory and tax base, continued the model of military conquest begun by Abu Bakr. But with Arabia firmly under their control there was now only one way to expand: north – straight into the armies of two of the world's most powerful empires, the Byzantines and Sassanians.

Fortunately for the Caliphate, both the Byzantines and the Sassanians had spent the better part of the past century beating each other senseless, and neither was able to offer much resistance to the fresh Arabian forces from the south. The Sassanian Empire was completely overrun within the space of a decade, ending more than a thousand years of Persian imperialism. Byzantium, with the indomitable Heraclius still at the reins during the initial invasion, was able to put up a greater resistance, ultimately preventing Muslim troops from taking the imperial heartlands of Asia Minor and the Aegean. Constantinople itself was blockaded for much of the 670s, but used its infamous 'Greek fire' – a kind of petroleum-spouting flamethrower – to hold back the Caliphate's navy. Even so, the Byzantine Empire was forced to concede much of its territory to their new rivals. The Levant was conquered by the Arabian forces in the 630s, with the spiritual centre of Jerusalem captured after a siege in 638. Egypt and Alexandria followed in the 640s. Byzantium's North African territories were under Islamic control by the 680s, which served as a base for the successful Muslim invasion of Spain in the early 8th century. By 732, a century after Muhammad's death, an Islamic Empire stretched from the Atlantic to the Indian Ocean, covering an area greater than either the Byzantines or the Romans before them had been able to amass. Byzantium, the last remnant of the Roman world, was reduced to the lands of Asia Minor, the Balkans and scraps of the Italian peninsula.

The remarkable speed of the Islamic conquests – by an unprofessional army, no less – is usually attributed to the proselytising zeal of the Arab warriors. The energy provided by the new religion was certainly an important factor, but we shouldn't neglect the possibility of more profane influences. Many Islamic troops were drawn from poorest parts of Arabia and saw the conquests as a chance to get their hands on the riches of the Byzantine and Sassanian Empires. Their leaders eyed the fertile fields of Egypt, the breadbasket of Byzantium, with equal interest. And just as the barbarian invaders in Europe two centuries earlier had often received support from Roman defectors, so too did the Islamic conquests find willing subjects among many of the Byzantines of Egypt, Syria and Palestine, who, as believers in a branch of Christianity deemed heretical in Constantinople, eagerly accepted the promise of greater toleration under Muslim rule.[16]

The establishment of a stable, multinational empire in the 7th and 8th centuries shaped the course of Islam just as much as the migration to Medina had – although at the local level you'd be forgiven for thinking nothing much had changed. Byzantine and Sassanian bureaucracy was kept in place; even their old coins were still being used. Moreover, Islam had yet to be widely adopted by the masses; at this point it was still known as 'the Arab religion': the strange new faith of a foreign elite who made up less than one tenth of the Caliphate's population. Jewish, Christian and Zoroastrian communities, which constituted the vast majority of the new empire, were usually left alone so long as they paid their taxes. Forced conversion was rare, partly because these taxes levied exclusively against non-Muslims were such a lucrative source of revenue.[17]

What had changed, however, was that these various communities now lived under a single, unified and increasingly centralised state. Road networks, shipping lanes, camel trails and even homing pigeons connected sub-Saharan Africa with the Mediterranean and Arabia with India. Understanding their importance, caliphs invested in these networks, improving roads and building way stations for travellers. Equally significant was their establishment of Arabic as the official language of imperial administration in the 8th century. For the first time, a single language connected the Mediterranean with the lands beyond

Asia Minor, opening up new channels of communication and exchange between previously distant people and groups. Rice, sugar cane, cotton, artichokes, lemons, limes, plantains, spinach, aubergines and bananas became common crops throughout much of the Old World. Explorers travelled throughout Africa and Asia, recording their experiences and observations of the people and customs they encountered. Scholars as far afield as Spain and Samarkand suddenly found themselves wrestling with new ideas and concepts: mathematical innovations from India, astronomical records from Persia, medical knowledge from Greece. And the new Chinese import of paper allowed them to write about these ideas much more easily than the expensive and bulky parchment they were used to. The stage was set for the Islamic Golden Age, a period of extraordinary artistic and scientific achievement that would last from the 8th to the 13th centuries and that ranks as one of the greatest intellectual blooms in human history.

The trigger for this Golden Age came from both Islamic scholars and their caliphs, who were keenly aware of the intellectual achievements of the empires they had conquered and were eager to acquire the fruits of Persian, Greek and Roman learning for themselves. From this desire arose the 'translation movement': a concerted effort by the Islamic Empire, beginning in the late 8th century, to acquire the world's knowledge and translate it into Arabic.[18]

It was an enormous undertaking. Simply locating the texts could be a serious challenge. Not so long ago, of course, classical Greek texts could be found in every monastery and schoolhouse in the Byzantine Empire. Following the crises of the 600s, however, the increasingly fundamentalist Byzantines turned their back on pagan learning, the suitably biblical scourges of death, war, famine and pestilence having been enough to convince them that they had strayed from their god's path. (A particular low

point for the Byzantines came in the year 811, when Krum, king
of the Bulgars, had the Byzantine emperor Nicephorus killed
and his skull fashioned into a goblet.) Faced with such trials, the
anti-intellectual strands in Byzantine society found a receptive
audience, and the Empire which had once considered it a matter
of duty to preserve ancient learning now left their Greek texts
to rot. Muslim scholars travelling to Byzantium reported finding
piles of disintegrating books locked away in Byzantine churches,
half-buried under dust and cobwebs. Beyond Byzantium, Islamic
scholars also ventured to Persia, India and perhaps even China in
search of valuable knowledge.[19]

The next step – of actually translating the hundreds of accu-
mulated documents into Arabic – was no less Herculean. It was
an international effort, requiring the skills of Greek, Latin, Persian,
Hebrew, Syriac and Sanskrit-speaking scholars as well as speakers
of Arabic. Muslim, Christian, Jewish and Zoroastrian translators
all contributed. Translation became big business, and capable
translators could achieve fame and fortune for their work, earning
up to 500 dinars a month – around £30,000 in today's money.[20]

The epicentre of the translation movement was Baghdad: the
purpose-built capital of the Abbasid Caliphate, the dynasty which
ruled much of the Islamic Empire from 750 to 1258. Then known
as Madinat al-Salam, the City of Peace, Baghdad was deliberately
built to rival Constantinople, which was still widely considered the
most splendid city in the known world. Rising to the challenge,
Baghdad quickly developed into a cosmopolitan metropolis of up
to a million residents and was adorned with gardens, fountains,
bath houses and state-of-the-art hospitals. During the early 9th-
century reign of the Abbasid caliph al-Ma'mun, perhaps the single
greatest patron of science in the Caliphate's history, it also became
an intellectual powerhouse, drawing scholars from across the

Islamic world. 'They come to Baghdad from all countries near and far,' wrote the geographer Ahmad al-Ya'qubi during al-Ma'mun's reign. 'There is none more learned than their scholars ... more poetic than their poets, and more reckless than their rakes.'[21] The city teemed with bookshops and libraries containing the latest translations (readers of Arabic in 10th-century Baghdad had about the same level of access to Aristotle as readers of English today), as well as state-funded schools, public academies and *majalis*, intellectual salons famous for their lively debates.[22]

Unlike the Byzantines, Muslim scholars weren't content to merely preserve ancient learning. Lacking the stifling deference to the classical past that their northern neighbours had once shown, they sought to challenge, re-interpret and build upon what they learned. As a result, the Islamic Golden Age led to scholarly advancements far beyond what the Byzantines had achieved. A clear example of this is in mathematics. The Byzantines insisted on sticking with the hopelessly clunky system of Roman numerals, which pretty much guaranteed their inability to advance beyond the achievements of classical mathematics. Even relatively simple calculations such as multiplication and division can be laborious using Roman numerals – try dividing CXLIV by XII and you'll get the idea. Islamic mathematicians, in contrast, were quick to adopt a revolutionary numerical system that had developed in India sometime in the 6th century. Known today as Arabic numerals – although Arabs themselves call them Indian numerals – this novel approach allowed any number to be represented by a combination of just ten symbols: 1, 2, 3, 4, 5, 6, 7, 8, 9 and 0. To this, Muslim scholars added the decimal point, a feature entirely lacking from Roman and Indian mathematics.

The flexibility and agility offered by Indian-Arabic numerals allowed scholars to look at old mathematical problems in a new light. Musa al-Khwarizmi, the man who did more than most to popularise Indian-Arabic numerals in the Islamic world, used them as the foundation of a new mathematical method for working out unknown quantities he called 'completion and cancellation'. Today we call it algebra, after its Arabic name *al-Jabr wa'l-Muqabalah*. (Al-Khwarizmi's name, meanwhile, gave us the word algorithm.) 'With al-Khwarizmi's algebra,' summarises science writer Ehsan Masood, 'scholars provided us with the single most important mathematical tool ever devised ... one that underpins every facet of science.'[23]

In astronomy, for instance, mathematical advances allowed astronomers, al-Khwarizmi among them, to calculate the positions of planets and stars and to predict eclipses with a greater accuracy than previous Greek, Persian or Indian attempts. These efforts encouraged astronomers to question the widely accepted geocentric structure of the universe, an ingenious but fundamentally flawed model that had been devised by the Greek astronomer Ptolemy in the 2nd century CE. Although Muslim astronomers unanimously rejected a sun-centred solar system – arguing that it would be impossible not to notice if the Earth was hurtling through space at more than a thousand miles a minute – their work would provide some of the mathematical proofs Nicholaus Copernicus needed to develop his heliocentric model of the solar system in the early 16th century. In his groundbreaking work of 1543, *On the Revolutions of the Heavenly Spheres*, Copernicus cites the work of the Islamic astronomer Muhammad al-Battani 23 times.[24]

Back on Earth, 9th-century geographers were able to use mathematics to test ancient calculations of the circumference of the planet (knowing full well, incidentally, that it wasn't flat). The previous best guess was around 28,900 miles, reached by the

Greek mathematician Eratosthenes, who measured the difference in shadow lengths in two different cities on the summer solstice of 240 BCE. In the 820s Caliph al-Ma'mun commissioned three of his court scholars to try again. Measuring differences in the position of the pole star at two locations, they arrived at an answer of 24,000 miles. Later Golden Age astronomers refined this figure to 24,835 miles, just 39 miles short of its current estimate of 24,874 miles: an error of just 0.16 per cent.[25]

Medicine was another field in which Islamic scholars made considerable advances by challenging academic orthodoxy. Nutrition, embryology, epidemiology, immunology and neurology were all explored, if tentatively. Ophthalmology, the study of the eye, became a particular speciality – understandable in an empire spanning many hot, dry and dusty environments, where diseases of the eyes were all too common. The first known anatomical drawing of the eye comes from the 9th-century physician Hunayn Ibn Ishaq, and words such as 'retina' and 'cataract' are derived from Arabic terms. Hospitals, too, underwent important developments. In the city of Córdoba, which easily rivalled Baghdad in academic output by the 10th century, hospitals were fitted with running water, baths, pharmacies and specialised wards for various conditions. The 10th-century Córdoban surgeon Abu al-Zahrawi is generally credited with laying the foundations of modern surgery, beginning its transformation from a barber's side job to a respected medical discipline. His 30-volume medical encyclopaedia, curiously titled *The Arrangement of Medical Knowledge for One Who is Not Able to Compile a Book for Himself*, remained one of the most important texts on surgery in Europe until the 18th century.[26]

As with medicine, practical needs spurred many other accomplishments of the Islamic Golden Age. Geography and astronomy were essential in the construction of mosques, which had to be orientated so as to allow Muslims to pray in the direction of Mecca. Al-Khwarizmi's algebra was devised to solve the everyday problems of 'inheritance, legacies, partition, lawsuits and trade', as he himself explained. Like any modern schoolbook, his *al-Jabr wa'l-Muqabalah* is full of practical demonstrations of the use of algebra – although his examples for calculating the price of slaves have thankfully lost their relevance.

Alongside these practical needs, however, there was also a clear love for the pursuit of knowledge in its own right. Many scholars demonstrated an innate curiosity about the world and a desire to solve its mysteries. Abu Bakr ibn Wahshiyya, a linguist from what's now Iraq, took the first steps towards deciphering ancient Egyptian hieroglyphics in the 9th century. The polymath Ibn Sina, also known by his Latinised name Avicenna, made significant contributions towards philosophy, medicine, geometry and astronomy, and even developed an embryonic understanding of the principles of geology more than 600 years before its modern incarnation. The 9th-century zoologist al-Jahiz expounded an early account of natural selection and evolution that is, in outline, remarkably similar to Charles Darwin's 19th-century theory. Given that the majority of scientific writings from the Golden Age are yet to be studied by modern scholars, it's possible that plenty more of its breakthroughs are still waiting to be rediscovered.[27]

It's true that many examples of Islamic scholarship would not be considered scientific today. Medieval Islamic chemistry, though taking tentative steps towards a systematic study of substances, was still firmly rooted in the magic of alchemy. Astronomy, for all its mathematical rigour, retained strong ties to astrology. Nevertheless, at its best the Islamic Golden Age could express a truly scientific approach to learning: a belief in the importance of rigorous, repeatable experimentation, and a deep distrust of wisdom from authority. Ibn al-Haytham, the father of modern optics, actively encouraged his readers to challenge his findings. 'Whosoever seeks the truth will not proceed by studying the writings of his predecessors and by simply accepting his own good opinion of them,' he declared. 'Whosoever studies works of science must, if he wants to find the truth, transform himself into a critic of everything he reads. He must examine tests and explanations with the greatest precision and question them from all angles and aspects.'[28] Yaqub al-Kindi, a leading light of the translation movement, summed up this spirit with equal vigour: 'we ought not to be embarrassed about appreciating the truth and obtaining it wherever it comes from, even if it comes from races distant and nations different from us. Nothing should be dearer to the seeker of truth than the truth itself.'[29]

The wealth of learning streaming out from cities like Baghdad and Córdoba exerted an enormous influence on scholarship throughout North Africa, Asia and Europe. Byzantium was rescued from its self-imposed academic exile and returned to its studies with renewed vigour, with a succession of scholarly emperors channelling significant funds into the reopened university in Constantinople. Well-established trade routes between China and the Middle East allowed consecutive Chinese dynasties to learn of Islamic innovations in astronomy, engineering, mathematics and medicine. The city of Timbuktu, in what's now Mali, absorbed these same innovations via the trans-Saharan trade routes to become a respected centre of mathematics and astronomy in its own right in the 15th and 16th centuries.

Europe was no different. Islamic scholarship had been making inroads north of the Mediterranean since at least the 10th century, if not earlier. Islamic Spain, in particular, had established itself as an internationally renowned centre for translation by the mid-12th century, attracting scholars from as far afield as Scotland, Hungary and Egypt. The earliest known Latin translation of the Koran, produced in Spain, dates back to 1143, and quickly became the medieval equivalent of a bestseller. Translations of Greek and Arabic works on philosophy, mathematics and astronomy soon followed. Even when the Golden Age ran out of steam in the 12th century, as weakening Abbasid authority allowed the Caliphate to splinter into rival states, its impact could still be felt far and wide.[30]

All of which begs the question: how could the centuries which followed the fall of the Western Roman Empire – a time of intellectual fervour, technical ingenuity and international cooperation and communication – ever have come to be described as a Dark Age?

As we've already seen, the notion of the post-Roman world as a time of darkness dates back to Petrarch, the 14th-century Italian poet and curmudgeon. Traditionally, Christians had regarded the time before Jesus as the age of darkness, and it was common consensus that things had been steadily improving since his time on Earth; to suggest otherwise was to flirt with heresy. Petrarch's obsession with ancient Rome was so great, and his misanthropy so boundless, however, that he flipped this paradigm on its head, declaring everything since the fall of Rome nothing but a 'sleep of forgetfulness'.[31]

The idea caught on, and successive generations of Italian writers continued to refer to the medieval era as a time of darkness. Lacking Petrarch's all-consuming despair for the modern world, however, they began to question whether they were still living in an age of ignorance. The historian Leonardo Bruni considered the retreat of the hated Holy Roman Empire from Italy in 1250 as marking the end of the Dark Ages. His contemporary, the antiquarian Flavio Biondo, put the date at 1410, exactly a millennium since the Goths' sack of Rome in 410. Whatever the preferred year, this new view of the past was, at heart, a celebration of the present. Bruni and Biondo were men of the Italian Renaissance, a time when scholars like themselves confidently set out to rescale the heights of classical civilisation. Consequently, many of the tropes about Dark Age ignorance were established by Renaissance writers as a way to boost their own standing: the more hopelessly ignorant their ancestors were, the more remarkable their own learning and erudition appeared.

With the dunce hat of the Dark Ages thrust firmly upon it, the Middle Ages have served as the foil for self-consciously enlightened people ever since. As a student at Cambridge, a teenage John Milton contrasted the edifying education of the 1620s with the 'blind illiteracy' of the medieval past, when 'nothing was heard in the schools but the insipid doctrines of the utterly stupid monks'. In 1697, the writer John Evelyn criticised medieval architecture as 'heavy, dark, melancholy, monkish piles, without any just proportion, use or beauty'. The chorus of condemnation reached a crescendo during the European Enlightenment of the 17th and 18th centuries, when philosophers like Voltaire, Condorcet and d'Alembert prided themselves on their reason, erudition, and familiarity with classical learning. The Dark Ages, in turn, became whatever they scorned: superstitious, irrational, authoritarian, unrefined and unscientific. In David Hume's *History of England*, for example, the philosopher described the Dark Ages as the long night of 'ignorance, stupidity and superstition' before the 'sun of science' rose in the 15th century. Historian and fellow Scot William Robertson, a critic of Christian fundamentalism, warned of how the unthinking medieval Church had 'degenerated ... into an illiberal superstition'. For the architect Robert Smirke, the 'vulgar and degenerate' ornamentation of Gothic architecture served only to highlight the 'noble simplicity' of contemporary neoclassical aesthetics.[32]

Of course, the glaring irony in all of this was that the great minds of the European Renaissance and Enlightenment owed much of their reason, erudition and familiarity with classical learning to the Byzantine and Islamic scholars of the Dark Ages. The intellectual ferment created by Spanish translations of Greek and Arabic texts helped transform Europe's cathedral schools and monastic schools, such as those in Paris, into universities. The Renaissance was kickstarted by an influx of Byzantine refugees into Italy in the 15th century, who brought with them many of the classical works that would fuel subsequent European scholarship. The Enlightenment, in turn, was based on the scientific and philosophical achievements of the Renaissance.

But these vital contributions were largely ignored by Europe's intellectuals. They didn't fit the narrative of the European Renaissance and Enlightenment – of bold scholars and artists rescuing 'lost' classical learning from the catacombs of medieval ignorance. And this is perhaps the biggest problem with the concept of the Dark Ages: it takes the particularly European experiences of decline and revival that followed the break-up of the Western Roman Empire and inflates them into a grand epoch of world history that can be applied with equal validity anywhere. Other perspectives that might contradict the story are dismissed or distorted. Of the few Renaissance scholars to write histories of the Turks and Arabs, most portrayed them as uncivilised barbarians. The Byzantine Empire, though spared the standard accusation of barbarism, was instead disregarded as a 'uniform' and 'tedious' civilisation, an unnecessary appendix to the Roman Empire that long outstayed its welcome on the world stage. At best, the Muslims and Byzantines were begrudgingly acknowledged as caretakers of classical knowledge, librarians whose sole purpose was to preserve ancient learning until a time when Europe might need them. The Dark Ages are both a product and an engine of Eurocentrism in their insistence on the primary importance of Europe in world affairs.[33]

This Eurocentric character of the Dark Ages has been present since at least Petrarch, whose fixation on ancient Rome was so single-minded that he considered regions beyond the Italian peninsula unworthy of study. 'For what is all of history but the praise of Rome?' he once sniffed.[34] The legacy of the Crusades of the 11th to 13th centuries, in which Christian and Muslim forces repeatedly clashed over control of the Holy Land, had encouraged this sense of separateness among Europeans. By the time of the Ottoman capture of Constantinople in 1453 – which finally brought an end to the thousand-year Byzantine Empire – European scholars had added to this dismissiveness an open hostility towards 'heathen' Muslims and their scholarship, which they branded 'Arab lies'.[35] European writers accused Muslims of appropriating classical knowledge, with the clear implication that such learning belonged to Europe. 'The Arabs had taken their knowledge from the Greeks and, like Harpies, defiled all that they touched,' cried the 16th-century Italian physician Bassiano Landi.[36] By the late 19th century, a significant number of archaeologists and historians had also adopted the concept of racial hierarchy to convince themselves that Arab and Islamic civilisation was biologically destined to be inferior to that of Europe.

Eurocentric approaches to the past inevitably provide us with a limited and skewed understanding of history beyond Europe. When centres of learning moved eastwards in the 5th century, a blinkered Eurocentric perspective can only assume that learning had vanished off the face of the Earth. With European civilisation accepted as the de facto pinnacle of human achievement, other civilisations can only be studied as backward and underdeveloped. A common criticism of Islam today is that it's 'medieval', implying that it's still stuck at a stage of history which Europe has since grown out of.

For the anthropologist Jack Goody, writing in 2006, these approaches represented nothing less than 'the theft of history' from places and people beyond Europe. At its most extreme, this theft has involved denying the very concept of history to regions with no obvious connection to Europe. Georg Wilhelm Friedrich Hegel, perhaps the most influential philosopher of history of the 19th century, famously opined that 'Africa has no history.' An American encyclopaedia from 1916 declared 'the Caucasian or white race' to be 'the only one whose history is important ... because it displays the most highly civilised type of mankind – that type whose progress and achievements are the true province of history'. These notions were still being spouted as recently as 1965 by the historian Hugh Trevor-Roper, who, as Regius Professor of Modern History at the University of Oxford, told his students that, as far as African history was concerned, 'there is none, or very little' to bother learning, on account of its 'irrelevance' to European history.[37] The fact that relatively few documents from the Islamic Golden Age have been studied, even today, is a testament to the continuing influence of this attitude.

Not only does the distorting lens of the Dark Ages dismiss the role of non-European civilisations, however: it obscures our understanding of Europe itself. While it's true that the civilisations of Byzantium and Islam led the way in science and technology following the break-up of the Western Roman Empire, it would be a mistake to assume, as the idea of the Dark Ages suggests, that Europe simply sat still for a millennium waiting for Petrarch and the Renaissance to arrive. As the historian Samuel Maitland wrote in 1853: 'darkness is quite a different thing from shutting the eyes; and ... we have no right to complain that we can see but little until we have used due diligence to see what we can.'[38] Yes, political fragmentation had deprived its scholars of many classical texts (as had Justinian's wars of conquest, for that matter), but in no way did the people living west of Byzantium suddenly lose their intelligence, inquisitiveness or imagination.

Certainly, there was never any 'collapse of the arts', as Condorcet and other Enlightenment pundits believed. The barbarian art of post-Roman Europe, though indeed very different from classical creations, included works of undeniable skill and beauty. In 5th-century Scandinavia, jewellers were experimenting with abstraction and surrealism in their depictions of animals and people. In remote corners of the British Isles, 8th-century monks were producing illustrated manuscripts of dizzying complexity. Even today, some 1,200 years later, the artwork and calligraphy in manuscripts like the Book of Kells and the Lindisfarne Gospels are remarkable for their psychedelic colours and hypnotic patterns.

Perhaps unexpectedly, the European Dark Ages also saw significant developments in literacy – thanks in no small part to the much-maligned monks of medieval Christendom. The 6th century witnessed the widespread adoption of punctuation in Europe, an innovation that has been compared to the invention of the printing press in its importance for the spread of literacy. Until then the literate had to make do with the *scriptura continua* of the Roman world, a breathless writing style that lacked not only punctuation but even spaces between words, making it virtually unintelligible unless read aloud. A number of historians have interpreted this shift to mean that the Dark Ages also saw the widespread introduction of silent reading, which, incredibly, appears to have been largely absent from the classical world. A further innovation came from the court of the Frankish king Charlemagne, who in the early 9th century promoted a neat, easy-to-read style of handwriting known as Carolingian minuscule. This script, which made use of recently invented lowercase letters, quickly spread throughout Western Europe. By the time Petrarch was moaning about his 'sterile-minded' brethren, increased schooling for the growing mercantile classes had pushed literacy rates in Italian cities as high as 70 per cent, far greater than the estimated 10–20 per cent of the Roman Empire.[39]

As historians shake off the illusions of the Dark Ages, it's becoming increasingly clear that many long-held beliefs about medieval ignorance in Europe are wrong. It wasn't widely believed, for instance, that the Earth was flat. As was the case with Islamic geographers, almost every European medieval writer and thinker knew that the Earth 'is but a little round ball', as a 15th-century compendium put it. The most popular astronomy textbook in European universities during the later Middle Ages was even called *On the Spheres*. And the church certainly didn't suppress such thinking as heretical; in fact, it actually condemned Flat-Earthers for promoting too literal an interpretation of the Bible. Similarly, the notion that the Dark Ages were obsessed with witch hunts is also false. A fear of witches certainly existed, but it was nowhere near the hysteria that erupted in the 16th and

17th centuries – ironically, medieval Europeans often showed a more reasonable and critical attitude to claims of witchcraft than their 'enlightened' Renaissance descendants. An edict from 9th-century France, for example, made it a capital offence to burn someone in the belief that they were a witch. In contrast, the witch hunts of early modern Europe often received the explicit support of the government.[40]

This isn't to say that the Middle Ages weren't superstitious times. Werewolves, demons and the evil eye were all, at various times, common fears. A traveller approaching a crossroads would need to be extra vigilant for ghosts and devils, and anyone who dared eat goose on the last Monday in April would surely die soon after. But let's not forget that the 21st century is just as superstitious. People *still* believe in werewolves, demons and the evil eye. Even the medieval fear of crossroads can still be found in contemporary blues numbers, where they serve as ideal locations for making a deal with the devil. In the United States of America, the 'mystical and psychic services' market makes an incredible $2.2 billion each year. A 2014 survey found that 55 per cent of British adults hold some superstition or belief in the supernatural, with one in five believing in UFOs, past lives or telepathy, and a full third confident in the existence of ghosts – and this, it's worth reminding ourselves, is in a country with compulsory science lessons for all children. Indeed, given the high rates of mandatory schooling in the modern world, it's almost certain that a far greater proportion of educated people today believe in astrology and Flat-Earthism – two of this century's more popular anti-scientific beliefs – than ever did during the Dark Ages.[41]

And so it's more than a little hypocritical of us to continue condemning the Dark Ages as a superstitious or anti-scientific time in order to congratulate ourselves on how enlightened we are today, as European scholars have been doing ever since the Renaissance. As the history of Byzantium and the Islamic Empire shows, learning has never been the property of any one group of people, whether they belong to a geographical region or a period in time. Our journey east could easily have been extended to include the numerous accomplishments of Persia, India or Tang Dynasty China, which was enjoying its own intellectual flowering around the same time as Islam. Likewise, this chapter could have been extended in time to incorporate the achievements of scholars living after the height of the Islamic Golden Age, such as the 12th-century philosopher Ibn Rushd, one of medieval Islam's and Europe's greatest authorities on Aristotle, or Ibn al-Nafis, a 13th-century physician who discovered the circulation of blood through the lungs.

Ultimately, the obscurity of the so-called 'Dark Ages' has nothing to do with any 'sleep of forgetfulness' that the world supposedly succumbed to between the fall of Rome and the rise of Renaissance Europe. The ignorance is our own: the assumption, still widespread today, that history beyond Europe is somehow less important, impressive or relevant to the modern world.

CHAPTER 5

Columbus didn't discover America

¡Tierra, tierra!'

The cry of 'land!' came at two in the morning on Friday 12 October 1492. It must have come as a welcome relief for the crew and captain of the *Pinta*, who, together with the ships *Santa Maria* and *Niña*, had been sailing west across the Atlantic Ocean for an unprecedented five weeks. Juan Rodríguez Bermeo, the sailor who first spotted the distant shoreline in the moonlight, was especially pleased: an annual pension of 10,000 maravedis – far more than he could earn in a year – had been promised by the King and Queen to the first person to sight land.

As the sun rose, the three ships dropped anchor just offshore. It was a beautiful morning. The azure water was calm and clear. The breeze was warm and light. Beyond the pristine white beaches a few huts and villages could be seen nestled among the deep green vegetation. Emerging from the captain's quarters, a tall, sun-burnt man, his red hair already turning white, descended the rope ladder hanging from the side of the *Santa Maria* and dropped into a rowboat waiting for him. Together with a few armed men he was taken ashore. Planting a royal banner in the sand, he declared this land to be the possession of Ferdinand and Isabella, King and Queen of Castile.[1]

Christopher Columbus had just arrived in the New World. But he certainly hadn't discovered it. Besides the obvious fact that the Americas were already inhabited by some 50 million indigenous people, we now know that Columbus wasn't even the first European to set foot in America. Nevertheless, it would be his story, with all its blunders and bloodshed, that would come to be celebrated as the discovery of America. It's a decision that's becoming increasingly contentious as historians bring to light the details of Columbus' exploits in the New World – details that are prompting ever-louder calls for his prominent place in US history to be re-evaluated.

~

Few figures from history are more enticing to the iconoclast than Christopher Columbus. The man has become so swaddled in lies and legends – many the result of his own tireless self-promotion – that virtually every widely held belief about the explorer is wrong in some way. He didn't discover America. He never even set foot in what is now the United States of America, the country where he's most celebrated today. And he didn't prove the world was round. In fact, as we'll see, he was perhaps the last educated European, until a resurgence of Flat-Earthism in the 19th century, to argue that it *wasn't* round.

He wasn't even called Christopher Columbus. The son of a weaver, Cristoforo Colombo was born in the fading Italian city of Genoa in 1451 (like many famous figures from the Renaissance, he's better known today by his Latinised name). Little is known about his early years, and Columbus himself rarely discussed them. His modest upbringing haunted him his entire life, and his desire to acquire wealth and status was the overriding motivation for almost everything he would go on to do. After a brief and unsatisfying stint as a weaver like his father, Columbus seized the opportunity to become a merchant sailor. This allowed him to see much of the world, sailing throughout the Mediterranean and along the western fringes of the Atlantic as far as Iceland and the River Volta in West Africa.[2]

Columbus, now in his mid-twenties, had grown into an awkward, unlikable young man. He was, by all accounts, obstinate, obsessive, paranoid and self-pitying, with a knack for turning friends into enemies. Nevertheless, his desperation to make a name for himself gave him a reckless, ruthless sense of drive and ambition that many of his contemporaries lacked. Most importantly, he quickly proved to be a gifted navigator with a rare instinct for the sea and an uncanny ability to reach his destination without the aid of equipment or calculations.

It was an exciting time to weigh anchor. Europe was entering its Age of Discovery, a period of global exploration and colonial expansion that would produce a revolution in geographic knowledge. In 1402 a ramshackle band of French adventurers kicked things off by launching the European colonisation of the Canary Islands. This was followed by the Portuguese discoveries of Madeira in 1419 and the Azores in 1427. By 1488 the Portuguese navigator Bartolomeu Dias had led the first European voyage around the Cape of Good Hope at the southern tip of Africa, opening up the Indian Ocean to further exploration by Westerners.[3]

Until now Europeans were reliant on wildly exaggerated and woefully outdated reports for information about the wider world. Study a world map from the time, such as the Borgia Map – made just a few years before Columbus' birth by an anonymous European cartographer – and you'd be forgiven for wondering whether you're looking at planet Earth. Only Africa, Asia and Europe are depicted, and even then in wildly distorted form: Europe is larger than Africa and Arabia combined, China is virtually non-existent, and imaginary mountain ranges criss-cross the continents. The cartographic tradition of putting north at the top had yet to be firmly established, with the result that Europe is found at the bottom of the map and southern Africa at the top. The landmasses are replete with biblical places, from the Garden of Eden to the evil land of Magog. Devils and dragons fill the map; Ethiopia is shown to be ruled by a dog-headed king named Ebinchibel. Such maps were, unsurprisingly, useless for navigation, and mariners had long ignored them in favour of their own sea charts. But navigation was never the purpose of medieval Europe's world maps: they were instead intended as visual displays of Christian theology – hence the biblical locations – as well as curiosity cabinets displaying the weird and wonderful corners of the world.

Things began to change in 1406, when a Byzantine copy of the 2nd-century geographer Ptolemy's writings – long since lost from European libraries – found its way to Venice and was translated into Latin. This translation, and its printing in 1477, reintroduced cartographers to the concepts of latitude, longitude and global coordinates, greatly improving the accuracy of their maps. In little more than 50 years after the creation of the Borgia Map, European cartographers were producing recognisable and increasingly precise depictions of the world.[4]

Despite these advances, Renaissance geography continued to mingle fact and fantasy – in part due to a lingering desire for the fantastic, but also because they knew no better. Entirely fictional rivers, seas and even whole continents festooned purportedly-accurate maps. There was the mysterious island of Taprobana, home to giant man-eating ants; the eastern land of Wak-Wak, where a certain tree produced fruit in the shape of screaming human heads; and the dreaded Isle of Demons in the frozen wastes of the north, from where the tortured cries of men were said to emanate. Such lands were inhabited by creatures including griffins, sphinxes and something called the bonnacon, a bull-like animal which could shoot scalding dung out of its rear end to a distance of 600 feet. Equally alarming were the many tribes populating the far corners of the Earth. These people were variously depicted on maps with six arms, four eyes, one leg or no head; mouths so small they could only drink through straws or ears so big they could be used to fly.[5]

More alluring were the tales of the fabulous wealth to be found in these distant lands. Africa and Asia were said to be overflowing with gold, jewels, spices and other expensive treasures. In addition to its macabre fruit harvest, Wak-Wak was said to have such abundant gold deposits that the metal was used to make chains and collars for dogs and monkeys. The palaces of India were rumoured to fuel their lamps solely with balsam, a tree resin similar to myrrh and frankincense that was highly prized as a perfume and medical panacea.[6]

These liberal spoonings of nonsense weren't damaging to European exploration. In fact, tall tales of foreign opulence provided perhaps the single biggest incentive for exploration in the 15th century. Bear in mind that Europe at this time was far from the world power it would later become. More than a century of unpredictable harvests and sporadic plagues had decimated the population and plunged the continent into a grim and long-lasting recession. Unrest in China and the collapse of Islamic unity in Central Asia had restricted the flow of silk and spices heading west along the once mighty Silk Road to a trickle. Particularly concerning was the exhaustion of Europe's gold deposits. By the time of Columbus' birth the continent's entire gold reserves had dwindled to little more than 200 cubic feet, an amount that could, were it not for its weight, easily be loaded into the back of a van.

Wages fell, banks folded and trade dried up. Mints across Europe closed, unable to source the metal to make new coins.[7]

So when legends of fantastically wealthy foreign lands reached Europe, they were met by an audience desperate enough to let greed and optimism outweigh any doubts. Numerous expeditions set sail from Europe's Atlantic coast in the hopes of finding mythical lands. Explorers usually returned empty-handed from these trips, but the geographic knowledge they gained in the process greatly added to Europe's understanding of the world. The discovery of the Azores came about during a Portuguese expedition to find the magical island of Antillia, where cities were paved with gold and silver nuggets could be plucked from the beaches. A number of English expeditions in search of the legendary island of Hy-Brasil (unrelated to the Brazil in South America) may even have reached the coast of North America years before Columbus crossed the Atlantic – but more on that later.

Columbus kept himself up to date with all the latest expeditions and discoveries. Working as a bookseller and cartographer in between trading voyages, he was also well aware of the many written accounts of fabulous wealth in the Orient. Keen to get involved in the action, by the 1480s he was devising his very own voyage of discovery. Quite what he hoped to discover wasn't clear. At various times Columbus considered captaining a trade mission, a voyage to find new lands and even a military expedition to recapture Jerusalem from the Mamluk Muslims. His only real aim was fame and fortune; how he achieved that was of secondary importance.[8]

Eventually he settled on a plan. Columbus was to 'go east by way of the west', as he put it: traverse the Atlantic to reach the eastern shores of China.[9] There he would load up on the country's bountiful treasures before sailing back home to a hero's welcome.

It would be quicker and simpler than travelling overland or navigating around Africa.

Atlantic expeditions were not, as Columbus later tried to make out, a bold new enterprise of his own devising. With the deteriorating situation in Central Asia making overland routes to the east inaccessible to most European traders, exploration of the Ocean Sea, as the Atlantic was then called, had become increasingly common in the 15th century. At least six expeditions to find rich fishing grounds in the North Atlantic were launched from the English city of Bristol in the 1470s and 1480s; no fewer than eight Portuguese voyages set sail between 1462 and 1487 in search of new islands west of the European mainland.[10]

What *was* unprecedented about Columbus' scheme was his proposal to cross the entirety of the Atlantic. No one before him had suggested such a plan, and with good reason: no ship could sail the many thousands of miles between Europe and East Asia without the serious risk of running out of supplies. Such a journey would easily take five months to traverse, and malnutrition had sounded the death knell for far less ambitious voyages before. And while a number of geographers confidently expected new lands and even entire continents to be discovered in the Atlantic (some cartographers were actually leaving blank spaces in their charts so that new discoveries could be added later), it remained foolhardy in the extreme to embark on such a long voyage in the mere hope that supplies could be topped up on as-yet undiscovered lands.[11]

In typical fashion, Columbus defied the academic consensus in favour of the fringe geography of Florentine astronomer Paolo Toscanelli, who argued, on the basis of grossly overestimating the size of Asia, that the distance between Lisbon and China was less than 3,000 miles – about one-quarter of the actual distance.

Columbus backed Toscanelli's miscalculations with his own faulty sums, which – owing to his schoolboy error in forgetting to standardise his units of measurement – underestimated the size of the Earth by a staggering 25 per cent. On the basis of these miscalculations, Columbus believed he could sail west to China in just a few weeks.[12]

It's worth stating that Columbus never proposed to sail to Asia to prove the Earth was round. As we discovered in the previous chapter, belief in a flat Earth hadn't been widely held by scholars for well over a thousand years, and no one rejected Columbus' plan on the basis that his ships would fall off the edge of the world. True to form, Columbus would actually go on to *reject* the spherical Earth in favour of his own, much weirder, hypothesis. 'I concluded that it was not round,' he wrote a few years after his first Atlantic voyage, 'but is of the same shape as a pear ... and at one point on its surface it was as if it had a woman's nipple put there; and this teat-like part would be the most prominent and nearest to the sky.' Not surprisingly, his nipple-tipped-pear-shaped Earth theory failed to find any supporters.[13]

Columbus would later claim that European powers were falling over themselves in a bid to be the lucky sponsors of his voyage to the Orient. This was another of his fabrications. When he first proposed his plan to the court of King John II of Portugal, it was roundly rejected once Portuguese scholars pointed out the obvious errors in his calculations. Undeterred, Columbus considered pitching his plan to English and French courts, his native Genoa and even the Pope, but none showed any interest. Nothing if not persistent, he then turned to the Castilian court of Ferdinand and Isabella. They were more receptive to his plan, but even then it took Columbus three attempts before they finally agreed to sponsor his voyage.[14]

Queen Isabella didn't pawn her jewels to fund the expedition, as popular legend has it. Indeed, neither Isabella nor Ferdinand expressed much interest or confidence in Columbus' scheme, and it was probably their lack of gold which finally pushed them to take a chance on the Genoese oddball. They provided just two ships, leaving it to Columbus to raise enough money to hire a third. Enthusiasm to take part in the expedition was so low that crew numbers had to be made up with prisoners, who were granted a royal pardon in exchange for joining the venture. Confident that Columbus wouldn't discover much, the King and Queen agreed to his inflated demands that he be made High Admiral of the Ocean Sea, entitled to claim one tenth of any treasure found out west and to rule over any new lands discovered in the Atlantic 'for ever and ever.'[15] It was a decision they would come to regret.

Columbus set sail from the Castilian town of Palos on Friday 3 August 1492. As well as the usual provisions of wine, water, beef and peas, his ships carried bells, beads and caps to trade at Chinese markets, passports addressed to the 'Grand Khan' of China (neither Columbus nor anyone else in Europe knew that the Mongol Khans hadn't ruled China for over 100 years), and an 'Oriental interpreter' who spoke Hebrew and Arabic.[16]

The first stop was the Canary Islands, which they reached after ten days' sailing. There they stocked up on supplies and repaired the *Pinta*'s rudder, which had come loose after just three days at sea. Three weeks later, on 6 September, the expedition ventured out into the Atlantic and the unknown. The story of Columbus' voyage is so familiar to us today that it can be difficult to imagine just how daunting this moment must have been. In the 15th century the Atlantic Ocean held a similar position in

European minds as outer space does today: no one on board knew what lay out there or whether they could ever return. 'Mankind then had no faster means of travelling than the sailing ship,' noted the writer Hans Koning, 'and these ships were leaving their world behind at all possible speed.'[17]

The crew of about 90, who didn't share Columbus' confidence in his calculations, were uneasy from day one. In order to allay their fears, Columbus started keeping two ship's logs: one for himself, in which he recorded his estimates of distance travelled, and another for the crew, in which the distances were noticeably shorter (as it happened, the falsified log turned out to be more accurate; Columbus' readings of latitude and longitude were often wrong by more than 100 per cent). As the days wore on, however, even Columbus grew surprised at the size of the Atlantic. It was taking weeks longer to cross than he had anticipated. Some of the crew, worried that this 'mad foreigner' had steered them so far west that they would never return home, even contemplated throwing him overboard and blaming the death on a freak astrolabe accident, which was presumably a more convincing explanation in the 15th century than it sounds today.[18]

For whatever reason, Columbus was never pitched overboard. And by early October there appeared, finally, signs of approaching land. Logs bobbed in the water; birds flew overhead. Then came the cry that land had been sighted, and crew and captain could at last breathe a sigh of relief. (Incidentally, Bermeo, the sailor who first saw land that moonlit night, never got his royal pension: Columbus later maintained that he had spotted land a few hours before Bermeo and claimed the reward for himself.[19])

On 12 October, as they set foot on dry land, Columbus believed that they must have arrived in some remote corner of Japan and, dismissing the native name of 'Guanahani', marked it down as 'San Salvador' on his map. Today we know that he was actually in the vicinity of the Bahamas, although we have no way of pinpointing exactly where the expedition made landfall, despite the many theories put forward; five centuries of shifting coast-lines, together with Columbus' vague descriptions, have made it impossible to be sure.

Most portrayals of Christopher Columbus' arrival in the New World depict the native inhabitants cowering in the bushes, fleeing from the new arrivals or being shooed away by crucifix-bearing churchmen. None of that actually happened. In truth, as Columbus himself recorded in his diary, the native Taínos appeared incredibly excited by the arrival of Columbus' expedition and were eager to greet them.[20] They crowded the beach, calling Columbus and his crew ashore. Those who couldn't wait dived into the sea and swam out to meet them. One old man even managed to haul himself into Columbus' boat as he was being rowed ashore. Once everyone was on land they readily exchanged gifts with the Europeans, swapping balls of cotton, parrots and handfuls of dried leaves for glass beads, red caps and hawks' bells. Others hurried to bring the visitors fresh water and food, surely a more welcome sight for the sailors after weeks of sour wine, foul water and brine-pickled pork. Other than their wooden spears, which they used for fishing, the Taínos appeared to have no knowledge of weapons; when Columbus showed them his sword, one of them tried to hold it by the blade and cut their hand.[21]

Columbus was impressed by the indigenous Taínos who welcomed him so warmly. They were tall and slim, 'with handsome bodies and very fine faces'.[22] None of them, he noted with some astonishment, appeared to suffer from rickets, unlike many back home in Europe. Most eye-catching for Columbus and his crew, however, were the small gold earrings and nose rings adorning a few of the natives. To the gold-obsessed mariners it was the first glimmer of hope in what had been a long, tiring and thoroughly unenjoyable journey.

Columbus' Hebrew and Arabic translator tried talking to the Taínos and claimed – somehow – to have understood that the Chinese city of Hangzhou lay a little further west. For the next three months the expedition zigged and zagged across the Caribbean in an increasingly frustrating search for the Grand Khan and his vast gold reserves. Hangzhou was never found, and Columbus suspected the Taínos had made up the story as a ruse to get rid of him and his men. An expedition into the Cuban interior, which Columbus believed to be mainland China, came back empty-handed. On 20 November the captain of the *Pinta*, fed up with the fruitless search, abandoned the expedition and set off back home. Then, as Columbus reluctantly agreed to follow, the *Santa Maria* ran aground off what today is Haiti and had to be abandoned. His voyage to the Orient, which had promised 'great riches and precious stones and spices', had managed to collect a few chillies, some low-quality cinnamon and several kidnapped natives (the gift of dried leaves from the Taínos had been thrown overboard by the crew, who were unaware that it was tobacco).[23] The expedition had been a complete failure.

But there was finally a silver lining for Columbus. Hispaniola, the name he gave to the island on which the *Santa Maria* ran aground, happened to have sizeable deposits of gold. This chance discovery allowed him to return to Europe with his head held high. 'This was the making of Columbus' mission,' remarks the historian Felipe Fernández-Armesto. 'Without it he would almost certainly have returned home to ridicule and obscurity.'[24] Realising the island's importance, Columbus ordered his crew to build a small stockade from the wood of the wrecked *Santa Maria* and left behind 39 men to guard it. After a miserable two-month voyage back to Europe, in which storms threatened to capsize the two remaining ships, Columbus returned to the Castilian Court to boast that he had indeed sailed east by way of west, and had the riches to prove it. It was, as he put it, 'the conquest of what seems impossible'.[25]

Isabella and Ferdinand were sceptical of Columbus' claim to have reached the shores of China, as were most people who heard of his expedition. Some suggested he had simply discovered new islands in the Canary Islands archipelago; others believed he had finally found the mythical island of Antillia, and still others correctly guessed that he had stumbled upon the fringes of a new continent. Wherever he'd been, the treasures and trinkets he brought back spoke for themselves: here was an opportunity for Castile to funnel an untapped source of wealth into its coffers. Preparations for a second, much bigger voyage began immediately.

~

Columbus would head three further return journeys across the Ocean Sea before his death in 1506. His second voyage, launched just six months after his return from the Caribbean, was an impressive seventeen-ship, 1,500-man fleet designed to establish a permanent Castilian presence on Hispaniola. In 1498 a much smaller expedition set sail with the aims of expanding the colonisation of Hispaniola and exploring more of the Caribbean, which Columbus still insisted on calling 'the Indies'. With his fourth and final voyage of 1502, Columbus hoped finally to track down the Oriental treasures that had eluded him back in 1492. Once at sea, however, what was to be his crowning achievement unravelled so disastrously that it would spell the end of his transatlantic travels for good.

So far it has been possible to follow Columbus' story without too much discomfort. He was nothing if not an underdog, and while it may be too much to expect anyone to actively like him it's certainly possible to root for him. All that changes with his three subsequent voyages. Whereas the first was little more than a glorified trade mission, these were undisguised colonial enterprises: get-rich-quick schemes designed to bleed the Caribbean dry. Then there's the character of Columbus himself. His self-righteousness, already grating for those who had to endure it, hardened in the face of growing criticism. His eccentricities soured into delusions. Most painfully, his utter rejection of the indigenous Americans' humanity, coupled with an emerging potential for psychopathic cruelty, ensured that Castile's first colonial ventures in the New World would be as heartless and destructive as possible for the indigenous populations ensnared by them.

Columbus' fall from grace began early into the second voyage. Returning to Hispaniola, he was shocked to discover that the stockade built from the wreck of the *Santa Maria* had been burned to the ground and all 39 of its men killed. The indigenous Taínos quickly confessed to the act, insisting they had acted in self-defence against the garrison's violent demands for gold and women. In retaliation, Columbus ordered the execution of a local chief and sanctioned hostilities against the Taínos, and within a year Hispaniola was engulfed in open warfare. Together with his brother Bartholomew, who joined him in Hispaniola in 1494, Columbus launched a series of military campaigns that are thought to have killed tens of thousands of indigenous people.[26]

Those who survived the slaughter were made the property of the Castilian colony and forced to work as servants, cooks and – for many of the girls and women – sex slaves.[27] As Columbus himself explained: 'the Indians were and are the wealth of the island of Hispaniola because it is they who mine and make the bread and all the rest of the Christian's food ... and perform all other duties and labours of men and of beasts of burden.'[28] The most destructive of these 'duties' was an edict forcing every native aged fourteen or older to deliver onerous tributes of gold or cotton to the colonists. Many died from exhaustion, and those who failed to fulfil their tribute, or refused to submit to the system, would face public mutilation or hanging.[29]

It seems unlikely that Columbus ever intended to exterminate the Taínos – they were, after all, his source of income – but the effects of his colonial management on the indigenous population were nothing short of genocidal. In the first two years of the establishment of slavery on Hispaniola, an estimated 50,000 natives died from disease, starvation and overwork. Tens of thousands more chose to take their own lives rather than endure the hellish system of enslavement established by Columbus. In 1492 Hispaniola was home to anywhere between 300,000 and 1 million indigenous people. By 1548 that number had dropped to about 500. An entire people were lost within a single lifetime.[30]

It's little use arguing that Columbus only reluctantly turned to slavery after failing to find enough gold to finance his voyages, or to excuse him as simply a man of his time, or to point out that he never personally owned slaves, as some have done. The unavoidable truth is that Columbus was obsessed with slavery, and as soon as he set eyes upon the Caribbean's native population he started plotting how best to exploit them. On 14 October 1492, just two days after meeting the Taínos for the very first time, he drafted an excited letter to Ferdinand and Isabella explaining how 'they would make fine servants ... should your Majesties command it, all the inhabitants could be taken away to Castile, or made slaves on the island. With fifty men we could subjugate them all and make them do whatever we want.'[31] In fact their Majesties had commanded no such thing, and Columbus had only been allowed to return to the Caribbean with the proviso that he 'try with all diligence' to convert the natives to Christianity.[32] This effectively ruled out slavery, as the enslavement of a Christian was an excommunicable offence for any Catholic. Economically, too, there was as yet no strong desire for a costly transatlantic slave trade: of the hundreds of slaves Columbus shipped back across the Atlantic during his second expedition, almost all died during the crossing or shortly after arriving in Europe, and his contemporaries deemed the enterprise unfeasible.[33]

Such concerns made little impression on Columbus, who cited unsubstantiated claims of cannibalism and incest among the indigenous population as grounds for shipping some 2,000 slaves back to Europe over the next five years. Even his fellow colonists, who had no qualms about slavery, complained that Columbus was singularly obsessed with establishing a transatlantic slave trade. By 1500 this all proved too much for Ferdinand and Isabella, who, never fully comfortable with the enterprise, commanded all indigenous Americans in Castile to be freed 'without any exception'.[34]

Despite this royal reprimand, Columbus' treatment of the Taínos only aroused very sporadic, if heartfelt, protests. What ultimately landed him in hot water was instead his treatment of the Castilian colonists. Columbus proved to be a woefully inept colonial governor: aloof and remote, cruel and paranoid, he quickly earned the nickname 'Pharaoh' among those who had to work for him. And while the plight of the colonists can't be compared to the devastation facing the Taínos, life on Hispaniola was undoubtedly miserable for all involved. Under the Columbus brothers' tyrannical rule, death sentences were handed out to colonists with alarming frequency, even for minor crimes. Other punishments included flogging and the confiscation of rations, which on more than one occasion led to death by starvation.[35]

It wasn't long before dissent among the Castilians erupted in outright rebellion, with half of them splintering off from Columbus' colony. Columbus attempted to suppress the uprising with arbitrary hangings, but he was unable to prevent colonists from sailing back to Castile to complain about his leadership. This they did in droves, with the first returning to Europe just months after the second voyage arrived in the Caribbean. By 1500 the chorus of complaints in the Castilian court was too loud to ignore, and Ferdinand and Isabella sent a royal administrator, Francisco de Bobadilla, to investigate.

Bobadilla was shocked by what he saw. The investigation began ominously when, pulling into the harbour, he was greeted by the spectacle of Castilian corpses dangling from gibbets. Stepping on land, Bobadilla discovered that the once paradisiacal island had been ravaged by six years of rule by Columbus and his brother. The landscape was scarred with mines and plantations. Vast stretches of land lay deserted save for the hundreds of gallows erected by the colonists. Disease was rife, food was low and fresh water scarce.[36]

Bobadilla had seen enough. Clapping Columbus and his brother in chains, he confiscated their property and ordered them back to Castile to stand trial for what he considered clear abuses of power. With their Pharaoh safely locked away, colonists lined up to denounce him to Bobadilla. 'For the love of God,' pleaded a priest stationed on Hispaniola, 'make sure that he or any of his countrymen never return to these islands.'[37]

Although his arrest and deportation marked the end of Columbus' colonial ambitions, part of him enjoyed the opportunity to wallow in self-pity. Holed up in prison while awaiting his trial, he finally looked to be as hard done by as he had always complained of being. For months he refused to have his shackles removed, despite being given repeated opportunities, and when he was summoned before Ferdinand and Isabella he made a great fuss of staggering up to them, chains clanking. The pity party worked, and the King and Queen, embarrassed by his condition, pardoned him. Notably, however, they refused to restore his status as High Admiral of the Ocean Sea – and with it his right to govern any lands discovered in the Atlantic.

Following his release in 1500, Columbus was permitted one final voyage to find the vast deposits of gold he insisted still lay out west, albeit with the explicit command that he never again set foot in Hispaniola. The distrust shown by the Castilian court was well-advised, for Columbus was by now betraying clear signs of delusion. He kept hinting that he had been sent to Earth by God and believed his discoveries had been prophesised in the Book of Isaiah. He took to dressing like a Franciscan friar, developed a habit of comparing himself to biblical figures such as Noah and Solomon, and on more than one occasion claimed to be guided by celestial voices.[38]

He also continued to insist, with increasing desperation, that his discoveries were Oriental and not of some previously unknown landmass, grasping at ever more tenuous evidence to make his case. Learning that some Caribbean natives called themselves Canibs, he convinced himself they were really saying *Khanibs*, which must surely mean they were subjects of the Great Khan. He asserted that the cotton headbands worn by the natives of Trinidad were in fact Moorish turbans. In Cuba he reported finding the footprints of a griffin, a mythical beast known only from the Orient. He claimed to have discovered the Garden of Eden in present-day Brazil, the mines of Solomon in the Panama Isthmus and the biblical land of Sheba in Hispaniola – locations all thought at the time to be somewhere in Asia. No matter how strenuous his wishful thinking, however, there were signs that Columbus' confidence was wavering. As early as 1494, during his second voyage, he forced almost every crew member in his fleet to swear an oath that Cuba was part of mainland China. Anyone who broke the oath, he threatened, would have their tongue cut out. The Oriental nature of his discoveries was the foundation of his entire reputation, and he would never accept any other explanation.[39]

It was in this increasingly unhinged state that Columbus once again sailed to the New World in 1502 with the intention of finally discovering the Chinese riches he had sought for ten years. He hoped this would be his 'noblest' voyage yet, a grand finale that would restore his tattered reputation and silence his enemies once and for all. Instead, it became the final proof that Columbus' ocean-going days were over. The voyage was a disaster – 'the most manifest failure of his life', in the words of one biographer.[40] Columbus remained an unusually adept navigator, but his journey was thwarted by a combination of hurricanes, malaria, hostile natives and worm-riddled ships, culminating in him and his crew being marooned on what's now Jamaica. Two of the castaways were able to raise the alarm after canoeing for five days back to the Castilian colony on Hispaniola, but even then Columbus was so despised by the colonists that they refused to launch a rescue party for seven whole months. Following his eventual return to Castile in November 1504, Columbus never again returned to the sea. He died, bitter and deluded, just eighteen months later at the age of 54. To his contemporaries it seemed that Columbus' story was well and truly over.

Each year, the second Monday in October sees thousands of people parade down Fifth Avenue in New York City. There are flags and floats, motorcades and majorettes. Members of the city's police troop past in dress uniforms. Local politicians and dignitaries, such as the city's mayor and the state's governor, join the procession. In the 2019 parade some 35,000 people marched past nearly 1 million spectators. The subject of this enormous celebration? Christopher Columbus.

The second Monday in October is Columbus Day in the USA, a time when millions of people across the country honour the cruel, selfish, deluded Genoese sailor who died, even by his own estimation, a failure. Even taking into account the increasing number of states and cities that have stopped celebrating Columbus Day – in response to growing opposition among sections of the American public – many areas of the country continue to observe the federal holiday. Clearly, in the 500 years since his death, Columbus has undergone one of history's more remarkable transformations. What happened?

Columbus didn't exactly die in obscurity, as is sometimes claimed, but he did quickly fade from public consciousness. The Florentine navigator Amerigo Vespucci, the first European to realise that America was a continent in its own right and not part of Asia, soon eclipsed Columbus thanks to the best-selling accounts he wrote of his voyages. When the cartographer Martin Waldseemüller decided to name the new landmass emerging from the Ocean Sea, he called it not Columbia but America, in Amerigo's honour, apparently unaware that Columbus had beaten him to its shores. Over the next three centuries Columbus was rarely discussed by historians; the centenary and bicentenary of his arrival in the Caribbean passed largely unnoticed both in Europe and America.[41]

And then Britain's thirteen North American colonies declared their independence in 1776. Now calling itself the United States of America, this young country suddenly found itself in need of a distinctly American origin story, one free from British influence. Today, the most obvious candidates for an American foundation myth would be the continent's indigenous inhabitants, who had already been there for over 16,000 years. In the 18th century, however, widespread contempt among European settlers for Native Americans ruled out that option. Perhaps the next best candidate was the Venetian mariner John Cabot, at the time thought to be the first European to set foot in North America. Annoyingly, however, Cabot had been sponsored by the English, so he couldn't be used either. The Portuguese-backed Vespucci had become the victim of a posthumous smear campaign by Spanish historians and was in no fit state to be idolised. That left Americans with the obscure Genoese navigator who had reached the Caribbean in 1492 – despite the unfortunate fact that he never found North America or knew of its existence. Christopher Columbus would have to do.

The reinvention of Columbus' first voyage as the Discovery of America rescued the mariner from the doldrums of obscurity and thrust him back onto the world stage. In the process he was transformed into the archetypal American pioneer: practical, level-headed and down-to-earth. His religious fanaticism and scientific illiteracy were swapped for a forward-thinking empiricism and a disdain for the antiquated views of the Old World. Columbus' status as a commoner, which he had tried all his life to shed, was now his greatest asset: here was a humble weaver's son who escaped the straightjacket of European life to make a name for himself out west.

The cult of Columbus was enthusiastically adopted in the USA. 1792 saw the first recorded celebrations in his honour, with dinners and drinks held in New York, Boston and Baltimore on 12 October to commemorate 'the greatest event in the history of mankind since the death of our Saviour'.[42] The name Columbia, despite missing out on the top job, was liberally bestowed upon cities, streets, schools, counties, parks and rivers throughout the country. The nation's capital was built in the District of Columbia. For over a century the song *Hail, Columbia* was the country's unofficial national anthem.[43]

This all-new, all-American Columbus received a major boost in 1828 when the author Washington Irving published *The Life and Times of Christopher Columbus*. Irving's best-selling biography showered Columbus with platitudes befitting of a national hero: he was dignified, forgiving and magnanimous; 'a man of great and inventive genius', whose 'quickness of temper was counteracted by the benevolence of his heart'.[44] Irving, who had found fame with his short stories *Rip Van Winkle* and *The Legend of Sleepy Hollow*, apparently struggled to keep the make-believe out of his 'faithful' history. His most enduring lie was that Europeans still thought the world was flat in 1492, a claim which the noted 20th-century historian Samuel Morison described as 'misleading and mischievous nonsense'.[45]

Irving's account isn't as sycophantic as some detractors have made out. He doesn't shy away from calling Columbus a bigot, for instance, and is critical of his treatment and enslavement of those who refused to convert to Christianity. However, these flaws are treated as aberrations from Columbus' natural compassion and generosity, times when he let the prejudices of his day lead him astray. Irving's intention with this book, as he openly admitted, was to create a patriotic role model for his compatriots. Consequently, he recasts Columbus' actions in Hispaniola as an attempt 'to civilise the natives', and shifts the blame for the resulting destruction of the Taínos from Columbus to his fellow colonists, a 'dissolute rabble' of thieves and pirates.[46]

Others went further than Irving in their praise of Columbus. The historian William Prescott claimed to find it 'difficult to point to a single blemish in his moral character'.[47] At the inauguration of the 1893 World Fair in Chicago, dedicated to the 400th anniversary of Columbus' first voyage (it opened a year late), he was celebrated in no uncertain terms as 'the greatest human benefactor of the human race'.[48]

Columbus' status as a national hero proved useful for Italian-Americans, who by the time of the World Fair had begun arriving in the USA in large numbers. By adopting Columbus as a kind of mascot they were able to present themselves as more American in the face of hostile anti-Catholic discrimination. The year 1882 saw the formation of the Knights of Columbus, an organisation to promote Catholic interests in the USA. High on their agenda was to have Columbus' arrival in the New World recognised with a national holiday. Early success came when President Benjamin Harrison declared 21 October 1892 as 'Discovery Day', notable for introducing the Pledge of Allegiance to American classrooms, where it's still recited today. By 1919 more than 30 US states had introduced some sort of Columbus-themed holiday, and in 1937 the Knights of Columbus successfully lobbied President Franklin Roosevelt to make Discovery Day an annual nationwide holiday, now called Columbus Day. It's principally as a celebration of Italian-American culture that Columbus Day continues today; despite the name, Columbus himself made only sporadic appearances among the flag waving and baton twirling of the New York parade.

As Columbus grew in popularity, however, so too did his critics. In 1874 the American diplomat Aaron Goodrich published
his scathing *History of the Character and Achievements of the
So-Called Christopher Columbus*, denouncing the Columbus
legend as 'but a gilded lie ... full of rottenness and dead men's
bones'.[49] In his wake there followed a series of critical – if more
measured – assessments from professional historians. In 1891
Justin Winsor, librarian of Harvard University, unapologetically
described Columbus as a man of 'overwhelming selfishness' with
'no pity for the misery of others', whose colonisation of Hispaniola
left a 'legacy of devastation and crime'.[50]

Other critics seemed more upset by Columbus' newfound
status as a champion of immigrants and Catholics. 'God's plan
was that Protestantism and not Catholicism should have its
chance in the New World,' fumed one historian.[51] Proof of God's
plan was therefore quickly sought, and the late 19th century
saw strenuous efforts to credit the discovery of America to a
more suitably Protestant explorer. Detractors gleefully pointed
to the Norse, whose ancient sagas described a series of expeditions to lands west of Greenland sometime around the year
1000 CE. True, the Norse weren't Protestants (many weren't even
Christians 1,000 years ago), but they were suitably Anglo-Saxon
enough to satisfy the anti-Catholic brigade. A full five centuries
before Columbus, the sagas claimed, the explorer Leif Erikson set
sail after hearing rumours of thickly wooded lands to the west –
an enticing prospect for someone living on treeless Greenland,
where timber was constantly in short supply. Living up to his
nickname 'Leif the Lucky', he found not one but three lands: the
barren Helluland, the wooded Markland and the fertile Vinland.
A subsequent expedition returned a few years later with the
aim of creating a permanent settlement in Vinland, but severe

winters and clashes with the natives eventually put an end to such ambitions.[52]

It was an exciting story, and not beyond the realms of possibility: the Norse were accomplished sailors, they were familiar with the North Atlantic, and Greenland was closer to mainland North America than Europe. The only trouble was in substantiating the claim. The sagas were too vague, too unreliable to be considered proof. They contradicted each other in places. Believable accounts of exploration were intermingled with clear strains of fantasy. Moreover, hard evidence was conspicuously absent. No shortage of purportedly 'Viking' discoveries had begun cropping up all across north-east USA, but none passed muster with professional archaeologists, who found them all to be either hoaxes or misidentifications. For some, this lack of evidence wasn't a problem: in 1887 the amateur historian Marie Brown argued that the Catholic Church, 'the foulest tyrant the world has ever had', had for centuries deliberately suppressed any evidence of the Norse discovery of America as part of its merciless quest for world domination.[53]

The difficulty in evidencing the Norse discovery of America did nothing to discourage similar efforts, and there soon began a veritable industry in 'proving' that Columbus wasn't the first person to discover America. In 1875 the folklorist Charles Leland introduced American audiences to the Chinese legend of the monk Hui Shen, who, at the venerable age of 90, is said to have crossed the Pacific Ocean to reach the shores of Mexico. The following year the clergyman Benjamin Bowen argued, on the basis of perceived (and since disproven) similarities between Welsh and various Native American languages, that the Welsh Prince Madoc sailed to North America in 1170. Then, in 1893, the genealogist Thomas Sinclair suggested that his ancestor, Scottish nobleman

Henry Sinclair, reached North America nearly a century before Columbus. Others pointed to the 5th-century Irish monk Brendan the Navigator or the 14th-century English astronomer Nicholas of Lynn as the continent's discoverers. All have since been discredited by historians.[54]

Even today, with the growing acknowledgement that the first explorers of the Americas were the ancestors of the continents' indigenous inhabitants, the urge to prove who 'discovered' America has lost none of its allure. The Phoenicians, Egyptians, ancient Greeks and Bronze Age Chinese have all been put forward as contenders. In 2014 it was suggested that Marco Polo may have ventured as far as Alaska on his famous 13th-century travels, which, given that there are doubts as to whether he even made it as far as China, seems unlikely.[55] That same year, Turkish president Recep Erdoğan solemnly declared that Muslims had reached the New World in 1178, citing the utterly false claim that Columbus discovered a mosque while exploring the Bahamas.[56]

Among the less fantastical notions entertained today is the suggestion that Bristolian fishermen stumbled upon the North American coast sometime in the 15th century as they searched for new fishing grounds in the North Atlantic. It's no secret that numerous expeditions were being launched from Bristol in the 1480s and 90s to find the cod-rich waters surrounding the legendary island of Hy-Brasil, which some historians have identified as present-day Newfoundland. Did they find it? A rival theory holds that they were beaten to it by the Basques, equally accomplished fishermen who were also scouring the Atlantic for untapped cod stocks in the 15th century. Intriguingly, when the French explorer Jacques Cartier 'discovered' the North American St Lawrence River in 1534 he found the waters were already full of Basque fishing boats.[57]

Another hypothesis suggests that the ancient Polynesians, the unrivalled mariners of the Pacific Ocean, reached the western coast of South America around 1000 CE. The presence of the South American sweet potato in Polynesia and the Polynesian bottle gourd in South America lend support to this possibility. There was excitement in 2007 when a Chilean archaeological dig uncovered bones of chickens – an animal previously thought to have been introduced to the Americas by Spanish Conquistadors – that were carbon dated to between 1321 and 1407. As this was well before Columbus' arrival in the Caribbean, could the chickens have been brought to the New World by Polynesian seafarers? Apparently not: subsequent DNA sequencing of both Pacific and American chicken populations has ruled out any contact between the two, casting doubt on those dates. Moreover, recent research has shown that the sweet potato and bottle gourd almost certainly crossed the Pacific naturally via ocean currents thousands of years before humans took to the waves. Add to that the absence in South America of the Pacific rat, which faithfully followed the ancient Polynesians on their other voyages, and the case for pre-Columbian contact via the Pacific remains contentious.[58]

In the end, it turned out that the Norse theory – once dismissed as 'nonsense' – was indeed correct, although it wasn't until the 1960s that evidence was found to support the adventure told in the sagas. The Norwegian archaeologist Anne Ingstad and her husband, the explorer Helge Ingstad, were convinced that there must be some truth to the legends, and in 1960 began scouring Canada's Atlantic coast for signs of Norse settlement. By 1962 they had arrived at the remote Newfoundland village of L'Anse aux Meadows, where a local fisherman pointed them in the direction of some curious rectangular mounds in the grass. Anne's interest was piqued: she knew what Norse building remains looked like,

she knew how Norse villages were laid out, and she knew the locations where the Norse liked to establish their encampments – and
the site of L'Anse aux Meadows ticked all three.[59]

Returning to the site with a team of international archaeologists, the Ingstads were delighted – if not entirely surprised – to
discover that the remains were indeed Norse. The settlement consisted of seven timber-framed, turf-topped houses, a 60-foot-long
hall, a smithy and a number of small outbuildings. The acidic soil
at the site had destroyed many remnants of life at the settlement,
but archaeologists were still able to recover enough artefacts,
such as iron nails and bronze ring pins, that proved definitively
that this was a Norse rather than a native village. Curiously, they
also found the husk of a butternut squash, a plant which could
never survive the bitter Newfoundland winter – suggesting that
the Norse may have gone on trading missions, and perhaps even
built other settlements, much farther south. Carbon dating provided the final piece of evidence needed, confirming that the site
was built around 1000 CE, just as the sagas claimed. 'This is the
first incontrovertible proof of Viking visits to North America in
pre-Columbian times,' announced the 16 November 1963 edition
of *Science News Letter*.[60]

~

Anne and Helge Ingstad's discovery was undoubtedly one of
the most remarkable archaeological finds of the 20th century.
However, to frame it in terms of dethroning Columbus, as many
have done, is something of a sideshow. For one thing, discovering
America was just about the one thing Columbus never claimed to
have accomplished, refusing to concede even the existence of the
Americas until his dying day. For another, it's an accepted fact that
the first people to reach America were the ancestors of today's

indigenous Americans, who did so long before any Castilians, Norse or any other suggested 'discoverers'. This isn't to say that we shouldn't challenge and question the history of exploration in the Americas – as L'Anse aux Meadows shows, our understanding of history can be wrong – but that we should stop framing such debates in terms of discovery.

Besides, regardless of who explored America first, it was Columbus who – for better or for worse – established a lasting connection between Europe and America in a way that the Norse never did. It was Columbus whose voyages became the founding myth of the richest, most powerful country on Earth. And it's Columbus who continues to be remembered and celebrated as the discoverer of America, even in the face of contradictory archaeological evidence.

The influence of Columbus' voyages can still be seen in a surprising number of ways. We still call the Caribbean the West Indies thanks to his bad geography and wishful thinking. Even more absurdly, we still refer to indigenous Americans as 'Indians', a name that makes as much sense as it would to call them 'Chinese', 'Japanese' or 'Malaysians' – all other places where Columbus suspected he may have landed. (As the etymologist Mark Forsyth notes, 'nonsense, under the tutelage of time, becomes geography.'[61]) Many of the other names Columbus bestowed on the Caribbean are still found on maps today, including Hispaniola, Trinidad, Guadeloupe and Dominica. His encounters with the Taínos brought us the words 'canoe', 'hammock', 'barbecue', 'tobacco' and 'hurricane', and his interactions with the neighbouring Canib people gave us the 'Caribbean', the 'cannibal' and Shakespeare's Caliban. Indeed, the popular image of the cannibal – a scantily-dressed jungle savage, usually with some bone stuck through their nose – remains a remarkably faithful visual account of the exaggerated descriptions given by Columbus of the Canibs in order to justify their enslavement.[62]

Columbus' ability to stir up controversy, more than five centuries after his death, is a testament to his enduring influence. The continued celebration of the explorer faces particular resistance from many Native Americans, who regard Columbus as the harbinger of the 'American holocaust', when as many as 50 million of the indigenous people died through a combination of the disease, enslavement, murder and war that came with European colonisation.[63] 'To celebrate the legacy of this murderer is an affront to all Indian peoples,' declared the American Indian Movement in 2000.[64]

Monuments to Columbus are coming under increasing attack in the USA by protesters who consider them 'symbols of hate' and 'monuments of genocide'. In 1989 three indigenous activists were arrested for pouring buckets of fake blood on a Denver statue of the explorer as a Columbus Day parade marched past. In 2017 a statue in New York's Central Park had its hands painted blood-red and the words 'hate will not be tolerated' spray-painted across it. That same year an obelisk in Baltimore, erected in 1792 and thought to be the oldest monument to the explorer in the country, was attacked with a sledgehammer by anti-Columbus protesters.[65] These efforts stepped up a gear in 2020, when widespread protests against racial inequality in the USA demanded the removal of Columbus statues. More than 30 memorials to the explorer have since been removed from various locations around the country. Most of these were ordered by local authorities, but a few dethronements came at the hands of protesters, with two statues being beheaded during the night and another set on fire and thrown in a lake.

In response to the explorer's growing unpopularity, an increasing number of US cities and states have chosen to replace

Columbus Day with a day celebrating indigenous Americans. The state of South Dakota, where almost one in ten people are Native American, was the first state to make the change when it replaced Columbus Day with Native American Day in 1990. The city of Berkeley in California soon followed suit, celebrating its first Indigenous Peoples' Day during Columbus' quincentenary of 1992. Today Indigenous Peoples' Day or some variant is celebrated instead of Columbus Day in more than 100 towns and cities throughout the USA, such as Los Angeles, San Francisco, Seattle, Minneapolis and Santa Fe, along with a current total of eleven states, including Minnesota, Vermont, Alaska, Oregon and Hawaii. Even the city of Columbus, Ohio, has abandoned its namesake's holiday, choosing in 2018 to commemorate Veterans Day with a public holiday instead.

Elsewhere in the Americas, 12 October has long been celebrated under a range of different, noticeably less Columbus-focussed, names. In Argentina it's known as the Day of Respect for Cultural Diversity; in Costa Rica it's the Day of Cultures; and in Venezuela it's celebrated as the Day of Indigenous Resistance. (Ecuadoreans, meanwhile, must make do with the leaden-sounding Day of Interculturality and Plurinationality.) In the USA, however, criticisms of Columbus Day have in turn faced resistance from many Italian-Americans, who see them as an attack on their heritage and community and accuse protesters of anti-Catholic bias. Columbus is also developing a loyal following among right-wing pundits who, annoyed by what they see as yet more 'multiculturalist and atheist' revisionism of American history, have leapt to defend the explorer's courage and Christian devotion.[66] Even Columbus' hare-brained scheme to launch a crusade against the Muslims of Jerusalem has found new support among the anti-Islam segments of the US right.

Ultimately, the question that's being discussed, debated, spray-painted and sledgehammered is: how do we commemorate the past? Do we celebrate it? Mourn it? Erase it? Ignore it? Do we commend the Age of Discovery as a time of daring exploration and geographic enlightenment, or condemn it as a prelude to imperialism and slavery? Do we praise Columbus as a champion of Italian-Americans or attack him as the murderer of indigenous Americans?

And it's here that the story of Christopher Columbus leaves the realm of history and enters that of politics. At best, the historian can present us with facts about the past. They can't tell us what to do with them. The facts about Columbus' life have been known for quite some time now – and yet virtually every widely held belief about the explorer is wrong in some way. He's *still* remembered as the man who discovered the New World, first set foot in North America and proved the world was round. His status as a national hero to some – and a villain to others – virtually guarantees that Columbus will continue to be subject to biased, exaggerated and inaccurate histories for the foreseeable future. It will come as little surprise if people are still trying to separate fact from fiction in another 500 years' time.

CHAPTER 6

The real housewives of the 18th century

For a few heady years, the French Revolution looked like it might become a women's revolution too. Beginning with the formation of a new government in the summer of 1789 – in defiance of the king's wishes – the shibboleths of the old regime came crashing down in such rapid succession that for a while it seemed as if anything was possible. France became a republic; press censorship was partially lifted; monarchy was abolished and slavery outlawed. From the ruins of the old way of life, France's politicians and philosophers set about building a new society: one founded on the principles of science and reason, the rights of man and – just perhaps – the rights of woman.

In 1790 the Marquis de Condorcet, who we last encountered decrying the so-called Dark Ages, published an essay demanding equal political rights for women while serving in the country's Legislative Assembly. 'Either no individual of the human species has any true rights or they all have the same,' declared Condorcet, 'and he who votes against the rights of another – of any religion, colour, or sex – has henceforth denied his own.'[1] The fight was taken up next by the playwright Marie Gouze, better known by her pen name of Olympe de Gouges. 'Women, wake up!' cried de Gouges in the *Declaration of the Rights of Woman*, her response to the Revolutionary government's famous *Declaration of the Rights of Man*. 'What advantage have you gained from the Revolution? A more marked contempt, a more noted disdain.'[2]

By now women had begun to organise themselves politically. In 1791 the writer, campaigner and spy Etta Palm d'Aelders led a female delegation to the government to protest against their 'secondary existence in society', demanding education for girls and greater legal rights for wives.[3] The spring of 1793 saw the establishment of the Society of Revolutionary Republican Women, a pugnacious political organisation that was halfway between a debate club and a goon squad. When not discussing the innate political and military capabilities of women, its members were busy shouting down political opponents in public meetings and harassing them in the street. Longer-term goals of the Society, as articulated by its two founders, chocolate maker Pauline Léon and actress Claire Lacombe, ranged from the prosaic demand for cheaper bread to the ambitious request that women be granted equal rights to bear arms and form military brigades.

For a while it appeared as if the Revolutionary government was listening. In September 1792 the National Convention, the country's new law-making body, not only made divorce legal but granted women the same rights as men to file for it. Both men and women took full advantage of this newfound freedom: over the next ten years close to 50,000 couples in France divorced. In some towns the annual divorce rate during this decade was 50 times greater than the rate of legal separation before the change in the law.[4] Women and girls were also granted greater inheritance rights; wives were promised equal control over marital property; and primary education for both boys and girls was in the works. A few politicians and publishers even began to voice their support for Condorcet, calling for the right of women to vote and to hold office.

Then, as suddenly as it had come in, the tide began to turn. In the summer of 1793 the violent Jacobin faction took control of government, ousting the moderate Girondins for what they

regarded as 'unfaithfulness' to the Revolution. The Jacobins instigated an eight-month period, subsequently termed the Reign of
Terror, in which dissent or criticism of the Revolutionary government was ruthlessly suppressed. Continued calls for gender
equality were ignored or quickly dismissed. The promises to grant
women equal control over marital property never materialised.
It soon became dangerous to speak out. On 20 July Olympe
de Gouges was arrested and imprisoned for 'attempting to per-
vert the republic with her writings'. Less than three months later
an arrest warrant had been issued for Condorcet.[5]

Trouble was also brewing for women's Revolutionary clubs. The
Jacobins had once been close allies of the Society of Revolutionary
Republican Women, but increasing disagreements over how best
to support France's poorest – with many of the Society's women
insisting that more be done to help them – left the Society politically isolated and vulnerable. On 29 October the club's members
were accused in the National Convention of neglecting their families by their involvement in politics. The theme was picked up the
following day by the politician Jean-Baptiste Amar, who argued
that 'it is not possible for women to exercise political rights' on
account of their innate lack of the moral and intellectual qualities
required. Indeed, for a woman to 'leave her family to immerse
herself in the affairs of government' would be to defy 'nature itself'.
All forms of political involvement, Amar concluded, must be forbidden to women. His speech finished, the Convention was ready
to vote on the matter, and on that same day all women's political
clubs in France were outlawed in a near-unanimous vote. Only one
member of the Convention had voted to keep them open.[6]

Women tried to protest the ruling, but on their first attempt
they were booed out of the Convention. On 17 November they
tried again, when a group of women led by Claire Lacombe

stormed a meeting of the Paris Council at City Hall. Again, however, their complaint was ignored; the decision was final. Before kicking them out of City Hall, the president of the Paris Council, Pierre Chaumette, denounced them as 'unnatural' women trying 'to turn themselves into men' by taking part in politics. 'Since when has it been decent for women to abandon their pious household tasks and their children's cradles?' he asked. 'In the name of nature itself, stay as you are. Instead of envying our perilous, busy lives, you should be content to help us forget all this at home in our families, where we can rest our eyes with the enchanting sight of our children made happy through your cares.'[7]

It's an appeal all too familiar to women today: that they should stay at home, look after their children, and leave the serious matters to men. At its heart is the belief that there's something natural about this arrangement – that women have always spent their days solely as wives and mothers: cooking, cleaning and keeping house. And yet every so often an event from the pages of history doesn't quite support this assumption. The very fact that a delegation of women were voicing their grievances to the politicians of the Paris Council – in the midst of the Revolution's bloodthirsty Reign of Terror, no less – should make us question the image of the housebound wife and mother, and invite us to look beyond the stereotypes of marriage and motherhood.

~

To appreciate just how mistaken the myth is that women are innately suited to domestic roles, we need to step further back in time for a moment. Imagine yourself in Europe around the year 1200, at a time known as the High Middle Ages. It is a rural world: forests and fields cloak the continent, where some 90 per cent of its 70 million inhabitants live out their entire lives in the countryside. Paris, the biggest city in Christendom, has a population of around 100,000 – about the size of Wakefield, England or Tuscaloosa, Alabama today. The continent is a mosaic of kingdoms and petty empires, often at war with one another. Europe at this time is still looked upon as something of a backwater by the empires of Islam and Byzantium: the intellectual fruits of the Islamic Golden Age had yet to transform European thinking, and Europe's globetrotting Age of Discovery was still three centuries in the future (although legends of mythical lands far out west are already common in the harbour towns of the Atlantic coast).

Politically, many Europeans lived under the socio-economic system of feudalism, whereby peasants were obliged to work the land for their local lord, who was in turn obliged to provide services, usually military, to the peasants and to the king. For the millions of women living as serfs under this feudal system, work was an inescapable part of life, and each year would bring with it the familiar cycle of agricultural jobs. Every spring the ground needed to be cleared and seeds sown. Summer was the time for haymaking, sheep shearing, muck spreading and the ever-tedious task of weeding. The end of summer saw the harvesting and processing of crops, and the fall of autumn leaves was met with the slaughter and butchering of livestock. Other jobs, such as milking, were carried out throughout the year. In all these tasks, women worked alongside men; only ploughing and sowing were considered to be typically manly jobs, but even here women would often help out when needed. Work began at a young age. Both boys and girls would help around the house and the lord's estate as soon as they could be trusted to work by themselves, looking after younger siblings, guarding geese, even working as carters or plough drivers on occasion. Others would be sent to work as servants within the manor itself.[8]

There was always work to be done in the countryside, but it was repetitive, exhausting and – even for those not slaving away as serfs – poorly paid. As a result, between the years 1000 and 1300 an increasing number of men and women made the decision to leave their homes in the country and start a new life in Europe's emerging towns and cities. Free from the straightjacket of feudalism, the various craft and mercantile industries that powered these urban centres offered new arrivals the prospect of higher wages and greater opportunity.[9] Fuelled by this migration, the High Middle Ages became a boom time for towns and cities, which expanded at a rate not seen since the height of the Roman Empire almost a thousand years previously. A number of urban centres doubled or tripled in size, both in terms of population and land area. Old Roman settlements like London, Paris and Cologne sprang back with renewed vigour, becoming the commercial, political and social centres of the medieval world.

Many young women arriving from the countryside took jobs as maidservants. The work paid poorly, but it was still more than they could expect to earn back home. Plus, there were always plenty of openings: thanks to the low wages it was quite common even for financially modest households to employ a few servants, and in the big houses of rich merchants and nobles there could be dozens of staff. When townswomen married (which, unless they joined a convent, was a virtual certainty), many of them stopped working as maidservants and instead learned their husband's trade. The typical medieval business was headed by a man, but most men relied on their wives working alongside them to make ends meet. As in the countryside, children would also lend a hand, and from a young age would either work in the family trade or be sent off to learn a new vocation as an apprentice to a craftsman or woman.[10]

Whether through family or apprenticeship, the sheer diversity of trades worked by women in the towns and cities of medieval Europe is remarkable. Records show them working as butchers, bakers, bookbinders and illustrators; as coopers, cobblers, shopkeepers and innkeepers. There were hatters and wig makers; waggoners and bucklers; moneylenders and currency exchangers; wire-drawers and cutlers; blacksmiths, brownsmiths and tinsmiths. Metalworkers made pins, needles, scissors and knives; leatherworkers made belts, straps, gloves and pouches. Even master craftsmen, who would spend at least seven years perfecting their trade, sometimes preferred working with their wives rather than hiring craftsmen. Thus we find women working as highly skilled professionals such as goldsmiths, jewellers and lapidaries.[11]

Although frequently referred to as helpers or assistants, the importance of women in these various crafts was far greater. In addition to learning a trade, women often performed the crucial job of selling the family's wares at shops, markets and fares. They might take charge of the business while their husbands were on out-of-town trips. And should their husbands die, the widows were entitled to run their husband's trade permanently, often proving themselves skilled workers and adept businesswomen in their own right.[12]

A woman's career wasn't necessarily dictated by her husband, however. As well as plying the family trade, many women took on extra work to boost the household income. The textiles and food industries in particular were dominated by women, to the point where they were widely regarded as feminine vocations. (In a refrain all too familiar today, the weaver's guild in Bristol complained that female competition had left men unable to find work.[13]) The most common tasks were spinning and weaving cloth, wool, linen and silk, as well as fabric dying, tailoring and

embroidery. Beer brewing was the second most common occupation for women after textiles work, followed by food-related jobs
such as making oils and condiments, growing and selling vege-
tables and freshwater fishing.

It would be a mistake, then, to think that women kept themselves to traditionally feminine roles such as sewing and cooking.
A job was a job, and women showed no hesitation seizing whatever opportunity came their way. In fact, with the exception of
the clergy, it's difficult to find any profession that was solely a male
preserve. Even trades still considered masculine today, such as
within the construction industry, were fair game, and there are
records of women in the Middle Ages working as carpenters, plas-
terers, masons, roofers and day labourers. Sometimes the number
of female construction workers outnumbered the men: workers
on building sites in the German town of Würzburg in the late
1400s, for example, were recorded as 750 men and 2,500 women.[14]

Professional medicine was another male-dominated discipline
that women took to. In addition to the many wives working alongside their husbands as medical assistants, a small but significant
number of women were licenced as physicians, surgeons and
apothecaries in their own right, especially in northern Europe.
Female doctors had a virtual monopoly on obstetrics and gynae-
cology, which male physicians, if they ventured near the subject
at all, treated as strictly theoretical disciplines. In some places,
such as Frankfurt, eye surgery seems to have been a particular
specialisation of female surgeons.[15] It would be a woman, Marie
Colinet, who first pioneered the use of magnets to remove metal
filings from a patient's eye.[16]

There were also a small number of women making a living
as merchants, a respectable trade for a medieval European. The
city of Bristol was home to some 50 female merchants in the later

15th century. One of them, Alice Chestre, became very wealthy running her late husband's trading network, using her own ships to freight iron, wool, wine and oil as far as Ireland, Flanders, Portugal and Spain. Others traded anything from sulphur to soap to arrows and crossbows. These women were invariably formidable traders, unafraid to protect their profits whenever necessary. When Coventry-based merchant Margery Russell learned that £800-worth of her goods had been stolen by Spanish pirates – an enormous sum worth many millions today – she obtained official permission to seize the equivalent amount back from Spanish merchants, which she promptly did. After the 14th-century trader Rose Burford had repeatedly tried and failed to get King Edward II to pay back a loan, she offered him a deal: the king could renege on his repayments if he waived the customary export tax for Burford's stocks of wool. The king, after inviting Burford to make her case before the royal court, accepted the deal.[17]

Women who lacked the personal wealth and authority of Russell or Burford were by no means defenceless when it came to protecting their livelihoods. In a number of European cities they formed their own all-female guilds to defend their industries, and at times monopolies in certain trades were granted exclusively to women. In London in 1368, female silk weavers petitioned King Edward III to stop a rival male trader from inflating the price of silk by hoarding resources. The following century, they successfully lobbied parliament to ban the import of silk goods into the country, which they argued was putting them out of business.

For many of these less well-off women, work didn't stop once they got home. Just as in the 21st century, women who worked full-time jobs were still expected to shoulder the majority of domestic chores. Servants were cheap and plentiful, it's true, but for many households there was still plenty of work to be done even with the help of a few servants. Chores included not only those familiar to us today – cooking, cleaning, shopping – but many other tasks now considered full-time jobs in their own right, such as spinning and weaving cloth, making medicines and brewing beer. For rural women the list was even longer: in the countryside it was considered a woman's responsibility to take wheat to the mill, churn cream and butter, make cheese, tend to the family's vegetable patch and look after any poultry or piglets they might own. Even property maintenance, such as thatching rooves and repairing roads, could fall under a woman's remit.[18]

Last but not least, a woman was still expected to be a mother on top of all her other duties. In a world before antibiotics and modern hygiene standards, heartbreaking rates of infant mortality (roughly one in three children would die before their fifth birthday), together with a lack of reliable contraceptives and a life expectancy for mothers of around 40, meant that women could reasonably expect to spend the majority of their adult lives either pregnant or with young children. Because of this, pregnancy and motherhood weren't considered reasons for a woman to stop working.

Indeed, nothing short of illness or injury would have prevented women outside the nobility from working, for the simple reason that their earnings were an essential source of income for many households. Even women from wealthy merchant families were encouraged to learn a craft as insurance against hard times and a defence against idleness – a deep-seated fear among medieval moralists – or simply to stave off boredom. In 1351 King Jean II of France went so far as to make it a crime for any healthy Parisian, male or female, to refuse work, threatening such idlers with expulsion from the city, a stint in the stocks or a spell in jail. The persistently workshy could even be branded on the forehead.[19] Pierre Chaumette's contention, 442 years later, that women should stay at home would have struck both women and men in the Middle Ages as nonsensical.

~

So what happened? If medieval women worked alongside men in a wide range of trades, why was Chaumette telling their descendants that they were fit only for domestic duties? The most straightforward answer to this question is, quite simply, that women were pushed out of the job market in the centuries following the High Middle Ages. Despite performing essential work in both the rural and urban economies of Europe, women had never been regarded as the equal of male labourers. They were certainly never paid the same as men, even for the exact same work. As a result, women found themselves at the vulnerable margins of the economy, the first to be dropped in times of crisis.[20] And Europe was about to be hit by two of the most destructive crises in its history.

The first of these arrived in the autumn of 1314, when torrential downpours across northern Europe were followed by a bitterly cold winter and a cool, wet summer. The same thing happened the following autumn. Then, to people's horror, it happened again the next year. Three years of extremely wet weather spelled disaster for farms across much of the continent: fields flooded, seeds washed away and crops rotted in the ground, while livestock, deprived of feed, starved or succumbed to disease. With crop yields falling by more than half in some countries and food prices skyrocketing, those unable to grow their own produce were also unable to buy anyone else's. In the space of a few years some 10 to 15 per cent of northern Europe – an estimated 4 million people – starved to death, in what has since become known as the Great Famine.[21]

As the effects of the famine receded in the 1320s, a new generation of Europeans began to pick up the pieces – unaware that a second disaster was already brewing in the far-off foothills of the Himalayas. There, a terrifying disease was spreading through the population. Symptoms began with a splitting headache, chest pains and stomach cramps, before internal bleeding turned the skin black and blotchy and fever rendered the helpless sufferer inconsolable. Death was inevitable. As people realised the danger of the disease they attempted to flee, but this only hastened its spread. By the 1330s it had appeared in China; the following decade it was in India and Persia, and by 1346 it had reached the Crimea. From there it went one of two ways: either taking the overland trade routes south through the Levant and Arabia or boarding the cargo ships heading west to the shores of the Mediterranean. The plague struck Constantinople and Sicily the following year before spreading to mainland Europe. It tore through the continent at a speed of two miles a day, taking less than three years to reach the Arctic Circle. It became known as the Black Death.

This wasn't the first time the disease had struck Europe – the same species of bacteria likely decimated the Eastern Mediterranean 800 years earlier – nor would it be the last. But the ferocity of the Black Death was unlike anything the Old World had experienced before or since. In China an estimated 35 million, a little less than a third of the population, succumbed to the plague over the next few decades. In Europe the toll was even higher: between a third and a half of the continent's population was killed by the disease, and it would take hundreds of years for many countries' populations to return to pre-plague levels. The population of England and Wales only reached this point in the 17th century, some four centuries later.[22] 'It made the country quite void of inhabitants so that there were almost none left alive,' reported a contemporary English chronicler. 'We see death coming into our midst like black smoke,' mourned the Welsh poet Jeuan Gethin, who would later die of the disease; 'a plague which cuts off the young, a rootless phantom which has no mercy or fair countenance'.[23]

For the women who survived both the famine and plague the economic consequences were mixed. On the one hand, the chronic shortage of workers throughout Europe not only meant that there were more job opportunities, but also allowed workers to demand much higher wages for their labour. In many places wages doubled in the wake of the Black Death, although it's revealing that the gender pay gap remained largely unchanged – even now, with more than a third of the work force obliterated, female labour was still looked down upon and women's wages never matched men's.[24]

On the other hand, the economic crises of the 1300s set in motion a long-term process of excluding women from professional work and pushing them towards poorly esteemed and badly paid jobs. Before the crises of the 14th century, economic power in towns and cities was concentrated in the guilds: exclusive groups of master craftsmen, craftswomen, workers and apprentices all specialising in a particular vocation, which might have been anything from basket weaving to longbow making. In the post-plague world, however, with the average worker newly empowered, the guilds closed ranks in an attempt to shut out the competition, making it more expensive for those without family ties to join and progress to the prestigious rank of a fully-fledged master craftsman or woman. The protectionism of the guilds wasn't aimed explicitly at the exclusion of female workers, but the precarious nature of female employment meant it hit them harder. A self-perpetuating cycle set in: as women found it harder to achieve master status in their professions, male guild members – who had consistently complained about female membership throughout the Middle Ages – began refusing to admit them on the pretext that they had proven themselves unable to master their crafts. As a result, job opportunities in respectable, well-paid trades slowly began to dwindle, and over the ensuing centuries industries once dominated by women, and even all-female guilds, were gradually taken over by men.[25]

This shift was justified by a range of excuses. Male workers argued that women were too weak, feeble-minded or ditzy to master a craft, or that it would be immodest for them to work alongside men. These claims had been made before, but they were heard with increasing frequency during the later Middle Ages. By the 15th and 16th centuries the prejudice against professional women had reached the point where it was considered questionable whether a man should even employ his wife and daughters in the family workshop. In the 1400s the wives of master fullers in Leiden were forbidden from taking charge of their husbands' accounts. Cologne's harness makers were banned from hiring female assistants in 1494. In 1556 a Strasbourg belt maker was forced to fire his own daughters after the other belt makers in the city protested against their employment.[26]

The male takeover of obstetrics provides a clear example of this societal shift. This discipline, for obvious reasons, had long been seen as a speciality of female doctors and healers. However, as medicine became increasingly academic from the 17th century onwards, training moved to medical schools and universities, from which women were almost always excluded (and would be until the late 19th century). By the 1700s male physicians and surgeons were openly attacking 'she-doctors' as untrained amateurs and dangerous quacks, even though female midwives often demonstrated better hygiene standards – such as washing their hands in water and vinegar – than their male contemporaries. Nevertheless, the smear campaign worked, and in the 18th century it gradually became fashionable for women to choose a male obstetrician to oversee their births.[27]

By this time an increasing number of women were either consigned to domestic tasks – cooking, cleaning or, for wealthier families, running the household staff – or plying trades considered feminine and therefore non-threatening to male workers, such as millinery and lacework. Not all women accepted these developments, of course, and there are records in the 18th century of female ironmongers, glaziers and sword makers. There also remained a sizeable number of wealthier women, especially widows, who owned property and worked as landladies. But such women were increasingly in the minority.

~

In and of itself, the idea that unpaid domestic jobs – what we would today call housework – was women's work was nothing new. In fact, evidence suggests that domestic chores were already a woman's burden in prehistoric times. Skeletal remains from some of the world's oldest farming communities show that as long ago as 9000 BCE women and girls were responsible for the majority of domestic chores, including the backbreaking work of grinding grain by hand. By studying the wear and tear on the skeletons of such women, archaeologists at the University of Cambridge found that the endless back-and-forth motion of grinding grain left these women with an upper body strength 16 per cent greater than the University's own female rowing team, who train for eighteen hours every week. A woman's household chores in early agricultural society demanded the equivalent effort of a twelve-mile row every single day.[28]

Historical evidence also supports a long-held belief in housework as somehow unsuited for men. The uneven division of labour first seen in early farming communities was later justified and enshrined by ancient philosophers and theologians. The ancient Greek philosopher Aristotle, for example, was clear that domestic chores were a woman's remit on the grounds that women should be subject to the rule of 'naturally superior' men in the home. It was a theme picked up by the early Christians, notably the apostle Paul, whose belief that women should be silent and submissive found pride of place in the New Testament.

Influenced by Aristotle and the Bible, such views remained commonplace in medieval Europe. Women were repeatedly encouraged by (male) writers to content themselves with domestic chores or – better yet – renounce the outside world altogether and join a convent. Given the scale and variety of female employment in the High Middle Ages, however, it's clear that most women roundly ignored such advice. And with good reason: in most households women were far too important economically to stop working. Only the nobility could afford such an extravagance, treating chronically bored noblewomen as little more than housebound breeders of male heirs.

This began to change with the growth of private business and the steady accumulation of capital in Europe's towns and cities in the centuries following the Black Death. By the 1600s a small but growing number of merchant families, particularly in Holland and England, had become rich enough to support unemployed family members. An 'idle wife' became the ultimate new-money status symbol, a sure sign that a merchant was rich enough to support a lifestyle once only available to the nobility.[29] Not everyone welcomed this new trend. 'The tradesman is foolishly vain of making his wife a gentlewoman,' grumbled the writer Daniel Defoe. 'He will ever have her sit above in the parlour, and receive visits, and drink tea, and entertain her neighbours, or take a coach and go abroad; but as to the business, she shall not stoop to touch it.' In his 1724 novel *Roxana*, Defoe has the title character complain about the 'life of perfect indolence' that the wife must submit to. 'The woman has nothing to do,' she explains, 'but to eat the fat and drink the sweet; to sit still, and look round her; be waited on, and made much of.'[30]

Defoe might not have approved, but in the decades following his death in 1731 the confinement of women to domestic affairs was endorsed by some of Europe's leading intellectuals. Indeed, it was central to the Enlightenment conception of the ideal family. Reacting against the widespread practice of arranged marriages among the upper classes, and the even more widespread practice of adultery, writers and thinkers like Jean-Jacques Rousseau and Denis Diderot began instead to describe marriage as not so much a religious duty as the natural and unassailable state of men and women. (Oddly enough, they rarely took their own advice: Diderot had numerous affairs, while Rousseau never legally married his mistress of 33 years and sent their five children straight to orphanages.)

At the heart of this new view of the family was the wife and mother, content – if not delighted – to renounce her career and devote her life to her children and husband.[31] For Enlightenment moralists, the shrinking economic freedom of women was a good thing, as it allowed women to focus entirely on family life – which was, they insisted, their natural inclination anyway – and allowed men to justify their monopoly of industry. The perfect wife had transformed from the competent business partner of the Middle Ages to a tender-hearted idiot, whose inherent lack of intelligence and patience rendered her unsuitable for anything but her instinctive desire to marry and have children. 'Woman was made specially to please man,' declared Rousseau; 'it is the law of nature.'[32]

The philosophy met with approval from the growing ranks of middle-class men wealthy enough to enact it. Nauseatingly saccharine depictions of doting mothers and blissful families saturated art and literature from the 1750s onwards, to the delight of Enlightenment dons like Diderot. Houses were transformed from public workplaces into private 'sanctuaries', where husbands – who were increasingly working outside the home – could relax after a hard day. Challenging the widespread employment of wet nurses by the middle and upper classes, mothers were encouraged to embrace their maternal duties by breastfeeding their own children. Rousseau, the most ardent champion of breastfeeding, praised it as the natural way to encourage maternal bonding, raise healthy children and (a little more optimistically) improve a nation's morals.[33]

Female education, in particular, reflected these changing views. In the Middle Ages a girl's education was geared largely towards learning a particular livelihood, whether that was the yearly cycle of agricultural tasks or the trade of an urban craftswoman. The only exception were the women of the aristocracy, whose education – in things such as chess, backgammon, singing, reading and falconry – was designed mainly to fill the long, lonely hours at home. By the 1700s, however, vocational training was being dropped among the middle classes. According to Rousseau, the whole purpose of a girl's education was to produce a woman eager to serve her husband and raise his children (the fact that this mindset was supposedly innate in women, and thus shouldn't have needed to be taught, seems to have escaped him). Any career aspirations on the woman's part would be 'to play the man' and abandon 'her natural state'. Instead, appropriate skills included the 'feminine arts' of needlework and dressmaking as well as 'the details of housekeeping', such as cooking, cleaning and shopping. Literacy was encouraged to a degree, as the Enlightenment mother was supposed to teach her own children to read, but excessive learning was frowned upon.[34] 'Laborious learning or painful pondering, even if a woman should greatly succeed in it, destroy the merits that are proper to her sex,' opined the philosopher Immanuel Kant. 'A woman ... might as well have a beard.' This hostility was keenly felt by women of the time. As the philosopher Mary Astell noted in 1694: 'girls who excel in learning ... are star'd upon as Monsters, Censur'd, Envy'd, and every way Discourag'd.' The writer Mary Wortley Montagu agreed, complaining in 1710 that 'there is hardly a character in the World more Despicable or more liable to universal ridicule than that of a Learned Woman.'[35]

Despite these criticisms, this new philosophy seemed to be having the desired effect: by the end of the 18th century the average age at which a woman tied the knot had dropped to 23, from close to 30 in the previous century, and the number of women choosing not to marry had halved. Moreover, wives were having more children than previous generations.[36] However, these changes probably owed more to the steadily shrinking job market for female workers, and the corresponding rise in poverty and unemployment among single women, than the urgings of Enlightenment philosophers. Technological advances meant that paid work was increasingly carried out in dedicated workshops which could easily out-compete the resources of individual craftswomen. In addition, the growing view of homes as private refuges from the working world meant that the lines of work women could still perform at home, such as sewing and food production, were increasingly disparaged as mere housework of little economic value. Even wet nurses found themselves out of a job thanks to Rousseau's breastfeeding drive.

There were positive consequences of the Enlightenment conception of the family. The focus on childcare encouraged middle-class families to recognise childhood as a stage of life in its own right, and to abandon the old view of babies as slightly sinister beings and children as simply imperfect adults. In connection to this was a concerted effort to lower the rate of infant mortality, which remained painfully high. The drive for 'natural' families also celebrated the idea of marrying for love, although it would be a mistake to assume that all marriages before the Enlightenment were loveless legalities – medieval accounts of fathers playing catch with their sons, or mothers curling their daughters' hair, for instance, give us glimpses into a surprisingly familiar family life. Nevertheless, the redefinition of women in the Enlightenment was in many ways an enormous step backwards, especially for the female worker. Olympe de Gouges questioned how, 'in a century of enlightenment and wisdom', a man could 'command as a despot a sex which is in full possession of its intellectual faculties'. It was a view echoed by Etta Palm d'Aelders, who repeatedly compared the new Enlightenment style of marriage to female slavery: 'our life, our liberty, our fortune are no longer ours.'[37]

These economic, social and philosophical developments formed part of the intellectual backdrop to the French Revolution, and help to explain the hostility to women's rights expressed by male revolutionaries like Jean-Baptiste Amar and Pierre Chaumette.

Jean-Jacques Rousseau, in particular, was raised up as a guiding light of Revolutionary thought. Rousseau's dictum that a new French republic must embody 'masculine virtues' of courage and strength if it was to avoid the fate that befell the 'soft and effeminate' royalist regime encouraged many Revolutionaries to reject female participation outright as political poison, and to dismiss Condorcet's calls for equality as dangerous nonsense. The Enlightenment idea of the family proved extremely useful in justifying this exclusion, as it allowed male Revolutionaries to charge that it would be 'unnatural' for a woman to leave her domestic duties to take part in politics. This was the most common explanation given in rejecting calls for gender equality; just as the Society of Revolutionary Republican Women was lambasted for not keeping busy 'with the care of their household', so was de Gouges told by the Revolutionary government that she 'would be better off knitting breeches'.[38]

Far from igniting a feminist uprising, the Revolution became the first time in French history when political rights were explicitly denied to people on the grounds of sex. Condorcet's ideas, despite being a more consistent exploration of the Enlightenment concept of human rights, remained a fringe view to which few were converted in his lifetime. The various Revolutionary governments that came and went never seriously considered giving women the right to hold political office or vote (and it wasn't until 1944 that French women were allowed to do either). The only true equality women enjoyed during the Revolution, as de Gouges acidly remarked, was 'the equality to ascend the scaffold'. It proved sadly prescient: four days after women's political clubs were outlawed, de Gouges was charged, in typical revolutionary hyperbole, of 'having composed a work contrary to the expressed desire of the entire nation', and sentenced to death by guillotine.[39] Time was also running out for

Condorcet: after months in hiding, he was eventually arrested and imprisoned on 27 March 1794 and found dead in his cell two days later, possibly by his own hand. The following month both Claire Lacombe and Pauline Léon were also thrown in prison. Léon was released after four months, but Lacombe had to wait over a year to be granted her freedom. Both women managed to survive the remainder of the Revolution, dying in obscurity decades later – but they did so only by abandoning their political ambitions.

The ideology of the Enlightenment wife also explains why these campaigners were unable to make many lasting changes to the status of women in European society. Continued protests by women only provoked greater restrictions of their freedom: two years after political clubs were disbanded in 1793, all women in France were barred from attending 'any kind of political assembly' or even congregating in public in groups of six or more.[40] The end of the Revolution and Napoleon's rise to power in 1799 brought no respite: France's new ruler was a firm advocate of the newly limited role of women in society, once commenting that they 'should stick to knitting'.[41] When he introduced his Civil Code, also known as the Napoleonic Code, in 1804, married women found their inequalities further entrenched. Whereas the Code ensured that widows and unmarried women enjoyed legal rights similar to men, a married woman was treated as a minor. Under the Code's laws, a husband had absolute authority over the running of his family, and in all his decisions – where they should live, how the children should be raised – his wife was legally obliged to obey. If a wife was convicted of adultery she would face between three months and two years in prison, whereas the husband could walk away scot-free. Moreover, if a husband caught his wife and her lover at home in the act he was legally entitled to kill them both; were a wife to try the same thing she would be charged with murder.[42]

The demise of Napoleon in 1815 brought no improvement in the status of women, followed as it was by the restoration of a conservative Catholic monarchy. A woman's right to divorce, already greatly reduced under the Napoleonic Code, was abolished completely in 1816, not to be reinstated until 1886. An increasing number of women were also coming to accept and endorse their role as housewives. Indeed, the 19th century saw the ideology of the housebound wife and mother reach its apogee in Western thought.

As before, this development was primarily driven by economic change. With the arrival of the Industrial Revolution at the turn of the 19th century, the social shifts that had been taking place among the upper and middle classes for the past five centuries – the separation of public and private lives, of 'masculine' work and 'feminine' housework, of the active husband and housebound wife – became even more pronounced. As the mechanisation of industry transformed workshops into factories, capable of producing goods at previously unimaginable speed and scale, it became even harder for the individual craftswomen, working by hand, to compete. The wealth created by the growth of industry, meanwhile, provided a greater number of families the means with which to keep their wives and daughters unemployed.[43]

Ideology, too, continued to play its part. The 19th century saw European empires and colonies spread to cover some three quarters of the world's landmass, making Europeans increasingly familiar with cultures other than their own. Convinced of their own superiority – this was, after all, the era of the Law of Progress – Europeans tended to view any differences to their own way of life as more primitive stages of civilisation. And one of the most striking differences they observed was that women outside Europe still worked. In Francis Parkman's *The Oregon Trail*, his account of a journey through the American West in 1846, he described how the old native women he encountered were shouldered with 'the heaviest labours of the camp ... they must harness the horses, pitch the lodges, dress the buffalo-robes, and bring in meat for the hunters'. These observations were matched in Charles New's recollection of his travels in East Africa, where 'the women are treated as beasts of burden ... while the men did nothing'. In light of such accounts, the housewife was no longer merely a symbol of a husband's wealth, but a mark of civilised society.[44]

These various factors combined to make a middle- or upper-class woman's life domesticised to the point of house arrest. Contact with the outside world should be limited from birth: if you could afford it, having your daughters educated at home was preferable to sending them off to school. Care must be taken not to overload them, of course, and few girls gained an education beyond secondary level. With the onset of puberty they were instead encouraged to 'reserve their energies for the development of their reproductive organs' in preparation for motherhood. Once married, a woman was expected to devote herself to raising her family and managing her household with patience, frugality and 'extreme activity and diligence'. Despite mawkish Victorian depictions of blissful domesticity, such as Coventry Patmore's wildly popular poem 'The Angel in the House', or Franz Winterhalter's famous painting of Queen Victoria and Prince Albert surrounded by five of their children, life as a housewife was hard work. In contrast to their medieval ancestors, most middle-class families in the 19th century could only afford one servant, and so many of the household chores still fell to the wife; the life of an idle wife was only available to the very richest. However, since it was a woman's 'feminine destiny' to become a housewife, as the German poet Friedrich Schiller put it, the endless chores must appear effortless. The housewife must never be heard to complain.[45]

For the girls and women forced to accept such seclusion, the life of the housebound housewife was no myth. But it was still the lifestyle of the few. During the 19th century no more than one in seven people could count themselves among the upper and middle classes; for the remaining 85 per cent of women who belonged to the working class, the cloistered life of a Victorian housewife was an unimaginable existence. 'To obtain a livelihood,' noted one Victorian doctor, 'females ... are obliged to work in excess.'[46]

The same economic developments that were allowing a greater number of middle-class women to spend their lives sequestered at home were also forcing working-class women to find work elsewhere. Many who had previously eked out a living at home – in cottage industries such as spinning, sewing, straw plaiting and leatherworking – were compelled to work in the factories that had put them out of business in order to feed their families. This was especially true for the textiles industry, which for centuries had been powered largely by women and was the first sector to become heavily mechanised in the early years of the Industrial Revolution. Women continued to dominate it, often outnumbering their male co-workers as they worked factory jobs such as picking, reeling, tenting, throstle spinning and power loom operating. Girls were often employed for the more nimble-fingered tasks, such as reconnecting broken threads. In the 1830s, two thirds of female factory workers in the United Kingdom were aged twenty or younger.[47]

Early factories were home to some of the most brutal working conditions people had ever endured. The fast-moving machinery was extremely dangerous, and there are numerous accounts of workers, children included, having their hair ripped out, their fingers sliced off or limbs wrenched from their sockets. Some injuries proved fatal. Even for those who avoided accidents, the machinery was quite literally deafening: many workers would eventually lose their hearing. The air, kept hot and humid to prevent threads from breaking, was so choked with cotton dust that it was often difficult to breathe. The appalling conditions, coupled with the long working day – thirteen-hour shifts were standard – meant that workers risked eye problems, lung disease and cancer if they stayed long enough.[48]

However, perhaps the most gruelling livelihood was coal mining, where women and girls worked hauling coals up to the surface on sledges or in baskets strapped to their backs. The 1851 UK census recorded some 11,000 women working in the mining industry. Conditions in the hot, dusty, filthy mines could fairly be described as hellish. In the early 19th century a civil engineer named Robert Bald was inspecting coal mines in the Scottish town of Alloa, appalled by 'the slavery and severity of the toil' performed by the women, when a female hauler emerged from one of the shafts and approached him. 'I wish to God the first woman who tried to bear coals had broken her back,' she said. 'None would have tried again.'[49]

Outside the cotton mills and coal mines, women could be found working in a wide range of other industries, from brick-works to paper mills to cement factories. Others were employed as potters, pen grinders and in the manufacture of buttons, chains and nails. However, as far-reaching as the Industrial Revolution would eventually become, in the mid-19th century its transform-ation of the working world was still in progress. Most Europeans still lived and worked in the countryside. Even in Britain, then the most industrialised country in the world, there were three times as many people working in non-mechanised industries as in mechanised ones, and the majority still worked as domestic servants and agricultural workers. Preindustrial jobs as cobblers, cooks, barmaids, laundresses, dressmakers and nurses were also still available to some women. Whatever their occupation, the economic and social status of female workers continued to decline, and working-class women were confined to the least prestigious and worst paid jobs available. They continued to be paid less than men, often receiving half or less of a man's wage for the exact same work. Nineteenth-century writers may have been quick to condemn other societies for burdening 'the tender half of humanity' with gruelling, thankless work, but they were often much slower to notice their complicity in the same thing in their own countries.[50]

If the image of female coal miners or factory workers strikes you as unusual or unexpected, it's a testament to the staying power of the Enlightenment conception of family and motherhood and its continuing influence on our understanding of the past – not to mention the class biases of historians who took the experiences of upper- and middle-class wives and mothers as typical for the majority of women. The emergence of modern history writing, both as a recognisable academic discipline and a mass-market hobby, took place in the mid-1800s, just as the cult of the housewife was reaching its zenith. What's more, its practitioners were almost entirely middle- and upper-class men, for whom the housebound wife and mother was an everyday reality and not an impossibility, as it was for the working class. As a result, 19th-century middle-class family values have been baked into our understanding of the past, often in defiance of evidence to the contrary. Assuming that women had always been confined to the home – and considering housework inherently unimportant – generations of male historians saw no reason to write about women or their experiences. With few exceptions, women were reduced to little more than historical backdrops: the wives and mothers of great men. Those who couldn't be presented in this way – working mothers, master craftswomen, cutthroat businesswomen – were sidelined, ignored or treated as unwomanly aberrations.[51] As Catherine Morland, the heroine of Jane Austin's novel *Northanger Abbey*, declared: 'History tells me nothing that does not either vex or weary me. The quarrels of popes and kings, with wars or pestilences, in every page; the men all so good for nothing, and hardly any women at all.'[52]

Something similar was taking place in the new discipline of archaeology. For much of the 19th and 20th centuries it wasn't uncommon for archaeologists to interpret finds and sites reaching all the way back to the Stone Age through this modern European lens. Women, it was assumed, had spent their time sequestered indoors, leaving men to embark on the great political, military and artistic endeavours of civilisation by themselves. The same artefacts would be given different interpretations based on where they were found. If pestles were unearthed in a female grave they showed that she cooked for her family; if they were found in a man's grave, however, they were taken as a sign that the deceased was a stonemason. The discovery of a set of scales in a male grave indicated that he was a merchant, but the same scales in a woman's grave meant only that she was married to one. Even when female graves were discovered loaded with goods indicative of power and wealth, it was taken to mean that the woman was the wife of a high-ranking man and not powerful in her own right.[53]

As academia becomes increasingly aware of its own presumptions and prejudices, historians and archaeologists see discoveries like the graves of prestigious women less as problems to explain away and more as valuable opportunities to learn about societies different to our own, perhaps gaining an insight into male and female roles in the past. Old discoveries are now being looked at again in a new light, often with surprising results. One such find is the grave of a 'high-status warrior' unearthed in Birka, central Sweden, in 1878. This remarkable 10th-century Viking tomb contained a skeleton together with the remains of two warhorses and a veritable armoury of weapons, including a sword, axe, knives, spears, shields and a quiver stocked with 25 armour-piercing arrows. On account of its military trappings – and the distinct lack of typically feminine items like jewellery or household items – the body was long assumed to be that of a man, and a particularly manly one at that. However, when a team of archaeologists re-examined the skeleton in the 1970s and noticed its suspiciously feminine build they began to doubt this assumption. These doubts were confirmed in 2017, when genetic analysis of the bones revealed the warrior was indeed female, calling into question many long-held assumptions about Viking society. What's more, the archaeologists who made this discovery suspect that other Viking warriors already excavated may also turn out to be women on closer inspection.[54]

Findings like this don't just allow us to reconsider the mores and customs of long-vanished societies, however, but of our own as well. It was 21st-century archaeologists, after all, who continued to assume that Viking warriors must have been men; for all we know the Vikings themselves may never have held such a prejudice. The same goes for any other historical or archaeological endeavour to learn more about the lives of women in the past, whether they were Iron-Age nobles or 19th-century factory workers. Each new detail uncovered helps furnish a richer, fuller understanding of their experiences, in all their diversity – and helps expose the myth of the eternally-housebound wife and mother for the man-made construct it is.

For those women who can afford to, the decision to stay at home is, of course, theirs to make. But any attempts to portray homemaking as a woman's 'true calling', or to suggest that the housebound lifestyle of middle- and upper-class Europeans from the 18th and 19th centuries can be applied to all women, is to ignore centuries of history. It's the same mistake Jean-Baptiste Amar, Pierre Chaumette and a thousand other Revolutionaries made over two hundred years ago when they invoked 'the law of nature' to deny women the right to join the French Revolution as anything other than wives and mothers.

History reveals this argument for the fallacy it is. Even as Chaumette uttered his condemnation of the Society of Revolutionary Republican Women, millions of women in France and throughout Europe were working for a living, as farmers, maidservants, tailors and in countless other trades. In previous centuries, before economic and social changes made the house-bound wife a realistic lifestyle for all but the richest families, even more lines of work were available to women, from the hard graft of metalworking to the precise art of gem cutting. The ancient world may hold even more surprises in store as archaeologists begin to look again at the roles of women in the distant past. Much is undoubtedly lost to time and anonymity, and we will probably never know the full extent of women's contributions to art and industry; as the writer Virginia Woolf once suggested, 'I would venture to guess that Anon, who wrote so many poems without signing them, was often a woman.'[55] But that doesn't mean there isn't more to unearth, and new finds are being made each year. If women were marching in the French Revolution, fighting as Viking warriors and labouring as medieval construction workers, what else is there to be rediscovered?

CHAPTER 7

How to invent a nation

For many of us, the first history lessons we're taught are about our own country's history: at school we learn of our nation's kings and queens, presidents or prime ministers; of births, deaths, battles and disasters. It's a subject many of us return to once we leave school. Bookshops teem with national histories. Documentaries focus on key events from our country's past. Dates such as 1066, 1776 and 1945 stay with us – even if their significance doesn't.

The fact that we learn about history this way – indeed, the fact that we learn about history at all – is largely thanks to the pioneering work of nationalist historians of the 19th century, who did much to promote the popularity of history and archaeology. Today, even in the age of 'the new nationalism', it's common to regard nationalism as an outdated ideology or a mere expression of discontent. To do so, however, risks overlooking the enormous influence it's had in shaping the modern world. The movements for national sovereignty and independence that came to dominate the 1800s not only gave us a world of nations, but sparked a widespread interest in national history that has stayed with us ever since.

In some respects, this is surely a good thing: the study of our country's past is not only fascinating but provides us with crucial context for understanding the machinations of modern politics. There is, however, a more questionable side to nationalism's legacy. In their eagerness to use history to foster national identity and pride, few nationalist historians were willing to let facts and evidence get in the way of a good story. As a result, many of our beloved national histories are riddled with inaccuracies, anachronisms, exaggerations and outright lies. Forget for a moment what you thought you knew about your country's past; Boudicca wasn't English, the Gauls weren't French, and the ancient Egyptians weren't actually Egyptian.

Nationalism has a lot to answer for.

~

We don't need to dig too deep to unearth the roots of nationalism, as the ideology only rose to prominence in the past two centuries. Before then, the idea that a nation – a group of people with a shared culture and territory – should have political power and rule as a nation-state was virtually unknown. Of course, culturally distinct groups have existed since prehistory. But a community's culture, traditions and language – today some of the most important building blocks of national identity – were by no means grounds for political autonomy or authority in the past. For the overwhelming majority of recorded history, beginning with the rise of the centralised states along the Fertile Crescent in the 3rd millennium BCE, political legitimacy instead rested on the twin pillars of monarchy and religion. More ambitious rulers attempted to roll these two authorities into one divine kingship, as was the case with the Egyptian pharaohs and, later, Japanese emperors – whose Japanese title of *Tennō* still translates as 'heavenly sovereign'.

This marriage between religion and royalty continued largely unchanged for millennia. At the height of the Inca Empire in the early 1500s, kings would regularly consult with their deified ancestors via oracles before making political decisions. Around the same time in Europe, the political theorist Machiavelli declared that 'there has never been in any country an extraordinary legislator who has not invoked the deity, for otherwise his laws would not have been accepted.'[1] As recently as the 18th century, the Holy Roman Emperor, who ruled a vast multinational expanse of Central Europe comprising more than 300 individual kingdoms, principalities, duchies and free cities, emphasised his political and religious might with official titles including 'Head of Christendom', 'Vicar of Christ' and 'Defender and Advocate of the Christian Church'.[2]

By this time, however, cracks were beginning to show in these ancient pillars of political power. In Europe and North America the development of scientific thinking and experimentation was steadily chipping away at heavenly authority by ascribing phenomena that were previously considered supernatural – the movements of the planets, the spread of diseases – to natural processes. Inspired by the successful application of the principles of reason and critical thinking to the natural world, philosophers started to apply them to the political world. Squarely in their sights were the venerable institutions of monarchy, aristocracy and the clergy, which they considered relics of an older, unreasoning age. Enlightenment thinkers like John Locke began championing the rights of the individual as a counterbalance to the whims of bigoted and despotic rulers. In France, Voltaire wrote scathing attacks against the previously unassailable Catholic Church. The Swiss-French philosopher Jean-Jacques Rousseau, in his political essay *The Social Contract*, not only identified the nation with its people – rather than its king as was customary for the time – but shockingly argued that the 'general will' of the populace should be allowed to govern the nation.

At first, these upheavals in political thinking retained a distinctly Enlightenment sense of universalism: a belief, born of scientific progress, that human reason and rationality would lead to worldwide peace and prosperity. The American and French Revolutions of the late 18th century clearly expressed this optimism with their grandiose invocations of the Laws of Nature and Rights of Man. Their idealism quickly inspired other uprisings. In the French colony of Saint-Domingue (now Haiti), slaves railed against the hypocrisy of being excluded from France's purportedly 'universal' rights, launching an ultimately successful revolution to overthrow their European masters and join the global 'empire of liberty'. In 1794 Antonio Nariño, one of the first proponents of Spanish American independence, generated support for his cause by translating the French government's *Declaration of the Rights of Man* into Spanish.[3]

Even as Nariño was printing his translation, however, challenges to authority elsewhere in the world were losing their cosmopolitan aspirations and taking on more distinctly national and culturally-grounded identities. This change could be first seen in Europe. Partly this was due to the increasing influence of Romantic philosophers such as Johann Fichte and Johann Herder, whose ideas came to dominate the European intellectual scene in the first half of the 19th century. At heart, the Romantic movement they championed was a rejection of what it saw as the cold, sterilised logic of the Enlightenment. Its artists and philosophers celebrated passion over reason, nature over civilisation and – crucially – the local over the international. The world citizenship that had been advocated by the likes of Voltaire left them yearning for a more personal, tangible sense of community.

Perhaps more important, however, was the growing conviction that the individual liberty sought by Enlightenment thinkers could only be secured through national liberty. This was especially true in Europe's multinational empires like the Holy Roman Empire, the Austrian Empire and the Ottoman Empire, where campaigners saw little hope of squeezing liberal reforms from their staunchly conservative rulers. Many began instead to advocate secession, citing cultural and linguistic differences – dismissed by rulers across Europe as politically irrelevant before the 19th century – as legitimate grounds for national independence. 'It is not true,' insisted the Italian nationalist Giuseppe Mazzini in 1850, 'that liberty and independence can be disjoined, and bargained for one after the other.'[4]

Mazzini's words signalled a new type of politics that was sweeping Europe. In contrast to the American and French revolutionaries of the previous century, who had attempted to ground their new republics in cosmopolitan ideals – even if they failed to live up to them – the 19th century saw secessionists increasingly frame their demands in terms of local culture, regional history and ethnic identity. A clear example of this shift could be seen taking place in the breakaway state of Belgium. When calls for Belgian independence from the Netherlands first spilled out into the streets of Brussels in the summer of 1830, protesters waved the French tricolour as an international symbol of their revolution. Within a matter of months, however, those same protesters had ditched the French flag, choosing instead to resurrect the disused red-yellow-black banner of a long-dead duchy as the new national flag of Belgium.[5] Liberty was no longer seen as some disembodied, universal concept, but as the property of individual nations. Nationalism, the politics of nationhood, was born.

Not that many Europeans noticed at the time. For much of the 19th century, nationalism was something of a nouveau riche preoccupation. It was a popular hobby among the continent's emerging middle classes – people such as writers, teachers and business owners – who had the time and money to study regional traditions and campaign for national independence. But the middle classes only accounted for about 5 per cent of Europe's population at this time. For the vast majority of Europeans – its 170 million or so agricultural and industrial workers – nationalism was an alien concept. The average European knew very little and cared even less about the nation to which they supposedly belonged; almost all of them identified first and foremost with local and more tangible ties, or with the age-old certainties of religion. When the political scientist Walker Connor studied US immigration records between 1840 and 1915 he found that most European immigrants identified themselves by their regional district, local parish, hometown or even their village, and only infrequently by nation. As recently as the First World War, local identities could still trump national allegiances throughout much of Europe. In 1918, a British observer in Ukraine – then in the throes of multiple nationalist uprisings – reported that locals would routinely give their nationality as Russian, Greek Orthodox or simply 'peasant' – but rarely, if ever, as Ukrainian.[6]

In short, most nations – in the sense of a body of people united by a shared territory and cultural and historical ties – simply didn't exist 200 years ago as they do today. This put nationalist pioneers in a curious position. On the one hand, they were advocating national self-determination on account of 'natural' and 'God-given' cultural identities; on the other, they were desperately trying to instil those natural and God-given cultural identities in their compatriots. It wasn't a question of 'reawakening' national sentiments in their compatriots, as nationalists loved (and still love) to say, but of inventing and imposing them outright. 'Italy is made,' declared the statesman Massimo D'Azeglio in 1861, following the unification of various kingdoms and states to make the Kingdom of Italy; 'now we must make Italians.'[7]

To shore up the cultural underpinnings of their respective nations, nationalists set to work documenting and compiling local folklore, village songs and regional clothing, which they amalgamated into an 'authentic' and immutable national culture. It was valuable ethnographic work – Europe's local cultures were already being lost to the sprawling slums and smokestacks of the Industrial Revolution. Unfortunately, nationalists felt no compunction about altering what they collected in order to better suit their purposes. Swiss nationalists collecting the folk music of their country were happy to edit songs, and in some cases rewrite them, if they were deemed 'not sufficiently patriotic'.[8] Hungarian musicologists, obsessed with defending the imagined purity of the 'Hungarian race', studiously *avoided* collecting Gypsy music, despite its overwhelming popularity with the Hungarian peasantry. Among them was the composer Béla Bartók, who once dismissed Gypsy music as nothing more than 'the melodic distortions of an immigrant nation'.[9]

An equally discriminating approach was adopted by those studying folk costumes, many of which received considerable overhauls to become the national costumes we're familiar with today. The Amalia dress, now the national costume for Greek women, was invented in 1838 by Amalia of Oldenburg, queen of Greece from 1836 to 1862, and owed as much to Western European fashions as it did to traditional Greek clothes. Women's national dress in Wales began life around the same time as an amalgamation and exaggeration of existing peasant outfits – not all of them unique to Wales – in the hope that it would provide young women with a 'respectable' alternative to the 'trumpery' of modern fashion trends. Many outfits were deliberately restyled to look older in a bid to bolster the venerability, and thus authenticity, of a nation and its people. The medieval-looking national dress of Sweden was invented in 1905 and was only made the country's official costume in 1983.[10]

Many folk traditions were also deliberately aged. In Wales, the 'ancient' arts festival known as the *Eisteddfod* dates back not to pre-Roman times as is sometimes asserted, but to the 1700s. Its creator, an antiquarian, forger and self-declared genius named Edward Williams, took a genuine but largely defunct medieval folk tradition and, with the help of frequent laudanum trips, reinvented it as an antediluvian Druidic celebration complete with cloaks, scrolls and swords.[11] In Scotland, similar endeavours in the late 18th century led to the resurrection of the Highland Games and the creation of pipe bands.[12] The kilt, adapted from the Highlander's belted plaid by an Englishman in the 18th century, was hailed as an equally ancient Scottish tradition, and the notion that different clans should wear different kilt 'setts', or tartan patterns – despite being nothing more than a Victorian marketing ploy devised by clothing manufacturers – was accepted wholeheartedly as genuine Highland heritage.[13]

Not to be left out, English nationalists also began promoting their own age-old traditions by revitalising old regional practices. The tradition of dancing around a maypole on May Day, which had been steadily losing popularity for 150 years, was revived as an 'old English custom', even though the style of dancing familiar to countless English schoolchildren today was a Victorian invention. The English folk tradition of Morris dancing – a sedate group dance usually performed by men – was likewise resuscitated from near-death in the Edwardian era largely by the efforts of the musicologist Cecil Sharp, who used his influence on the British Board of Education to promote folk dance as 'a wholly national' tradition.[14]

In some cases traditions were simply invented outright. The Japanese national sport of sumo, rather than enduring 'since time immemorial', was only formalised in the early 20th century, as the nationalist government sought to cultivate a distinct Japanese culture to counter the growing Western influence in the country. The same nationalising drive saw judo, invented in 1882, hailed only years later as a 'traditional' form of martial arts. In China, the tradition of worshipping the Yellow Emperor, the mythical founder of Chinese civilisation, was established by nationalists in the early 20th century. The 'traditional culture' on display at Uzbekistan's annual *Navroz* festival, billed as an organic national awakening following decades of colourless Soviet bureaucracy, only assumed its current form in the 1990s at the hands of the country's Ministry of Cultural Affairs. As the philosopher Ernest Gellner observed in 1983, 'it is nationalism which engenders nations, and not the other way round.'[15]

As important as these cultural elements were for nation-building, it was history that nationalists really desired. 'History was a crucial element with which to construct nations and national identity,' writes Stefan Berger, a nationalism scholar at the Ruhr University of Bochum in Germany. 'Nation-builders everywhere agreed: their nation had to have a history – the longer and the prouder the better.'[16] A noble and venerable history lent authenticity to claims of national identity and gave weight to demands for national self-determination – think back to the efforts of newly-independent Americans to resurrect Christopher Columbus as a (distinctly un-English) national hero. By linking their current efforts to achieve national independence to older, unrelated struggles, nationalists added greater prestige to their endeavours.

Pro-independence campaigners also hoped that a rousing, feel-good national past would inspire the as-yet indifferent masses to join their cause. 'We were a great people, therefore we are a great people,' as the Portuguese nationalist Augusto Aragão put it.[17]

Fortunately for the nationalist cause, many 19th-century historians were enthusiastic adopters of nationalist movements, more than willing to cite glorious episodes from their respective nations' pasts as proof that these countries had what it took to achieve statehood. 'Nobody versed in history can possibly doubt the former sovereignty and independence of the government and land of Bohemia,' declared the Bohemian historian and nationalist František Palacký in a statement typical of the time.[18] Elsewhere, scholars like Poland's Joachim Lelewel penned hugely popular history books encouraging their compatriots to take up the nationalist mantle. Many historians went further, employing the old standby of historical inevitability to argue that national independence was not only possible but inevitable, an inescapable product of the gears of capital-H History. The Romanian scholar and nationalist Mihail Kogălniceanu described the past as 'a prophecy which foreshadows the future' – a future in which Romanian unification and independence was destined to happen.[19] The German historian Johann Droysen claimed that the calls for German unification were an inevitable expression of 'the primordial spirit of the united German people'.[20] Mazzini even argued that nations were predestined by God, and that to deny their independence was to 'violate … the Design of God on Earth'.[21]

It worked. Over the course of the 19th century, aided by the promotion of national history, nationalism became an increasingly popular way of framing political issues. A sign of its growing importance came in 1848, the 'Spring of Nations', when a firestorm of liberal, republican and socialist revolutions, many of them explicitly nationalist in character, tore through Europe. By February, the streets of Paris were choked with barricades, manned by republican revolutionaries fighting against the monarchy 'for the glory and liberty of the homeland'.[22] By March, protesters in Berlin were calling for Europe's German-speakers – then divided between 39 different states, such as Prussia, Bavaria and Saxony – to unify into a single Germanic nation. By April, mass demonstrations in Budapest had forced the Austrian Empire, a 270,000-square-mile state covering much of Central Europe, to grant Hungary its own national parliament. As one panicked Russian aristocrat scribbled in his diary that year, 'the revolutionary contagion is everywhere!'[23]

The spread of nationalism meant that, by 1848, concepts of personal freedom and national self-determination had become almost irretrievably tangled. The universalism of the previous century – the Enlightenment cosmopolitanism that had shaped the American, French and Haitian revolutions – was increasingly abandoned, and to champion liberty without championing nationalism had become nothing short of an anachronism. When Charles Mackay, a Scottish writer and free-trade advocate, called for the establishment of a United States of Europe in early 1848, he was roundly rebuffed by political campaigners on the continent. 'Modern civilisation,' he later brooded, 'is, unfortunately, yet too young for peace.'[24]

And yet, for all their single-mindedness, the revolutions of 1848 failed to achieve many lasting gains. The conservative and illiberal rulers of Europe managed to keep the loyalty of their armed forces, and by the summer uprisings were being suppressed by force. Absolute monarchy was quickly reinstated in Italy and Austria. The liberal accomplishments that had been made in Prussia – an unfettered press, freedom of assembly and universal male suffrage – were revoked in 1850. In France, the newly created Second Republic lasted less than four years before being replaced by the hereditary empire of Napoleon III.

In another way, however, the 1848 revolutions did spark a fundamental change in politics. The host of kings, princes and emperors the protesters were fighting against were deeply impressed, and more than a little frightened, by the power of nationalism to mobilise the masses. Aware that the old appeals to thrones and altars were rapidly losing this ability, they began to wrap their own ideals – conservatism, monarchy, imperialism – in the new language of nationalism. King Frederick William IV of Prussia drew cheers from advocates of German unification when he rode through the streets of Berlin under their black, gold and red flag instead of the usual black-and-white Prussian flag. Napoleon III of France stoked Gallic pride by publicly honouring the history of the Gauls, the Iron-Age inhabitants of the land now occupied by France. Until 1848 Europe's monarchs had shown little interest in their subjects. Royal ceremonies were private affairs. Now that public opinion meant something, however, monarchy became an open-air performance. Rulers were anxious to be seen visiting the people, attending local events and sponsoring societies. State rituals were transformed into elaborate spectacles designed to awe the assembled crowds. It was the birth of the modern monarchy: the smiling, waving, ribbon-cutting institution familiar to us today.[25]

It was a prescient move. Nationalism and national history proved as staunch an ally for established states as it did for emerging ones – if not more so. By emphasising the similarities between their present regimes and their countries' glorious national pasts, conservative governments used history to promote continuity rather than revolution. By stressing national unity and integrity

above all else, they could condemn protesters as divisive antagonists who didn't have the national interest at heart. And with the
apparatus of the state at their disposal, they were able to instil their
state-approved version of nationalism into their citizens and subjects. The introduction of compulsory education throughout much
of Europe in the 19th century meant that children could be taught
the importance of patriotism and of the willingness to fight for one's
country. The instigation of mandatory military service throughout
much of Europe around the same time allowed the state to drill
similar 'cultural education' lessons into the continent's peasantry,
instructing them to place the nation above all other interests –
self-preservation included. Meanwhile, the growth of nationwide
media, communications and transport – newspapers, telegraphs,
steam engines and the like – made it easier for compatriots to
envisage themselves as members of the same national community.[26]

All this meant that, by the dawn of the 20th century, nationalism had triumphed across the political spectrum. Within the
space of a century it had ballooned from an obscure middle-class
interest into the lingua franca of politics. Conservatives and
liberals, monarchists and republicans: all found the nation and
national history to be the most captivating way of expressing their
ideas and garnering support. Even the staunchly anti-nationalist
communists would eventually give in during the first half of the
20th century, transforming themselves into die-hard patriots by
the outbreak of the Second World War.

Geographically, too, nationalism had spread rapidly out from
Europe. A burgeoning nationalist movement in India was citing
the subcontinent's historic independence as evidence that Indians
were capable of governing themselves without the foreign over-
sight the British Raj insisted upon. In the short-lived Republic
of China – which was struggling to hold together its imperial

possessions against internal rebellions and external encroachment – a renewed sense of pride in Chinese antiquity was promoted to the country's 475 million inhabitants by the ruling Nationalist Party as being essential for 'saving the state'.[27] In Mexico, the dictator Porfirio Díaz went to greater lengths than any previous leader to promote national archaeology, ordering archaeologists to survey and collect the country's enormous wealth of ruins and artefacts in the hope that the wonders of Mexico's precolonial history would boost the country's international standing and esteem. Japanese nationalists, meanwhile, appealed to the country's 'glorious past' to justify their government's aggressive imperial expansion in East Asia. Similar stories could be found all around the world. Ironically, it was Romantic nationalism, not Enlightenment internationalism, that achieved the status of a worldwide political ideology.

~

The desire to establish a glorious history shown by the various nationalisms of the 19th century was nothing new, however. Throughout the Middle Ages and into the Renaissance, European scholars spent considerable time and energy trying to prove that their royal and aristocratic employers were the descendants of ancient and noble ancestors, such as the ancient Egyptians, biblical patriarchs or – by far the most popular choice – the mythical Trojans. In the 3rd century CE, the founder of the Sassanian Empire, Ardashir I, tried to channel the glory of the earlier Persian Empire by adding new inscriptions, artwork and monuments to ancient Persian sites. A similar tactic had been used almost 2,000 years previously by the Egyptian pharaoh Thutmosis IV, who added an engraved stone slab to the already ancient Sphinx, describing his heaven-sent mission to excavate and restore the monument, which had become half-buried by the Saharan sands. In fact, it's now thought that the earliest known example of history writing – a 4,000-year-old stone tablet engraved with a list of Sumerian kings – was yet another expression of this yearning for a grand history; archaeologists suspect that it was commissioned by a usurping monarch who, anxious to legitimise his reign, had himself depicted as the rightful heir to a long list of earlier, respected rulers.

Nevertheless, the level of interest in the past that was sparked by the rise of nationalism in the 19th century was something that had not been seen before. Clearly, the study of history had always had a political dimension to it; now, however, it was central to political legitimacy. European cities saw a boom in the number of historical archives, libraries and history courses available at their universities. The continent's monarchs, as part of their new man-of-the-people charm offensive, opened up their royal treasure vaults – now rebranded as national museums – to the public. National histories, that bookshop staple, emerged as the most popular form of history writing as a new generation of nationalist historians began writing for the mass market. History was no longer the preserve of the upper classes.

The effect on archaeology was even more profound. Until the mid-19th century archaeology had been little more than an excuse for the wealthy to see the sights and rob a few graves. In 1801 the British diplomat Lord Elgin bribed the Ottoman authorities into letting him ship marble sculptures and friezes from the Parthenon in Athens to the British Museum, where they still reside to this day (and where, you may recall, they were stripped of their original colours by chisels and acid baths). The demand for ancient souvenirs was so great during the early 19th century that Giovanni Belzoni, a former magician and circus strongman, made a career out of selling purloined Egyptian artefacts (acquired with the aid of dynamite and battering rams) to wealthy Europeans. With the advent of nationalism, however, the desire to uncover a glorious national past pushed archaeology towards becoming a more rigorous academic discipline. Governments around the world began to bankroll excavations, giving researchers the time and money to begin cataloguing their finds systematically. 'Since its inception, archaeology has been deeply involved in nationalist enterprises,' write the archaeologists Philip Kohl and Clare Fawcett. 'The development of archaeology as a scientific discipline in the 19th century can only be understood in the creation of a national history ... directed at legitimising the existence of a nation.'[28]

Nationalism also led to a newfound respect for the past and its remains that's still with us today. During the 19th and 20th centuries archaeological sites previously considered unremarkable were designated as national monuments. At the same time laws banning the exportation of antiquities were established as authorities began championing archaeological relics as a source of national pride. For the first time in history, the idea of historical preservation and restoration became widespread. Until the mid-1800s, historic sites had been routinely demolished to make way for roads, railways and new buildings, or simply left to crumble through neglect. In the 1830s the Egyptian government even considered plans to demolish the pyramids of Giza for use as building stone. Such attitudes quickly changed once ruins and relics gained political power as 'ready-made national symbols'.[29] Nationalists could be found rebuilding ruined castles in Germany, renovating Renaissance churches in Italy and recreating Aztec temples in Mexico. It's difficult to overstate just how influential nationalism was to the development of history and archaeology, both as academic disciplines and popular hobbies.

Unfortunately – though perhaps unsurprisingly – the influence of nationalism on the study of history and archaeology hasn't been entirely positive, as the insistence on an august and awe-inspiring national history requires a very selective and simplistic approach to the past. Victories are inflated; accomplishments exaggerated. Episodes of defeat or dishonourable conduct tend to be skipped over or denied altogether. Those who don't easily square with the national story, such as immigrants and other minorities, are frequently written out of existence, and the long-standing subjugation and inequality they endured are likewise downplayed or dismissed. With occasional exceptions, women have been reduced to bit-parts in their country's history. On top of this, unsupported fringe theories that promote national greatness – such as the Korean claim that ancient Koreans invented Chinese writing, or the belief that the Welsh are descended from the Trojans – are given greater credence than their shaky evidence warrants. Facts are forced to fit the story, and discarded if they can't be bent into shape.[30]

Consider the efforts of nationalists in newly independent Greece in the early 19th century. In 1830 the country had just emerged victorious from a gruelling eight-year war of independence against the Ottoman Empire. Keen to bolster their claims to statehood, Hellenic politicians and historians worked hard to hammer the history of the Greek peninsula into a proud and coherent national story – with their newfound independence as the climactic and inevitable culmination. Scholars deliberately archaised the spoken language, reverted place names to their ancient spellings and embraced neoclassical architecture so as to position the new state as the rightful heir to the glories of the ancient Mediterranean. Outdated classical Greek names like Pericles, Themistocles and Xenophon were revived and bestowed on unsuspecting children. At the same time, any non-Greek elements in the nation's history – its Frankish, Slavic and Venetian influences, for instance – were dismissed as aberrations or erased. Local folklore was stripped of its Ottoman accents; Athens was 'purified' of its non-Greek architecture, and the Greek language was purged of Turkish 'impurities'. Centuries of Ottoman rule were disregarded as 'four hundred years of slavery', even though the era had seen increasing wealth for many Greeks. Over time, Greek citizens – most of whom neither knew nor cared about ancient Greece in 1830 – began to see their new state as the direct descendant of ancient Sparta and Athens. It's a view still passionately held to this day.[31]

At least the Greeks had some history to mangle. Many emerging nations of the 19th century, equally confident that history would support their claims to independence and sovereignty, were disappointed to discover that there was scant evidence of ancient grandeur within their new national borders. Historians determined to tell a grand national narrative were thus forced to be a little more creative: postulating the existence of illustrious civilisations from shards of pottery, constructing national histories out of snippets of folklore, or simply fabricating evidence outright. In Finland, archaeologists felt compelled to invent non-existent Finnish Vikings in order to compete with Denmark, Norway and Sweden, which all viewed their Viking heritage as a source of national pride. The 'medieval' *Königinhofer* and *Grünberger* manuscripts, detailing the patriotic exploits of the Czech warrior-minstrel folk heroes Záboj and Slavoj, were later exposed as 19th-century hoaxes. A similar fate awaited the supposedly 3rd-century Scottish epics *Ossian* and *Temora*, which were revealed to be 18th-century forgeries by the Scottish poet James Macpherson – a man dismissed by his contemporary Samuel Johnson, who took a more discerning view of the poems than many members of the British literati, as 'a mountebank, a liar, and a fraud'.[32]

Such imaginative approaches to history were taken to extremes by Turkish nationalists following the establishment of the Turkish state in 1923. Compensating for their lack of scholarly rigour with sheer ambition, they claimed that Turkey was not only the cradle of civilisation and the birthplace of writing, but that the Turkish nation had somehow found the time to establish the Hittite, Sumerian, Assyrian, Egyptian and Aegean civilisations during its purportedly 7,000-year history. Even more impressively, an official government announcement from 1935 declared that the first word ever spoken by humans was in Turkish.[33]

These historical narratives become even more far-fetched when you consider how young most countries are. Nationalism, as we saw, was not so much the reawakening of ancient nations as it was the deliberate creation of them out of scraps of local culture. Consequently, most countries today have remarkably recent origins. Take a look at a world atlas from the turn of the 20th century to see how much the world has changed politically in little more than 100 years. Turkey, Mongolia, Pakistan, Bangladesh, Belarus, Indonesia and dozens of other countries are nowhere to be found. Central and Eastern Europe are home to just seven sovereign states, as opposed to today's 22. Much of Africa is unrecognisable, with a handful of colonial powers dominating a continent that's today home to 54 countries. Indeed, at the time of writing, more than half of the world's countries are less than 100 years old. The majority of African countries are just 60 years old – younger than their average head of state.

Despite this, most countries extend their national histories deep into the past, well beyond their emergence as recognisable political units. Accounts of Iraqi history, for instance, frequently portray the country as the natural heir to the ancient kingdom of Babylonia that once inhabited the same land. The Iraqi dictator Saddam Hussein even rebuilt one of the country's ruined Babylonian palaces in 1987 to celebrate and reinforce this connection. (In a suitably megalomaniacal touch, Hussein ordered bricks used in the recreation to be imprinted with his name – a deliberate imitation of Babylonian king Nebuchadnezzar II, who gave the same order for the construction of the original palace in 605 BCE.) And yet Iraq's roots reach no deeper than the 20th century: the country was cobbled together by the British from largely unrelated fragments of the defunct Ottoman Empire in 1920, a full 2,500 years after the demise of Babylonia.

Similar architectural tricks are currently being played in North Macedonia. The North Macedonian state was first established, as a Yugoslav republic, in 1945, taking its name from the ancient Greek kingdom that had once inhabited the same region. Following the demise of the kingdom there elapsed a thousand-year period in which no sign of a distinct Macedonian nationality existed; indeed, until 1945 Macedonians generally referred to themselves as Bulgarians. Despite this, since 2010 the North Macedonian government has sought to position the country as the direct descendant of the ancient kingdom of Macedon and its most famous son, Alexander the Great. In a remarkable parallel with Greek nationalists of 180 years earlier, they have instigated a sweeping programme of architectural 'antiquisation' in the capital, Skopje. A budget of more than €600 million (in a country that spends less than €800 million on healthcare each year) has transformed the brutalist architecture of the city into a gaudy neoclassical Disneyland, complete with Corinthian columns and triumphal arches. Skopje is now festooned with over 120 statues, monuments and facades evoking ancient Greece, including an 80-foot-high bronze statue of Alexander the Great. Greek nationalists have, predictably, accused the country of 'stealing' and 'embezzling' their national heritage, even though Greece's claims to ancient Macedon are hardly less tenuous than those of North Macedonia. Perhaps they needn't be too worried, however: after just ten years, the hastily built refurbishments, some of them constructed using plywood and Styrofoam, are already beginning to crack and moulder. Analogies to the flimsiness of the historical claims behind these renovations are, if anything, too easy.[34]

This national appropriation of the pre-national past is more common than you might think, even in countries widely regarded as ancient. Present-day Egypt, for example, has no reservations about boasting of its long and fabulous history. 'Egypt and history are synonymous,' proclaims the historian Hussein Bassir.[35] And yet the modern state of Egypt was only founded in 1802 (by an Albanian, nonetheless), some 2,000 years after Egypt had last existed as an independent entity. As a result, 21st-century Egypt has virtually nothing in common with its ancient namesake – not its language, borders, religion or culture. And, if we're being honest, they don't even share the same name: ancient Egyptians called their land *Kemet* (and present-day Egyptians call their country *Misr*).

Alternatively, consider the case of Boudicca, the Celtic warrior-queen who stood up to the might of the Roman Empire. Following the English rediscovery of her story in the 16th century with the translation of Roman texts, Boudicca was quickly lionised as an 'English heroine' who 'exemplifies the very spirit of England'.[36] The image of a fierce woman standing up to foreign oppression proved very convenient for the court of Elizabeth I, which – at a loss to find any other suitably heroic female figures from English history to bolster the queen's reputation – encouraged comparisons between the Tudor monarch and Boudicca.

By the 19th century, with Queen Victoria on the British throne, Boudicca had achieved the status of a national icon, featuring regularly in Victorian paintings, engravings, murals and poems celebrating 'the glory of the country'.[37] In all the excitement, people seemed to have overlooked the rather obvious fact that Boudicca wasn't English. After all, no such political entity as England existed when Boudicca was alive, and it wouldn't be until nearly 900 years after her death that a kingdom called *Englaland* began to emerge. As a result, Boudicca didn't speak English – no such language existed – nor did she express any hint of English identity in the accounts we have of her. (Incidentally, she almost certainly didn't slather herself in blue woad dye, either, as modern representations suggest: as any Iron Age reenactor knows, woad produces a dye so dry and crumbly that it is useless for body painting.)

A similar story can be found in other European countries that have adopted opponents of Roman rule as symbols of national pride. Just as Boudicca's statue stands today outside the UK Houses of Parliament, so there are monuments to the French national hero Vercingetorix (who wasn't French), the Belgian figurehead Ambiorix (who wasn't Belgian) and the Spanish heroes Indibilis and Mandonius (neither of whom was Spanish). In 1875 German nationalists erected a colossal 175-foot-tall monument to the tribal leader Hermann, the 'saviour of Germany', even though Germany didn't exist until after Hermann had been dead for 1,800 years. The Gauls, despite enjoying an important place in French history – after all, there could be no Gallic pride without the Gauls – stopped being a significant cultural and political force centuries before the kingdom of *Francia* was founded in the 5th century CE.

National histories, in short, are some of the most confusing compilations of fact and fantasy ever assembled. As the historian

Christina Bueno succinctly put it in 2016: 'national histories are inventions.'[38] It's the inevitable result of forcing the past to serve a political purpose, of making it tell a feel-good tale rather than the truth. These distortions can only come at the expense of academic rigour and intellectual honesty. The more patriotic the past becomes – the more it's forced to fit an inspiring national narrative – the less room there is for historical complexity and nuance. 'To get one's history wrong,' sighed the French historian Ernest Renan in 1882, 'is an essential factor in the making of a nation.'[39]

～

All of this might be considered a purely academic issue were it not for the fact that these historical myths are promoted and accepted as historical facts by many people around the world. Parties have been founded, protests instigated, policies enacted and people killed on account of them. 'National narratives time and again have led to intolerance, xenophobia, violence, war and genocide,' writes Stefan Berger. Or, as the historian Eric Hobsbawm puts it: 'historians are to nationalism what poppy growers are to heroin addicts; we supply the essential raw material for the market.'[40]

The distinctly un-English Boudicca, for example, has been adopted in some circles of the English far-right, who champion her as a poster girl for their anti-immigrant views (conveniently overlooking the fact that her rebellion killed far more native Britons than Romans). In France, Vercingetorix has likewise become the object of nationalist veneration: in 2016, ex-president Nicolas Sarkozy, hoping to capitalise on growing anti-immigrant sentiment in his short-lived bid to run for president again, told prospective citizens that they must first accept 'the Gauls and Vercingetorix' as their true ancestors if they wanted to be granted citizenship.[41] A few months later the far-right National Rally chose to launch their 2017 election campaign in Lyon because it was 'the capital of the Gauls'.[42] Finland's non-existent Vikings, meanwhile, have become mascots for the country's far-right vigilante group, Soldiers of Odin.

In Greece, the national myth of an unbroken Greek nation reaching back to the classical past, uncontaminated by foreign cultures, has been swallowed whole by modern-day nationalists. The neo-Nazi Golden Dawn party, in particular, bases its ideology on the entirely false 19th-century assertion that the Greek nation represents a genetically pure and distinct group of people. Ignoring the fact that the Balkans are in reality the most genetically diverse region in Europe, the Golden Dawn see it as their mission to defend the 'Greek race' with openly racist policies. Comparing themselves to ancient Spartan warriors, and immigrants to the 'wretched' Persian invaders of the 5th century BCE, they have repeatedly incited and committed violence against non-Greeks living in the country. In 2012 the party even proposed that the Greek-Turkish border be laced with landmines in order to deter would-be immigrants. Such is the power of historical myth that, when believers like the Golden Dawn are faced with evidence that contradicts their convictions – such as the presence of ethnic minorities in their country – they would sooner change reality to fit their beliefs before changing their beliefs to reflect reality.[43]

Similar interpretations of history can be found in Hungary, where the increasingly right-wing government of prime minister Viktor Orbán justifies its refusal to accept refugees from North Africa and the Middle East by citing the country's historic opposition to the Ottoman Empire. Orbán likes to claim that Hungary is once again the only country defending European Christianity from a Muslim 'invasion', even describing himself as a modern-day János Hunyadi, a medieval nobleman and Hungarian national hero who successfully held back Ottoman advances into Central Europe in the 15th century. The history lessons that Orbán cites, however, are the concoctions of 19th-century nationalists trying to boost Hungary's standing in Europe. In truth, European resistance to Ottoman invasions was multinational, drawing men and resources from across much of Central and Eastern Europe. Even János Hunyadi (who was Transylvanian, not Hungarian, by the way) led an international force against the Empire.[44]

In many other instances, racial and ethnic tensions have been deliberately exacerbated through the endorsement of demonstrably false national histories. In 1992, a Hindu mob in the northern Indian city of Ayodhya destroyed a 460-year-old mosque, believing it to have been built on the site of a sacred Hindu temple. An estimated 2,000 people lost their lives in the communal riots which followed. And yet there's no evidence that a Hindu temple ever stood on the site, let alone – as Hindu nationalists claimed – that it had been destroyed by Muslims. The story first appeared in the 1850s and was deliberately spread by Hindu nationalists looking for excuses to demonise India's Muslim minority, whom they described as 'foreign invaders'.[45]

At the same time as the Ayodhya mob was taking axes and hammers to a 16th-century mosque, Yugoslavia was tearing itself apart along national lines. During the Yugoslav Wars of the 1990s, Catholic Croats, Orthodox Christian Serbs and Muslim Bosnians all supported their military campaigns by appealing to the past. Croatian forces attempted to validate their claims to enormous stretches of Bosnian territory by citing the existence of Catholic communities there in the Middle Ages. The Serbian leader Slobodan Milošević repeatedly justified his genocidal aggression against Bosnian civilians by claiming that he was seeking retribution for the 1389 Battle of Kosovo, a medieval bloodbath between

Christian and Ottoman forces. The Bosnians, in turn, looked back to the 14th-century conquests of the Bosnian king Tvrtko I to argue that they were entitled to chunks of Serbian and Croatian land. In all these cases, the national histories being appealed to were not objective reconstructions of the past but the imaginative creations of earlier generations of nationalists. In the Battle of Kosovo, for instance, a significant number of Serbs fought *for* the Ottomans, while a substantial Bosnian force joined the multinational Christian army.[46] 'The myth of the battle that was created in the 19th century was more important than what actually happened,' explains Gëzim Krasniqi, a scholar of nationalism and national identity at the University of Edinburgh. 'It's what people *believe* that matters. Forget the facts.'

Indeed, when the facts failed to support the historical myths being peddled during the Yugoslav Wars, nationalists simply destroyed the evidence. For politicians and soldiers professing to 'reclaim' ethnically homogenous states for their people, evidence of the Balkans' deeply rooted ethnic diversity – mosques, churches and synagogues on the same street, for instance, or Serbian and Bulgarian graves lying side-by-side – proved a perennial source of irritation. Consequently, buildings, bridges, archives, libraries and archaeological sites of no military significance were dynamited by enemy forces for belonging to the 'wrong' ethnicity. In Bosnia alone some 300 mosques and 30 Islamic cemeteries were destroyed.[47]

The line between farce and tragedy is a thin one. On paper, the wild historical claims of nationalists can make for entertaining reading. But when these fantasies are politicised – when people are taught to invest their national pride and their personal worth in them – they can quickly turn sinister. Krasniqi, who grew up in 1990s Kosovo, is keenly aware of the dangers. 'When elites want to use history for political ends – to justify a political order, to mobilise hatred against minorities – they will do it,' he tells me. 'These people are not stupid. They know exactly what they're doing.' All the more reason, he insists, that we question and challenge our national narratives. 'If we continue to allow the past to be exploited for political gain, then the consequences could be very dangerous.' History, after all, has a habit of repeating itself.

~

In 1945, a slim volume was written by the political scientist Edward Carr titled *Nationalism and After*. Having surveyed 'a world bewildered by the turmoil of nationalism and war,' the author looked ahead to what the post-war world – 'the aftermath of the age of nationalism' – might hold. Carr, by no means an optimist when it came to human nature, was nevertheless fairly convinced that the chaos of the 1940s represented 'the final bankruptcy of nationalism', and that people would soon 'rise above the national hatred and conflicts of the past'. It was almost inconceivable that a world so exhausted from two titanic nationalist conflicts could do anything else. 'The movement for national toleration,' he concluded, 'will spring from the destructive 20th-century wars of nationalism.'[48]

Carr joins a long list of writers and thinkers who have prematurely predicted the demise of nationalism. Perhaps the earliest such forecast comes from Karl Marx and Friedrich Engels, who wrote in *The Communist Manifesto* that industrialisation 'has stripped [the proletarian] of every trace of national character'.[49] This bold assertion was made, incredibly, in 1848, the very same year that deeply nationalistic revolutions were sweeping across Europe. Later, the anarchist Emma Goldman declared nationalism to be losing steam in 1911, just three years before the outbreak of the First World War. As recently as the 1980s historians were still making confident predictions that nationalism would soon be 'past its peak'.[50]

All have proved woefully optimistic. Nationalism has stubbornly refused to bow out from the political stage. Indeed, it has only grown in geographic scope and political legitimacy since Carr wrote his book. In 1945, our planet was home to just 51 sovereign states (Carr already considered that too many). Today that number has nearly quadrupled: as of 2020, the United Nations recognises 193 national states, and there are many more unrecognised nations – such as Catalonia, Kurdistan and Transnistria – vying for the distinction. The concept of the nation remains central to 21st-century politics. 'Nationalism is the mainstream,' writes the political theorist Tom Nairn, 'and it's time we recognised that fact.'[51]

As a result, the political manipulation of the past for nationalist purposes is still very much with us, and national histories continue to be written and rewritten to justify contemporary beliefs and ideologies. Since 2018, the Polish government, as part of its bid to make Polish history a guilt-free discipline, has threatened legal action against anyone who suggests that Poles may have collaborated with Nazis during the Second World War (the same government also made it a crime to utter the phrase 'Polish death camp').[52] In India, successive pro-Hindu governments, undeterred by the violence at Ayodhya, have spent millions changing the country's place names in an attempt to erase memories of the subcontinent's British and Muslim rulers – memories which refuse to fit with their image of India as a glorious and uniquely Hindu civilisation. Bombay has become Mumbai, Madras has changed to Chennai and Allahabad renamed Prayagraj. Dozens of other cities are also slated for similar rebranding as Hindu nationalists vow to 'connect the current generation to our glorious past' and 'erase the deep scars of subjugation'.[53]

Elsewhere in the world, history textbooks have been doctored to better suit official narratives. In 2017 the Chinese government, seeking to strengthen anti-Japanese sentiment among the population, extended the Second Sino-Japanese War by six years by moving the official start of Japanese aggression from 1937 to 1931. In 2019, the pro-military Brazilian government announced a 'progressive shift' in school textbooks whereby the country's 1964 military coup will now be described as 'a sovereign decision by Brazilian society' that instigated 'a democratic regime'. Meanwhile, in the USA, the conservative Republican Party has made repeated efforts in recent years to remove the 'liberal bias' from the country's school curriculum, which it argues 'emphasises negative aspects of our nation's history' by giving 'undue emphasis to topics such as slavery and the treatment of Native Americans'. Since 2015, a new edition of state-approved textbooks in Republican-dominated Texas no longer mention either Jim Crow laws or the existence of the Ku Klux Klan. Other textbooks in the same state have described slaves as 'workers' and downplayed the role of slavery in inciting the US Civil War. There's no reason to suspect this sort of meddling will end any time soon: as long as nations continue to dominate politics, national politics will continue to interfere with our understanding of the past.[54]

To say that nationalism has a complicated relationship with history and archaeology is to put it mildly. On the one hand, the 19th-century craze for national history helped transform these subjects from elite pursuits into academic disciplines with wide public appeal. On the other hand, that same craze has bequeathed later generations of researchers a lot of shoddy scholarship and a fair amount of nonsense – nonsense which continues to be promoted, and added to, by today's nationalists. More worrying still, nationalism has weaponised history in a way never before seen. It encourages people not only to celebrate and preserve the past but to demonise and destroy it as well. Libraries have been built, and burned to the ground, in its name; archaeological sites have been discovered and subsequently demolished in bursts of nationalistic enthusiasm. All too often, innocent people have been caught up in these conflicts.

Ultimately, nationalism likes its history lessons a little too trim and tidy. History is a mess. How could the record of billions of people over thousands of years be anything else? Those neat national narratives we learned at school – those lists of kings and queens and presidents and prime ministers – do their best to hide this fact, but they can only do so at the cost of the complexities and ambiguities of the past. Such a price is rarely, if ever, worth paying.

CHAPTER 8

The curse of the crystal skulls

Item 1898-1 stares back at me, grinning. I've been steeling myself for this encounter: of all the archaeological artefacts I've come across while researching this book, the crystal skull housed in the British Museum is the only one that comes with a health warning. Those who have found themselves face-to-face with this enigmatic artefact, and the handful of others like it housed in museums around the world, have reported a range of disconcerting experiences: some have smelled strange odours, others are struck with a painful thirst, and others still claim to have been visited by hallucinations or crippled by pangs of pure terror. The skulls are frequently described as having a 'sinister, mysterious power', a 'primaeval darkness' that crashes computers and leaves people unable to sleep. Unearthly growling, chanting and chiming are said to emanate from within them. They will emit light, change colour, grow cloudy or blacken completely with no apparent cause. And before you scoff at such claims, it has been said that the skulls will strike dead any who mock them.[1]

Their very creation is an enigma. They are carved out of quartz, a hard and brittle crystal – so brittle, in fact, that any attempt to carve against the crystal's natural axis would surely shatter the entire block. This leaves the creation of complex, three-dimensional objects like these skulls a mystery. Examinations of the surface of the artefacts have found few clues to the riddle of their creation, as it's said to be impossible to find a single tool mark or scratch that would suggest a method of construction, even under microscopic analysis. 'It appears to be an imposs- ible object,' marvels one enthusiast, 'which today's most talented sculptors and engineers would be unable to duplicate ... Modern science is stumped as to how to explain it.'[2]

Who could have created such remarkable artefacts? According to some accounts, they were crafted thousands of years ago by the ancient Maya, and later copied by the Aztecs, where they were worshipped in sinister rites. Others place their origins within the mythical island of Atlantis, or even somewhere in the depths of outer space. Wherever they came from, it's said that legends of the crystal skulls have been told by people around the world for millennia, from the Babylonians to the Egyptians to the Knights Templar. 'There are very few legends that cross over cultures and times the way the crystal skull legends do,' explains another admirer of the skulls.[3]

It's with these claims ringing in my ears that I find the crys- tal skull in a corner of the British Museum one rainy Thursday afternoon. In reality it's not at all sinister. Large, circular eye sockets and a simplistic, toothy smile make it quite endearing, really. Trying to hide my disappointment, I look deep into the sockets and attempt to channel some of its mysterious energy, but a gaggle of schoolchildren soon swamps the exhibit, scup- pering my hopes of building a psychic rapport with the skull. No sense of dread, no unearthly chanting, no flood of unexplained emotion. My phone hasn't been fried by the encounter nor my sleep disturbed. As of writing this, I am still waiting to be struck dead by the skull.

There's a very good reason why I've lived to tell the tale: the crystal skull at the British Museum – along with every other crystal skull in existence – is a modern fake, and the ominous mythology surrounding them a pack of equally modern lies. Welcome to the world of pseudoarchaeology.

~

The story of the crystal skulls began in 1867, when a French antiquarian and a specialist in pre-Columbian artefacts named Eugène Boban set up a stall at the International Exposition in Paris. Boban's exhibit showcased artefacts he had discovered while serving, he claimed, as the official antiquarian to Mexico's Emperor Maximilian. Among the necklaces, pottery, terracotta figurines and weapons on display, visitors could find two crystal skulls. These weren't the lifelike skulls famous today, but much smaller – less than two inches high – and more crudely carved. Nevertheless, they quickly caused a stir in the antiquarian community, and over the following two decades Boban managed to fuel the growing interest by acquiring a number of other crystal skulls, each one larger and more impressive than the last. He was an enthusiastic promoter of the artefacts, describing one as a 'masterpiece' and 'unique in the world'.[4]

Archaeologists were intrigued by the crystal skulls and keen to acquire them for their own collections. In 1874 the National Museum in Mexico City bought one for 28 pesos, a significant sum of money at the time. Twelve years later the Smithsonian Institution managed to obtain a different skull from a Mexican collector. When the Musée d'Ethnographie du Trocadéro opened in Paris in 1878 it managed to acquire another from the French ethnographer Alphonse Pinart, who had himself bought it from none other than Eugène Boban.

Boban was also responsible for bringing to light the crystal skull I encountered in the British Museum. It first appeared in his collection sometime in the 1880s, while he was living in Paris, and came with him when he relocated to New York in 1886. That same year the skull was bought by the jewellers Tiffany & Co. – along with a mysterious 'crystal hand', which has since vanished – who sold it to the British Museum in 1898 for £400, the price of a small London house at the time.[5]

As the price tags suggest, many archaeologists in the late 19th and early 20th centuries accepted these items as genuine and important Aztec artefacts. Writing in 1890, the geologist George Kunz described the carving of the skull now on display in the British Museum as 'very characteristic of Mexican art'. These comments were echoed by the ethnologist Hermann Braunholtz, who wrote that the artefact was 'in accordance with the general character of ancient Mexican art' and likened it to 'Aztec stone masks and figures of deities'. In 1936 an archaeologist at the British Museum described the same skull as lacking 'any trace of identifiable tool marks' and bearing 'no traces of recent (metal age) workmanship', concluding that the question of forgery 'may almost certainly be dismissed'.[6]

By the 1930s more sinister comments were also being made about the crystal skulls. Much of the mythology surrounding these artefacts can be traced back to an English collector and self-styled explorer named Frederick Mitchell-Hedges, who claimed to have discovered a particularly well-crafted crystal skull while exploring Maya ruins some years previously. The artefact, he divulged to a local newspaper in 1949, had been used by the Maya to curse their enemies thousands of years ago. Three years later he elaborated in his autobiography *Danger, My Ally*, stating that the skull – now called 'the Skull of Doom' – was used in sinister Maya rituals as early as 1600 BCE. 'According to legend', he continued, the skull 'was used by the High Priest of the Maya when performing esoteric rites. It is said that when he willed death with the help of the skull, death invariably followed. It has been described as

the embodiment of all evil.' Mitchell-Hedges was also the first
to claim that the skull would strike down its detractors. 'Several
people who have laughed cynically at it have died', he warned.
'Others have been stricken and become seriously ill.'[7]

Mitchell-Hedges was uncharacteristically reticent about how
he had acquired the skull. 'How it came into my possession, I
have reason for not revealing', he wrote. It wasn't until the Skull
of Doom fell into his daughter Anna's possession in 1959 that
more details would emerge. Anna claimed to have accompanied
her father to Central America in 1924, where, on 1 January that
year – her seventeenth birthday, as it happened – she personally
discovered the skull among the ruins of a Maya temple. 'I saw
something shining in the sunlight', she recounted. 'I got the Maya
people to help me clear the ground and … we found the top of the
crystal, the head. Three months later we found the jaw.'[8]

By the 1970s Anna Mitchell-Hedges was making a living
from promoting and touring with the crystal skull. She expanded
considerably on her father's description of the skull's powers,
describing it in more positive terms as containing 'a benevolent
divine magic' and 'protection from heaven' that 'defeats all evils
of witchcraft'.[9] (Even so, its jealous streak remained as strong
as ever: one young lady who had laughed at the skull, Anna
confided to William Shatner in a 1976 documentary, died just
months later, and on her deathbed had pleaded with her friends
to never mock the skull.) Whether deliberately or not, Anna had
chosen the perfect time to embark upon her career as the skull's
intermediary: the 1970s saw the emergence of the New Age movement in many Western countries, and her talk of ancient secrets
and supernatural powers found an eager audience. Skull lore
exploded. Miracles and prophecies were ascribed not only to the
Mitchell-Hedges skull but to the ever-expanding number of other

skulls appearing around the world. Enthusiasts claimed to find references to artefacts not just among the legends of the Maya and the Aztecs, but also the Egyptians, Babylonians, Phoenicians and Native Americans like the Cherokee.[10] Others searched further afield, arguing that the skulls were created using such advanced technology that their origins must be extraterrestrial. By 1998 the Mitchell-Hedges skull was described in no uncertain terms by the author and crystal healer Phyllis Galde as 'the most fascinating, mysterious artefact ever unearthed'.[11]

As the fame of the crystal skulls grew, however, the scientific community became increasingly sceptical of the artefacts. Although crystal skulls had been purchased and displayed by the British Museum and the Trocadéro, among others – and despite the confident assessments of the British Museum staff – a small number of experts in Mesoamerican art had long expressed doubts about the items. Indeed, the crystal skull purchased by the British Museum in 1898 had already been rejected as a fake by the National Museum of Mexico and the Smithsonian when Boban tried to sell it to both of them.

For starters, there were niggling issues with the skulls' designs. Human skulls certainly feature in pre-Columbian art, but no authenticated artefacts shared the style of the crystal skulls, with Mesoamerican artists generally preferring a more stylised, blocky aesthetic – as seen in the ruined Maya city of Chichen Itza, for example – compared to the naturalism of the crystal skulls. Moreover, a number of the skulls' features – particularly the neat, straight lines separating the teeth – looked to have been cut with a rotary wheel, a tool unknown to the pre-Columbians. Even the crystal itself was a cause for concern: the Aztecs and Maya carved their skulls from basalt, not quartz, as neither had access – either directly or through trade – to blocks of quartz large enough to carve a life-size human skull from. There were also growing suspicions around the fact that crystal skulls could only be found on the market and not in the field: not one shard of one skull had been uncovered in an archaeological investigation or been found in the possession of the contemporary Central American tribes who were said to still worship them. Added to the fact that the artefacts had only started appearing in the 1860s, a boom time for the archaeological fakes industry in the Americas, things had begun to look decidedly fishy.[12]

Despite these doubts, it wasn't until 2008 – when Anna Mitchell-Hedges' widower brought her crystal skull to the Smithsonian Institution for examination – that scientists were able to prove beyond doubt that it and other crystal skulls weren't authentic artefacts but modern forgeries. The investigation was led by Jane Walsh, an anthropologist at the Smithsonian and an expert on Mexican archaeology. She and her team used an electron microscope, capable of magnification thousands of times greater than that of the light microscopes previously used to inspect crystal skulls, to examine tiny marks on the surfaces of several of the artefacts. The results were unequivocal. Disproving the fringe assertion that no tool marks could be found on the skulls – and the consequent interpretation that they must have been created using highly advanced (and possibly alien) technology – the skulls were all found to have parallel scratches running along their surfaces, indicative of having been carved using rotary wheels. When Walsh and her colleagues examined authentic Mesoamerican quartz artefacts including beads and a small goblet under the electron microscope, they found that these entirely lacked machine-made striations, consistent with them having been chiselled with stone and copper tools and polished with natural abrasives such as sand and bamboo.[13]

Even the provenance of the quartz used to make the British Museum skull could be roughly determined by matching the chemical makeup to known rock deposits around the world. Confirming earlier suspicions of geologists, the quartz used to make the skull came not from Central America but from either Brazil or Madagascar – neither of which was within reach of Mesoamerican trade routes. Further studies on a crystal skull at the Smithsonian discovered traces of an abrasive called carborundum, an incredibly rare substance in the natural world that was virtually unknown in stone working before the 20th century. Similar investigations have produced similar results; to date, every purportedly ancient crystal skull to undergo scientific examination has been shown to be a 19th or 20th-century fake.[14]

The knowledge that the skulls were in fact modern forgeries prompted Walsh to investigate the history of the artefacts. And wherever she looked, Eugène Boban's name soon surfaced; at least five of the crystal skulls that appeared in the 19th century could be traced back to him. Did Boban know he was selling fakes? It seems almost certain. He had a track record in dealing in forgeries and had acquired a reputation in Mexico as a fraudster. (His attempted sale to the Smithsonian was foiled when a fellow antiquarian wrote to the Institution warning them that Boban had probably bought the skull, newly made, in Germany.) There's also no evidence that he was ever Emperor Maximilian's official antiquarian, as he claimed; he simply added 'Antiquarian to His Majesty the Emperor' to his business cards after Maximilian purchased some items from him in 1866.[15]

Boban lacked the necessary expertise to create the crystal skulls himself, but the available evidence suggests that he did indeed purchase at least some of them from German craftsman, as the Smithsonian's tipster indicated.[16] Walsh suspects that the two small skulls he exhibited back at the Paris Exposition in 1867 – the very items which helped spark the crystal skull craze – may also have been fakes, possibly reworked Aztec quartz beads.[17] Boban himself even hinted at his deception in a 1900 interview with the *New York Tribune*, noting how 'numbers of so-called rock crystal pre-Columbian skulls have been so adroitly made as almost to defy detection, and have been palmed off as genuine upon the experts of some of the principal museums of Europe.'[18]

There are good reasons to doubt that the Mitchell-Hedges were any more honest in their accounts of crystal skulls than Boban. In his lifetime Frederick was known as something of a charlatan. He reported that he discovered the Maya city of Lubaantun in the 1920s, despite the fact that the doctor and amateur archaeologist Thomas Gann was already there in 1903. In 1927 he claimed to have been attacked by assailants who stole six shrunken heads in his possession; when the *Daily Express* charged that he had orchestrated the event for publicity he sued them for libel and promptly lost. (The judge even concurred with the defence's description of him as 'an imposter'.) His autobiography – which alleged, in addition to the claims made about the Skull of Doom, that he had worked as a US spy, lived as an outlaw with Pancho Villa and bested J.P. Morgan out of £4,000 in a game of poker – was so overblown that he was panned by one reviewer as a 'facile scribbler in pseudo-science'.[19]

Anna, meanwhile, was strangely inconsistent in her accounts of discovering the skull. As well as insisting to have unearthed it in 1924, on her seventeenth birthday, she also told reporters that she found it in 1926, 1927 and 1928. In some retellings she uncovered the skull from the ruins of a temple, in others from beneath a stone altar, and in others still from a cave deep within a pyramid. She also seemed unclear about the skull's name, variously referring to it as the 'Skull of Doom', the 'Maya Skull of Divine Mystery' and the 'Godhead Skull'. Equally suspicious was that fact that she only started claiming to have found the skull in 1964, a full 40 years after the discovery supposedly took place – by which time, notes Walsh, 'all the people involved in her … father's expeditions to Lubaantun were dead' and therefore unable to contradict her.[20]

It turned out there was a good reason for Frederick's reticence and Anna's uncertainty when it came to the skull's provenance. When investigators Joe Nickell and John Fischer researched the item's history in the 1980s they came across a handwritten note in the British Museum archives, dated October 1943. 'Bid at Sotheby's sale, lot 54', it read. 'Sold subsequently by Mr Burney to Mr Mitchell-Hedges for £400.'[21] Lot 54, it turned out, was the Mitchell-Hedges skull. Neither Frederick nor Anna Mitchell-Hedges discovered it in some forgotten Maya city. It was bought by Frederick in London in 1943. The 'Mr Burney' from the archived note was Sydney Burney, a well-known art collector and dealer who acquired the skull from an unknown source sometime around 1933. Mitchell-Hedges even admitted as much in a letter to his brother two months after the purchase, noting that he had recently 'acquired that amazing Crystal Skull that was formerly in the Sydney Burney Collection'.[22]

It isn't just the skull's discovery that has since been exposed as a fabrication. Contrary to the claims of the Mitchell-Hedges, crystal skulls are nowhere to be found in mythology of the Maya, Aztecs or any other civilisation. Historians have yet to find any legends that extend further back in time than the 1930s, when they first began appearing in pulp fiction adventure stories – the same tales of square-jawed heroes, exotic locations and unearthly treasures that one would day inspire Indiana Jones' adventures.[23]

One of the earliest examples was the 1930 novel *The Moon of Skulls* by Robert Howard, the author who would later create Conan the Barbarian. In *The Moon of Skulls*, hero Solomon Kane travels to Africa where he finds a sinister tribe worshipping a crystal skull which is revealed to be none other than the skull of an Atlantean wizard. The following year Paul Claudel included a prophetic crystal skull in his historical play *The Satin Slipper*, in which King Philip II of Spain foresees the destruction of the Spanish Armada when he gazes into the Aztec relic. This was followed in 1936 by Jack McLaren's *The Crystal Skull*, the story of a double-dealing ethnologist who steals the eponymous skull only to discover that it has the power to read people's minds. Frederick Mitchell-Hedges is known to have been an avid reader of pulp fiction, and it seems very likely that he borrowed from stories like these when fabricating his minatory account of the Skull of Doom and its unearthly powers. The description of the skull in his autobiography is suspiciously similar to the one given in *The Moon of Skulls*.[24]

As for the other commonly reported mysteries surrounding the crystal skulls – both the Mitchell-Hedges skull and the many others now in existence – none has withstood scientific scrutiny. There's simply no evidence that they can produce light, sound, smells or any other phenomenon. None has ever been observed to change colour or project images. No computer, including the mountains of hardware required to power the electron microscopes which have studied them, has been shown to crash in their presence. Perhaps the most stubborn myth – that crystal skulls are impossible to replicate, even with modern technology – is also the most easily disproved. Although it's true that an inexperienced hand could shatter a crystal like quartz, a little practice is all that's needed to carve against the grain without fracturing it.

The proliferation of crystal skulls in recent decades – thousands are now made every year for the New Age market – is a testament to their replicability and to their profane origins.[25]

~

The mythology that has built up around the crystal skulls is just one example of the bewildering variety of alternative ideas that dot the archaeological landscape. There are the 'ancient astronaut' theorists, who maintain that many of the ancient world's greatest achievements – Stonehenge, Machu Picchu, the Easter Island statues – were created with the help of visiting aliens. There are others who instead argue that ancient civilisations had access to highly advanced technology, including electric lighting, powered flight and even nuclear weapons. Biblical literalists try to prove that humans and dinosaurs coexisted just 4,000 years ago; Hindu nationalists claim that Indian civilisation is at least 10,000 years old. Advocates of the Phantom Time Hypothesis, meanwhile, insist that the very dating system used by archaeologists is a Jesuit conspiracy, and what we call the 21st century is actually the 10th century. This is just a small sampling of pseudoarchaeological claims. The rabbit hole is bottomless.

This variety is a testament to the enormous popularity of pseudoarchaeology in the 21st (or 10th) century. Today its advocates can choose from hundreds of 'alternative history' books discussing everything from sunken cities to ancient Antarctic civilisations. (Swiss author Erich von Däniken's 1968 *Chariots of the Gods?*, the book that sparked the ancient astronaut craze, has sold an astounding 65 million copies and continues to sell.[26]) Alternatively they can tune into the dozens of televisions shows or check out the hundreds of thousands of sites dedicated to fringe interpretations of the past. An online search for 'suppressed history' (a favourite phrase in pseudoarchaeological circles) returns a staggering 64 million results.

It's not hard to see why pseudoarchaeology is so popular. As with Mitchell-Hedges and the so-called Skull of Doom – and in contrast to the measured and cautious writing of professional archaeologists – many of its proponents display an undeniable flair for the dramatic, using bold, exciting and eye-catching language that even the most excitable academic would steer clear of. Who wouldn't want to learn about an 'amazing new discovery' that will 'rewrite the history books' and 'change everything we thought we knew about human history'?[27] The claims made by Semir Osmanagić, a US-Serbian business owner, are typical in this regard. In 2005 Osmanagić announced that he had discovered that Visocica Hill, a sandstone promontory in the Bosnian countryside, was in fact the remains of a pyramid. This in itself would be an incredible find, but Osmanagić went further: the structure – which he's dubbed the Pyramid of the Sun – is not only the oldest and largest of its kind ever discovered, but part of a colossal 12,000-year-old temple complex created by a previously unknown civilisation. If true, it would be the most remarkable archaeological discovery ever made.[28]

Archaeologists and geologists have been quick to challenge Osmanagić's claims – insisting that Visocica Hill really is just a hill – but these efforts have done little to dampen the enthusiasm among his supporters. Indeed, many of them have proudly touted these criticisms as evidence that Osmanagić's shocking discovery has ruffled the feathers of the academic elite – an elite who would rather not have their history books rewritten. 'The idea of ancient pyramids in Europe throws a significant wrench into schoolbook history', explains one believer in the Bosnian pyramid, 'and orthodox academics are outraged that they might have to learn something new'.[29] Herein lies another secret to pseudoarchaeology's popularity: by positioning themselves as outsiders and underdogs daring to challenge the 'establishment dogmatists' of professional archaeology, its advocates lend an edge of intrigue and danger to their ideas. 'It gives the reader a feeling of being included in a great mystery,' recalls the former pseudo-archaeologist Katherine Reece. 'I wanted to be on the side of the freethinkers, the open-minded, and the curious. What could be better than to join the quest for the true and hidden knowledge of human history?'[30]

As Reece's question reveals, people are ultimately drawn to pseudoarchaeology for the same reason others are drawn to archaeology: a fascination with the past and a desire to uncover its secrets.[31] For those trying to refute the claims of the fringe, the frustrating thing is that so much of what makes pseudo-archaeology popular – amazing discoveries, audacious theories, ancient mysteries – can also be found in genuine, mainstream archaeology.

Take the curious case of the 4,000-year-old writing system of the Indus civilisation, a society that once flourished along the banks and tributaries of the River Indus in what's today Pakistan and India, between the years 2500 and 1900 BCE. The civilisation was home to grid-plan cities, remarkable artwork and a sewerage system the likes of which most people wouldn't enjoy until the 20th century. It also appears to have been a literate civilisation, and since the 1870s archaeologists have uncovered thousands of artefacts containing the civilisation's striking script. The only problem? No one has been able to decipher them. The 400 or so symbols in the Indus script bear no resemblance to anything else being written at the time, such as the hieroglyphs of Egypt or the cuneiform of Sumer. The inscriptions are also maddeningly short

– the longest found so far contains just twenty symbols – making it difficult for epigraphers to detect patterns that might suggest how the language was structured. Many samples of text are accompanied by illustrations of animals, both real and imagined, or what appears to be a human-animal hybrid practicing yoga, but these have been little help to those trying to decipher the script. Perhaps most intriguingly, about 50 of the script's symbols bear an uncanny resemblance to Rongorongo, the (also undeciphered) writing system used by the inhabitants of Easter Island in the 19th century. Could the writing system of the Indus civilisation have survived undetected for four millennia, only to reappear some 12,000 miles away on a remote Pacific island? It seems incredible, but the truth is that we simply don't know.[32]

Or consider the mysterious fate that befell the English colonists of Roanoke, a small island off the North Carolina coast. Unlike the Indus civilisation, archaeologists have plenty of information regarding the Roanoke Colony. They know that it was established in 1587, when 118 men, women and children arrived on the island in an attempt to establish a permanent English presence in the New World. They know that the colony struggled to eke out a living in the unfamiliar surroundings and sent their governor, John White, to return to England for much-needed supplies. What they don't know – what no one knows – is what happened next. By the time White had managed to return to the island in 1590 the colony was deserted. Every single colonist had vanished without a trace. The only clue to their possible whereabouts was the word 'Croatoan' – the name of another small island 50 miles to the south – carved into a wooden gatepost, but storms prevented White from reaching Croatoan to see if the colonists had indeed moved there. In the years since, archaeologists have unearthed a handful of the colonists' artefacts on both islands, including a sword hilt, crockery and a slate writing tablet, but the fate of their owners remains unknown.[33]

Archaeologists across the globe are working to solve these and thousands of other mysteries. In addition to Rongorongo and the Indus script there are the curious hieroglyphs of the early Minoans, the clay tablets of ancient Elam, and the Zapotec and Isthmian scripts of Central America all awaiting decipherment.[34] And while some archaeologists search for clues to the disappearance of Roanoke's colonists, others are trying to work out why hundreds of cities across the Levant suddenly vanished around 1200 BCE in what's known as the Late Bronze Age Collapse, an event that has been described as 'one of the greatest puzzles in Mediterranean archaeology'.[35]

In every one of these cases, professional archaeologists are the first to admit that they don't have all the answers. It's a modesty often lacking among pseudoarchaeologists. Fringe theorists, for all their talk of 'unsolved mysteries', never actually present the past as either unsolved or mysterious. Every code has been cracked, every cypher solved, every script deciphered.[36] Anna Mitchell-Hedges never entertained any other interpretations of her crystal skull and its alleged supernatural powers. Semir Osmanagić has always been certain that his hill is an ancient pyramid – even claiming to know what it was called – regardless of what others say or even what his own digs uncover.

This unshakeable faith in their beliefs, so typical of the fringe, reveals the fundamental difference between archaeology and pseudoarchaeology. Although both approaches attempt to explore and explain the past, fringe theorists are free to voice any interpretation of history no matter how speculative or unevidenced. Archaeologists, guided by the scientific principles of their profession, must instead evaluate all the available evidence – regardless of whether it supports their personal preferences – and only then see what conclusions, if any, can be drawn. 'Archaeologists, as scientists, can no more select what data to consider than a chemist can select which laws of chemistry to follow', explains the archaeologist Kristina Killgrove.[37] Pseudoarchaeologists, in contrast, turn this process on its head, beginning by choosing a conclusion they like the look of – aliens built the pyramids, prehistoric civilisations possessed nuclear weapons – and then look for evidence which supports it. More than any other characteristic, it's this rejection of the scientific method that defines pseudoarchaeology.

Of course, people have always held beliefs about the past that are now considered unscientific. Classical historians were happy to attribute past events to fate or the will of the gods. In the Middle Ages it was suggested that Stonehenge had been built by the wizard Merlin or a race of giants. As recently as the 18th century Christian historians were still insisting that giants had lived on Earth before the Great Flood, as reported in the Bible.

However, it would be unfair to group any of these beliefs with modern pseudoarchaeology, as they were all genuine attempts to make sense of the world with the limited information available at the time. It wasn't until the 19th century that there began to appear interpretations of the past deliberately refuting the evidence-based conclusions of mainstream scholarship; after all, archaeology had only just adopted an evidence-based approach for fringe theorists to take issue with. Inspired by the scientific principles of making observations, forming hypotheses, testing those hypotheses and drawing conclusions – and funded by national governments suddenly interested in their country's pasts – 19th-century archaeologists were transforming themselves from treasure hunters into disciplined academics. Rather than seeking out only the rare and the valuable, and discarding the rest, they started collecting and describing all artefacts uncovered at a dig, regardless of their financial value. The dig sites themselves were carefully and systematically mapped to ensure that an artefact's context – the specific place where it was found – could also be studied. (It makes a great deal of difference whether a dagger is found in someone's grave or in someone's back, for example.) Archaeologists also began publishing their papers and reports in academic journals, allowing their findings and conclusions to be scrutinised by fellow scholars. This process of peer review, which remains the backbone of scientific publishing today, prevented archaeologists from making unevidenced claims, greatly improving the study's accuracy and credibility.

Perhaps surprisingly, however, 'the enlightened 19th century' was also a time of rampant mysticism and anti-intellectualism in Europe and North America. This was partly a reaction against the rapid spread of scientific thinking that was transforming archaeology and many other disciplines. Just as new innovations are often greeted with suspicion today, so too did the rapid scientific and technological advances of the 1800s – telegrams and telephones, photographs and phonographs, theories of evolution and electromagnetism – inspire a backlash among those concerned that something was being lost in an increasingly industrial, automated world.[38]

It was thus a time hungry for alternative ideas – anything that might impart a deeper sense of meaning to people's lives. Cults, prophets and religious revivals swept through the USA. In the West a growing awareness of Eastern religions like Buddhism and Hinduism introduced millions to the concepts of reincarnation, meditation and karma. There were also plenty of opportunists willing 'to excite the wonder-loving faculties of the ignorant and superstitious', as the US journalist Eliab Capron put it in 1855.[39] In 1848, two teenage girls in upstate New York launched the spiritualist craze when they claimed they could communicate with the dead by knocking on wood. Around the same time the medical quack Robert Collyer was claiming to cure 'nervous disorders' with the help of magnets.[40] When not attending seances or being prodded with magnets, the gullible were busy undergoing hypnosis to cure their ailments, buying books to hone their telepathy skills, or gazing into crystal balls in the hopes of divining the mysteries of the universe. The spirit of the age was encapsulated in the new religion of Theosophy, a heady potpourri of existing faiths and occult beliefs. Its founder and figurehead, the Russian aristocrat Helena Blavatsky, claimed to receive 'ancient knowledge' from a secretive brotherhood of higher beings known as The Masters.

It was out of this melee of science and mysticism that pseudo-archaeology emerged. At first it was largely indistinct from other occult practices. Clairvoyants would claim to receive knowledge from ancient civilisations by channelling long-dead spirits or regressing back through their past lives. In Edwardian England the architect Frederick Bond and medium John Bartlett developed 'psychic archaeology', using Bartlett's supposed ability to commune with the spirits of medieval monks to locate dig sites at Glastonbury Abbey, until they were banned from doing so by the Church of England in 1921.[41]

The person who helped popularise pseudoarchaeology as its own distinct field was the US politician Ignatius Donnelly, whose 1882 book *Atlantis: The Antediluvian World* attempted to show – without recourse to mysticism – that the fabled island was not only real but home to a remarkably advanced civilisation. Moreover, argued Donnelly, the Atlanteans went on to lay the groundwork for all future civilisations, from the Egyptians to the Phoenicians to the Maya, as they escaped the cataclysms that destroyed their island. This was one of the first examples of genuine pseudoarchaeology: an attempt to explain the past in the style of a scientific investigation, but without going to the effort of actually testing its arguments using the scientific method. Donnelly makes a great show of drawing together many disciplines to make his case, from archaeology to linguistics to geology to metallurgy (none of which he had any training in), but in each instance he fails to subject his ideas to true scientific scrutiny, allowing weak evidence and flimsy conclusions to stand unchallenged. Donnelly's real skill was to mask this laziness with an engaging and authoritative style and to write for the mass market rather than professional academics. *Atlantis: The Antediluvian Word* was nonsense, but it was exciting and dramatic nonsense, and it quickly became a runaway bestseller, forging a whole new genre of popular history writing prioritising spectacle and mystery over substance and proof. Donnelly's book – which hasn't been out of print since 1882 – remains the model used by pseudoarchaeologists to this day.[42]

One group of people not impressed by Donnelly's wild theories were professional archaeologists, who were quick to point out the unscientific nature of his arguments. 'So far from a large continent or large mass of islands being depressed into the Atlantic Ocean, the facts are directly the reverse,' noted the historian Hyde Clarke in 1886; 'there is no evidence that such a continent ever did exist, nor is it even possible that it could.'[43] It was to be the first of many debunkings that would take place throughout the late 19th and 20th centuries, as an increasing number of ever more fantastical claims were made about the past.

In the years since Donnelly and Clarke sparred over Atlantis, archaeology and pseudoarchaeology have left us with very different legacies. Since adopting a scientific mentality in the 19th century, archaeologists have revolutionised our understanding of the past. Epigraphers may not yet know how to read the Indus script, but in the past century they have uncovered the secrets of Maya glyphs, Ugaritic cuneiform and the Minoan syllabary, each discovery unlocking a wealth of new information about the past. And although archaeologists may not yet know the whereabouts of Roanoke's lost colonists, they do now know the locations of the tomb of Tutankhamun, the Inca citadel of Machu Picchu and the ancient Assyrian library of Ashurbanipal. After more than a century of careful excavation, painstaking study and critical evaluation we can peer into previously inaccessible times and places, from the depths of the Ice Age to the heart of the Amazon. There are still many more archaeological mysteries to solve, of course – that's part of the fun – but the progress achieved over the past 150 years is undeniably impressive.

Pseudoarchaeology, on the other hand, remains virtually unchanged since the Victorian era. Many of its 'bold new theories' are in essence identical to those first put forward by Donnelly back in 1882.[44] New archaeological discoveries might be incorporated into its worldviews – Göbekli Tepe is currently the subject of much fringe fantasising – but these additions merely furnish pseudo-archaeologists with new ways to restate the same old arguments. 'One of the oddities of pseudoarchaeology is that it is so lacking in truly original or fantastic imagination,' remarks the marine archaeologist Nicholas Flemming. 'The same reworked themes are repeated continuously or in cycles, with nothing going out of date.'[45] The crystal skulls are a clear illustration of this: whereas professional researchers have used scientific techniques to reveal that these remarkable items, for all their artistry and intrigue, were nothing more than forgeries, many pseudoarchaeologists continue to promote them as marvels of the ancient world in a manner largely unchanged since the days of Eugène Boban and Frederick Mitchell-Hedges. Fringe theorists may like to portray professional archaeologists as inflexible dogmatists, but the latter's science-based approach has proven itself far more open to new evidence and ideas, and for those with a genuine interest in history it offers a far more rewarding and fruitful way to explore the past.

~

Even if scientific methods are by far the most productive when it comes to investigating the past, does it matter that some people choose not to believe in them? Is it really something that ought to concern anyone outside of professional archaeology? To many people, discussions of crystal skulls, hidden pyramids and the lost continent of Atlantis sound so bizarre that it can be difficult to think that such oddball beliefs could be important in the real world.

For those of us tempted to laugh off pseudoarchaeology, it's important to remember just how popular it's become in recent years. With the rise in shows, sites and forums dedicated to promoting crank theories, what was once comfortably dismissed as the 'lunatic fringe' by professional archaeologists is now threatening to become the mainstream opinion among the public. In a 2018 survey of ordinary US citizens by Chapman University, two fifths of those questioned believed that 'aliens visited the Earth in ancient times', and a dizzying 57 per cent agreed that 'civilisations like Atlantis once existed' – an increase of 17 per cent since the same question was asked by the university in 2016.[46] The flip side of these statistics, of course, is that less than half the people surveyed still believe professional archaeologists when they insist that there's no evidence of highly advanced civilisations like Atlantis ever existing. Ultimately, archaeology and pseudoarchaeology are both trying to answer the same questions about history and humanity: support for one can only come at the expense of the other. Thus the growing public endorsement of fringe beliefs is to the detriment of a rational, science-based understanding of history, and of the ability of non-professionals to distinguish between fact and fantasy in the past. If things continue at this rate, warns the archaeologist Mario Liverani, 'ancient history will become a minor branch of science fiction.'[47]

Pseudoarchaeology isn't the most pressing problem facing the world today, it's true. But that doesn't mean that its growing popularity ought to trouble only those who study the past for a living. If truth matters, then pseudoarchaeology's rejection of truth matters. If the story of humanity's time on Earth is important, then pseudoarchaeology's distortion of that story is also important. The rise of pseudoarchaeology matters because it is robbing us of our ability to understand our past and thus ourselves. History, when honestly pursued, allows us to learn from our mistakes, recognise our strengths and understand the world around us. Pseudohistory provides us with none of that. When we discover that supposedly 'primitive' Stone Age hunter-gatherers were capable of building a site as large and as complex as Göbekli Tepe, for instance, we're forced to reassess our old notions of who is and isn't civilised. But if we accept one of the many fringe interpretations of the site – that it was built by aliens, or by highly advanced Atlanteans – then we continue to treat our ancestors as passive simpletons and so miss an opportunity to learn more about ourselves.

Indeed, for a group of people who frequently claim to have a unique appreciation of the wonder of the past, much of pseudoarchaeology is founded on a remarkably condescending treatment of ancient people. All too often fringe theorists seem incapable of granting people skills or knowledge that they themselves lack. They can't personally explain how the Great Pyramid of Giza was built, so they ascribe the achievement to the handiwork of passing extraterrestrials. They don't know how Inca masons carved such incredibly well-fitting stone blocks for their buildings, so they insist that the Inca couldn't have known how to carve them either and must have instead enlisted the help of advanced beings from Antarctica (I promise I'm not making this stuff up).

Often there's an edge of racial prejudice to this condescension. Ancient European sites are rarely subjected to the same level of suspicion and fantastical reinterpretation as American, African and Asian sites. For example, the same theorists who are convinced that the Inca lacked the skills to build their mountaintop citadel of Machu Picchu, or that the ancient city of Meroe in present-day Sudan couldn't possibly have been built by Africans, seem to have no problem accepting that the Parthenon was built by the ancient Greeks, or the Pont du Gard aqueduct by the Romans.[48] When the archaeologist Kenneth Feder surveyed all the archaeological sites that Erich von Däniken (godfather of the ancient astronauts craze) argues could have been built with extraterrestrial help, he found that a third were in Africa, a quarter in Asia, but only 4 per cent in Europe.[49] Indeed, the very premise of the ancient astronaut hypothesis rests on the assumption that ancient people – usually non-European ancient people – were incapable of developing sophisticated art, science or technology by themselves. By denying ancient societies outside of Europe the same skills and knowledge granted to ancient Europeans, pseudo-archaeologists like von Däniken cast white Europeans as more advanced than other groups of humans.

Occasionally the damage caused by pseudoarchaeologists is physical as well as intellectual. In 2014 two pseudoarchaeologists managed to break their way into the Great Pyramid of Giza and scrape away at a red pigment inscription – significantly damaging it in the process – in a failed bid to show that the pyramids are in fact 20,000-year-old Atlantean power stations.[50] Back in Bosnia, Osmanagić's digs on Visocica Hill provoked outcry from archaeologists when excavations damaged medieval, Roman and pre-Roman archaeological sites on the hill. Particularly galling for academics was that these digs had been sponsored by the Bosnian government, which sees the Pyramid of the Sun as a symbol of Bosnian national pride and an important source of tourist revenue. Unimpressed, the European Association of Archaeologists has described the digs as 'a cruel hoax' and 'a waste of scarce resources that would be much better used in protecting the genuine archaeological heritage'.[51]

The desire of many pseudoarchaeologists to find evidence for their beliefs has even created a market for hoaxers and forgers, who create fake artefacts – or deface genuine ones – to sell to the fringe. A particularly disturbing incident of this emerged in 2015, when ancient astronaut advocates announced the discovery of mummified aliens in Peru by a band of 'treasure hunters' (a local archaeologist has alternatively described them as looters). Although professional archaeologists have been denied access to the bodies, they strongly suspect that the aliens are in fact ancient human remains deliberately disfigured to look otherworldly. In one case, of a suspected mummified child nicknamed Maria, it's thought that the grave robbers chopped off four of the child's fingers and toes, and sliced off her ears and nose, in order to give the body the classic three-fingered, three-toed alien look.[52]

There's another reason to be wary of pseudoarchaeology's growing popularity and authority – one that extends beyond the study of history. Unfortunately, archaeology isn't the only academic discipline currently being accosted by the fringe: researchers from just about every scientific field are accused of being 'establishment dogmatists' working to protect the 'academic orthodoxy'.[53] Zoologists take heat from Bigfoot hunters and Loch Ness Monster enthusiasts for refusing to accept the existence of such cryptids. Physicists who refute those who claim to have built free energy or perpetual motion machines (on the fairly rock-solid grounds that such inventions would defy the laws of physics) have been called 'ignorant' and a 'cabal of fossil fuel pushers'.[54]

Indeed, science itself is undergoing a crisis of trust in the 21st century as people increasingly reject it in favour of any number of unscientific, if not overtly anti-science, beliefs. In the USA, a growing number of farmers are adopting 'biodynamic agriculture', a pseudo-pagan hodgepodge of alchemy, astrology and homeopathy in which growers cast spells and sprinkle potions over their crops. Hundreds of 'Flat Earth' conspiracy theorists compete with pseudoarchaeologists and paranormalists for YouTube views. And an increasing number of people are rejecting science-based medical practices for demonstrably worthless and potentially harmful practices like cupping and colon cleansing. Even Robert Collyer's magnet therapy has made a comeback – despite being as useless now as it was in the 1800s – with the global sale of 'therapeutic magnets' topping $1 billion each year.[55]

There's no way this rejection of science can end well. The philosopher Bertrand Russell, writing back in the 1940s, warned of a 'vast social disaster' that would result from the 'madness' of rejecting the scientific method.[56] Already we can feel the foreshocks of this disaster. Diseases like measles and mumps that were on their way to eradication have returned because parents refuse to let their children be vaccinated. Unfounded opposition to drought-resistant genetically modified crops is condemning millions of people to hunger and starvation. Irrational rejection of climate science has, for decades, stalled increasingly urgent needs to de-carbonise the world's economies.

Pseudoarchaeology feeds into this emerging disaster. A certain hostility towards the scientific community has been simmering away in pseudoarchaeological circles ever since the revival of mysticism in the mid-19th century; Blavatsky, for instance, repeatedly mocked 'modern science' for its ignorance of ancient wisdom.[57] With the emergence of self-reinforcing online communities in recent decades, however, this hostility has boiled over into out-right antagonism. 'The primary driver behind pseudoarchaeology today is the belief in a conspiracy by "mainstream" archaeology to cover up and deny some inconvenient truth,' explains Brian Dunning, a science writer who's spent the past thirteen years investigating unscientific and conspiratorial beliefs. 'It's little dif-ferent from the Flat Earth belief or 9/11 Truthism,' he tells me. 'As long as your alternative view of history includes belief in this conspiracy, you're in the club, regardless of the validity of your alternative view.'

For anyone troubled by the rising tide of fake news and alter-native facts, such conspiracy mongering ought to arouse concern. Particularly when considering that fringe attacks against aca-demics and their advocates are often personal, and often savage. Everyone I spoke to while researching this chapter has received hate mail for questioning pseudoarchaeological beliefs. 'Death threats and online harassment are very much a standard part of the game,' states Dunning.

Nevertheless, Dunning remains clear on the threat posed by pseudoarchaeology through its contribution to a broader distrust of science. 'The lack of basic science literacy and the lack of criti-cal thinking in pseudoarchaeology should concern everyone,' he tells me. 'We have children dying needlessly in measles outbreaks worldwide right now because of exactly these same failed beliefs. Every time a show like *Ancient Aliens* persuades a single viewer that mainstream science is lying to them, we're another step closer to another measles outbreak, the rejection of AIDS drugs, rejection of drought-resistant crops, rejection of climate science, the whole thing. Every bit of promotion of any pseudoscience is ultimately harmful.'

I left item 1898-1 to the crowd of schoolchildren and made my way to the museum's exit. In the end I wasn't surprised that I'd failed to establish any spiritual communion with the skull. After all, the curse of the crystal skulls isn't that they can summon death or drive you mad with visions of pure terror, but that they have contributed, perhaps more than any other type of artefact, to the spread of bogus historical thinking – and, through this, to the growing distrust of science in general.

I can't help wondering what Eugène Boban or the Mitchell-Hedges would make of their collective legacy. Frederick and Anna would probably be delighted simply to know that their skull, and the legends they wove around it, continue to be talked about (Frederick Mitchell-Hedges even gets name-checked in the fourth *Indiana Jones* movie). Boban, however, I suspect would have more mixed feelings. On the one hand he would no doubt be pleased to know that the skull he sold in 1886 is still on display in the British Museum, even if the museum now very clearly presents it as a modern forgery. On the other hand he might be surprised, and more than a little dismayed, by the extent to which crystal skull lore has established itself around the world. Boban was a swindler but he was no crank, and never suggested that the crystal skulls he sold were anything other than works of art. He also had a genuine enthusiasm for archaeology and antiques, and the knowledge that his deception is now undermining his life's passion would surely be uncomfortable.

Can the curse be lifted? Of course. All that's required is the realisation that the past needs no help from Maya curses, Machiavellian conspiracies or extraterrestrial architects to make it exciting, mysterious or rewarding. As any archaeologist will tell you, it already is.

CHAPTER 9

How the West wasn't won

I had to keep rewriting this chapter's introduction. When I started investigating the history of guns in the United States, I planned to open with an account of the latest mass shooting from that country. At the time this was the Las Vegas massacre of October 2017, when a lone gunman killed 58 people and injured 851 as he fired on a music festival from a nearby hotel. Fewer Americans died in the battles of Lexington and Concord. And yet, only 35 days later, this had become old news: a 26-year-old ex-serviceman, using a rifle he bought despite having a criminal record, killed 26 and injured twenty more at a Texas church. Then, on Valentine's Day 2018, seventeen students and teachers were killed at a high school in Florida. Ten more students and teachers were murdered at a high school in Texas three months later. Then eleven were shot dead at the Tree of Life Synagogue in Pittsburgh in October, making it the largest mass murder of Jews in US history. In 2019 there were more than 400 mass shootings, the most yet recorded in a year, including the murder of 23 people in El Paso in what's believed to have been a deliberate massacre of Latinos. That record looks set to be broken in 2020, a year that has seen an unprecedented surge in gun sales and a significant rise in mass shootings across the country. There will almost certainly have been more by the time you read this.

The seemingly endless cortege of mass shootings in the USA looks set to be a fixture of the 21st century. And yet it represents only the tip of the iceberg when it comes to the country's 'gun violence epidemic'.[1] A total of 15,363 people died from gunshot wounds in the USA in 2019, an average of 42 a day. Mass shootings – defined here as when four or more people are shot or killed in the same incident – accounted for little more than 3 per cent of these deaths, meaning that for every person who died in a mass shooting that year, 33 more were killed by what's almost dismissively referred to as 'background violence'. All the while, gun ownership continues to rise. In the past decade US citizens have bought well over 100 million new guns, bringing the total number of privately-owned firearms to more than 400 million. There are now more guns than people in the USA, and sales figures show no sign of slowing; in 2019, the guns and ammunitions industry netted a total revenue of $16 billion.[2]

Why should this be? Why is it that the United States, the richest, most powerful country on Earth, suffers from levels of gun violence found in places like Panama and Iraq? US debates on firearms understandably revolve around the country's Second Amendment, the constitutional guarantee that US citizens have a right to bear arms. By itself, however, the legal endorsement of gun ownership doesn't explain the passion generated by these debates – especially when compared to the lack of discussion surrounding most of the USA's 26 other constitutional amendments – or the country's extraordinarily high rates of gun violence. Finland has one of the highest rates of gun ownership in the world and yet has suffered just four deadly mass shootings in the past two decades. The Swiss government actually *gives* its male citizens an automatic rifle on their twentieth birthday, the age they become eligible for military service, and Switzerland still has a firearm homicide rate just one fourth that of the USA.[3]

So what makes American gun culture different? Plenty of

reasons have been offered by politicians, journalists and academics, from a fondness for hunting to a fear of crime and armed invasion. Many gun enthusiasts, however, frame their motivations not just in practical terms of pastimes and personal protection but also in the symbolic language of freedom, dignity, identity and independence. 'The gun', writes American sociologist Paul Froese, 'brims with symbolic power far beyond its physical utility.'[4]

And it's here that history takes centre stage. For many Americans, gun ownership, personal liberty and their country's past are all inextricably intertwined. 'It's about ... our culture, our heritage and our freedom', argues the current National Rifle Association Chief Executive Wayne LaPierre.[5] One episode of American history in particular is routinely held up as emblematic of this independent, freedom-loving heritage: the Wild West. That lawless frontier land of cowboys and Indians, outlaws and gunslingers, shoot-outs and duels, where men took care of their problems and government knew its place. Out of this Hobbesian crucible modern America was forged – a country steeped in the heritage of self-governing, violent, gun-wielding men.

Or so, at least, goes the story. But what truth is there to it? Can modern-day attitudes towards firearms trace their origins back to the American West? When we look beyond the Spaghetti Westerns to the real history of the frontier – and the violence that supposedly plagued it – a surprising picture begins to emerge from the gunsmoke.

~

What we tend to think of as the Wild West – the cowboys, the duels, the whiskey-soaked saloons – was in truth only a very short episode in the long history of western North America. This vast area west of the Mississippi River, stretching from the sun-seared deserts of Mexico to the wind-blasted prairies of Canada and the rain-drenched Pacific coast, has been inhabited by humans for thousands of years. Estimates vary, but it seems likely that the indigenous inhabitants of both North and South America can trace their origins back some 16,500 years, when bands of hunter-gatherers crossed the Bering land bridge that once connected Asia and North America. It would be another 16,300 years before any cowboy ever set foot in the region.

Much of this history is unrecorded and unknown. But the fragments that have survived reveal a world that is difficult to square with the USA's narrative of pioneers and progress. It's not widely known, for instance, that the very first Europeans to arrive in the West did so as slaves of Native Americans. And yet that's precisely what happened to a band of Spanish conquistadors in the early 16th century.

We know about the disastrous fate of the Narváez expedition because one of the very few survivors, an accountant named Alvar Nuñez Cabeza de Vaca, managed to return to Spain and write down his experiences. The resulting travelogue, describing how a headstrong imperial voyage of five ships and 600 men was reduced to four half-starved survivors, is remarkable for its sheer scale of misery and misfortune. De Vaca relates how he and his fellow explorers were battered by hurricanes, ambushed by natives and felled by disease. An inland expedition from the Florida coast (in search of gold, of course) succeeded only in separating the Spaniards from their supply ship, forcing them to build makeshift boats out of wood, dead horses and their own tattered shirts. When these broke apart in storms, the few remaining survivors were washed up on the shore of what would one day become Texas, 'nearer death than life', as de Vaca put it. For the next seven years he and three other survivors were forced to work as slaves among various indigenous tribes, before finally escaping captivity and crossing the American Southwest on foot – a journey of almost 4,000 miles – to reach Spanish forces at Mexico City.[6]

The West would prove equally hospitable to other outsiders for many years to come. Esteban de Dorantes, one of de Vaca's three surviving companions, would later be killed by indigenous Zunis in the deserts of the Southwest. Juan Rodriguez Cabrillo, the first European to sight California, died slowly and painfully of gangrene following another native attack. French attempts to establish a colony in the Gulf of Mexico, meanwhile, proved as luckless as the Narváez expedition. Originally bound for the lower Mississippi, navigational errors dumped the French colonists on the Texan coast, where they were beset by disease, desertion, infighting, hostile natives, Spanish soldiers and an axe-wielding murderer. The ruinous affair finally ended – perhaps unsurprisingly – in mutiny, when the colony's leader was shot and killed by the few remaining settlers.[7]

Even the might of the Spanish Empire suffered a major defeat at the hands of the Pueblo people of New Mexico, who arose in rebellion in 1680 after nearly a century of brutal oppression and religious persecution. Spanish forces found themselves outnumbered 25 to one as some 2,500 Pueblo warriors laid siege to Santa Fe, the capital of Spanish New Mexico, cutting off the water supply and killing hundreds. The Pueblos took particular delight in erasing all traces of the Spaniard's hated Christianity, burning churches, killing friars and annulling their Christian marriages, mockingly singing the Catholic liturgy in Latin as they did so. After an eleven-day siege the Spanish were forced to retreat and were unable to retake the territory for another twelve years.[8]

During all this time the West was 'American' only by virtue of being in America. It wasn't until the 19th century – three centuries after Europeans first washed ashore in the region – that the idea of the Wild West familiar to us began to take shape. And it happened almost by accident. In April 1803, president Thomas Jefferson dispatched a handful of diplomats to Paris with instructions to offer up to $10 million for the ramshackle port of New Orleans and the surrounding countryside. They were astonished when their French counterparts, who were both cash-strapped and increasingly preoccupied with European affairs, offered their entire North American empire of Louisiana for just $5 million more. Worried that Napoleon's government might change its mind, the American negotiators quickly accepted.[9] The resulting Louisiana Purchase has gone down in history as one of the most incredible bargains ever struck.

The United States had just doubled in size. The Louisiana territory was enormous: at 530 million acres, it ranged from the Mississippi River in the east to the Rocky Mountains in the west and from Mexico to Canada (then known as 'the Canadas'). An area larger than Spain, France, Germany, Italy and Poland combined – but with a population of around 100,000, 50 times smaller than that of the USA at the time – had been acquired for less than three cents an acre.[10] For millions of Americans, a life beyond the Mississippi now beckoned.

People pushed west for various reasons. Farmers were encouraged by the promise of better land. Misanthropes were enticed by the prospect of fewer people. The Panic of 1837 caused many to flee from plunging wages and soaring unemployment in the east. The Mormons, widely despised wherever they travelled, began a self-consciously biblical exodus into the wilderness of Salt Lake Valley following the murder of their leader Joseph Smith in 1844. The growing craze for top hats, meanwhile, lured a few intrepid trappers as far as the Rockies in the early 19th century, where they caught the beavers whose fur was used to make the iconic headgear. But perhaps the most glittering enticement came in 1848, when vast deposits of gold were discovered in California. The population of California ballooned from 20,000 to more than 200,000 in the space of four years as hopeful prospectors raced to the Far West.[11]

Before the transcontinental railroad connected North America's east and west coasts in 1869, emigrants reached the territories west of the Rocky Mountains by overland wagon trails, such as the 2,000-mile Oregon Trail. Whatever their motivation, the journey across the continent was, for most, a long, uncomfortable and boring test of endurance. The 'forlorn and dreary monotony' of the landscape inspired little enthusiasm.[12] The food supplies they brought with them were dull and unvaried – consisting largely of flour, bacon and coffee – and in constant danger of running out. 'Anything you see as big as a blackbird,' one westbound party was advised in 1843, 'kill it and eat it.'[13] And the progress was painfully slow: wagon trains rarely covered more than fifteen miles a day, meaning the whole journey west would easily take four or five months. The wagons (pulled by oxen and not horses as is commonly thought) swayed so much as they lurched across the plains that many travellers suffered from seasickness. Far more serious were the periodic outbreaks of cholera that littered stretches of the overland trails with hastily-dug graves.[14]

Neither disease nor drudgery could stem the rising tide of settlers, however; by 1870 an estimated 400,000 had set out for the frontier.[15] Almost all of them were misinformed about the West, and many were shocked by what they found. For one thing, there was no inland sea called the Timpanogos, as their maps confidently claimed. Nor did the Pacific Northwest enjoy a 'tropical

climate', despite the assurances of one Eastern senator. And the
slopes of the Rocky Mountains they would have to cross certainly weren't 'almost imperceptible', as promised by New England
newspapers.[16]

Perhaps even more shocking was the state of frontier towns,
which had quickly acquired a distinctive character. 'Saloons –
saloons – liquor – everywhere,' gasped a scandalised visitor to
the mining town of Aurora in 1863. 'It is so unlike anything East
that I can compare it with nothing you have ever seen.'[17] He wasn't
exaggerating: the enormous popularity of alcohol out West meant
that the average town had an inordinate number of watering
holes. Within one month of its foundation, the Oklahoma town
of Guthrie already had 50 saloons: one for every hundred citizens,
a ratio equalled in the east only in the more disreputable quarters
of New York City.[18]

However, drinking wasn't the only diversion on the frontier.
Wrestling and walking races were particular favourites, and skiing
was a popular pastime for miners in the Sierra Nevada mountains
of California. Many miners also owned shares in mining companies and avidly followed the stock market. Newspapers, political
clubs and restaurants sprang up almost as quickly as the saloons.
Even the saloons could accommodate the more discerning cus-
tomer, offering not just whiskey but French brandy, imported
wines and Havana cigars.[19]

New arrivals to the West would have also been struck by its
diversity. The opportunities promised by the frontier attracted
immigrants not just from the eastern USA but from all over the
world: as well as hundreds of thousands of black, Hispanic and
indigenous people, there were Austrians, Basques, Bohemians,
Chileans, Chinese, Danish, English, Finnish, Flemish, French,
Germans, Greeks, Hawaiians, Irish, Italians, Norwegians,

Peruvians, Polish, Portuguese, Russians, Serbians, Slovenians, Spanish, Swedish and Welsh all making their homes on the frontier.[20] By 1860 almost one in ten Californians were Chinese. In the copper mines of Butte, Montana, the 'no smoking' signs had to be written in fourteen different languages.[21] Whether they came from the eastern states or further afield, migrants plied just about every trade the West could offer: barkeepers, shopkeepers, sheriffs, lawyers, farmers, ranchers. One frontiersman, the Chinese-born Sam Chung, worked variously as a farmer, police interpreter, landlord and restaurant owner in the Californian mining town of Bodie.[22]

It was a very different story for the indigenous inhabitants of the West, whose shrinking freedoms during this time closely mirrored the growing opportunities for new settlers. For the uncomfortable truth about the West is that the classic frontier narrative of westward expansion only occurred through the systematic displacement, subjugation and sometimes annihilation of Native Americans by European and later US forces. When Cabeza de Vaca was staggering through the Southwest in the 1530s there were an estimated 5 million indigenous people living in what would become Canada and the USA. By the closing of the American frontier in the 1890s – by which point all of the USA's continental acquisitions had been incorporated into states or territories – there were fewer than 400,000.[23] Most died as a result of diseases brought by Europeans, which colonists could neither have known about nor prevented when they first arrived (although some later exploited the situation by sending smallpox-infested blankets to indigenous groups in an attempt to 'extirpate this execrable race').[24] But warfare also played its part. For much of the 19th century Washington was engaged in a long series of 'Indian Wars' – comprising over 60 separate conflicts and some 600 battles – against the continent's indigenous population.

Between 1850 and 1890 an estimated 15,000 Native Americans were killed in conflicts with the US military and volunteer units in the West. Some of these were more traditional battles between soldiers, such the famous Battle of the Little Bighorn. Others were nothing short of slaughter, such as the infamous Sand Creek Massacre, where 150 Cheyenne and Arapaho men, women and children were killed and mutilated by US volunteer troops.[25]

To justify its aggression the US government dismissed or ignored earlier treaties and Indian reserves (the earliest of which had limited US westward expansion to the Appalachian Mountains, 1,300 miles east of the Rockies). The 19th century saw more than 100,000 Native Americans forcibly relocated to ever smaller, ever ecologically poorer lands, until by 1890 not a single indigenous person anywhere in the USA lived freely on their own land.[26] 'I once thought that I was the only man that persevered to be the friend of the white man', expressed the Cheyenne leader Black Kettle in 1865, less than a year after many of his people were slaughtered at Sand Creek, 'but since they have come and cleaned out our lodges, horses, and everything else, it is hard for me to believe white men anymore.'[27]

Women were another group for whom the frontier wasn't a land of opportunity. During the 19th century the economic prospects of the West were answered largely by men. Consequently, in many towns – especially those centred on industries like lumbering and mining – women were vanishingly rare, sometimes making up less than 10 per cent of the population. Miners would travel 40 miles just to catch a glimpse of one of these 'petticoated astonishments', as they were fawningly known. 'Got nearer to a female this evening than I have been in six months,' noted one awestruck man in Nevada City, California. 'Came near to fainting.'[28]

For the men of the American West, women usually fell into one of two very distinct categories. On the right side of frontier morality were the 'respectable' wives and mothers, who were routinely praised, in typical 19th-century terms, for their domestic virtues and for their volunteer work in schools, church groups and social clubs such as temperance societies.[29] Such women were generally treated with courtesy. 'One of the striking features of all mining camps in the West', recalled one frontiersman, 'was the respect shown even by the worst characters to the decent women and children ... I do not recall ever hearing of a respectable woman or girl in any manner insulted or even accosted by the hundreds of dissolute characters that were everywhere.'[30] When the English writer Isabella Bird decided to travel solo through the Rocky Mountains in the 1870s she found she could 'ride alone in perfect safety'. In one incident a burly lumberjack did approach her, only to bashfully offer her a bouquet of freshly picked mountain pinks.[31]

Women like Bird – wealthy, white, independent – were exceptions, however. For the 'disreputable' women who fell foul of the frontier's Victorian morality, the West offered very little in the way of respect or independence. This was especially true for the frontier's many prostitutes, who could be found throughout the camps, towns and cities of the West. Some women, like the professional gambler Eleanor Dumont, turned to prostitution when other sources of income dried up; others, such as the majority of Chinese women who arrived in the United States during the 19th century, were kidnapped, tricked or sold by their impoverished families into the sex trade and shipped across the Pacific especially.[32]

The Hollywood image of the bawdy 'painted lady' is a far cry from reality. 'They look so charming in the movies – the dancehall girls, the borderline prostitutes wearing those colourful clothes', remarks Patricia Limerick, a professor of history at the University of Colorado Boulder. In actuality, however, 'the stories seem to be close to pure misery: squalid living conditions, risk of physical violence every working moment, wretched rate of pay, drug addiction, alcoholism. Suicide was a common way for a prostitute's life to end.'[33] Frontier society was unmoved by their condition. Newspapers of the day treated prostitutes as figures of fun and the violence they endured as unworthy of censure. Men convicted of assaulting prostitutes were given much lighter punishments than if they had committed the same crime against 'decent' women. The stigma stayed with them even in death: the historian Roger McGrath reports that prostitutes in the mining town of Bodie were buried outside the town graveyard.[34]

Hollywood has a lot to answer for when it comes to another famous frontier figure: the cowboy. For many people the word still conjures images of Stetson-topped actors like John Wayne and Burt Lancaster, but such depictions are often far from the truth. Significantly, up to half of America's cowboys weren't white. One in three cowboys were Mexican vaqueros, who had already been driving cattle for centuries, and on certain trails another one in four are thought to have been black.[35] As for the cowboy's distinctive Stetson hat: John Stetson's upmarket headwear was much too expensive for the majority of westerners, and most opted for a bowler or slouch hat instead. The cowboy's heroic, action-packed life is another product of the silver screen. In contrast to their cinematic alter egos, genuine cowboys had a specific and largely uneventful job: they were paid solely to drive their herds of Texan longhorn cattle from southern ranges to Midwestern cow towns like Abilene, Kansas, where the cattle were sold to eastern states for ten times the price they could fetch in Texas. 'Most of the time it was dull work, lonely work, dirty work and hungry work,' write the historians Joe Frantz and Julian Choate.[36] It was also time-consuming work, and would easily take three months – covering an average of ten miles a day – for even experienced cowboys to reach the cow towns.[37]

The cowboy's modern-day status as America's folk hero would have struck most early westerners as laughable. For one thing, they were hardly the most familiar face on the frontier: even at the height of the cattle trade there were never more than 10,000 cowboys in the entire West, and for every cowboy riding the Texas trails there were a thousand farmers ploughing the plains.[38] For another, cow punching (as cowboys called their job) wasn't considered an exciting or glamorous occupation. In fact, cowboys were widely disliked by those who had to share the frontier with them. They were notorious for burning through their pay on alcohol, gambling and tacky clothes, and generally disturbing the peace of quiet towns like Abilene. Indeed, the citizens of Abilene were so sick of their yobbish behaviour that in 1872, just five years after the first cowboys had arrived, they sent notice to Texas that they would no longer accept cowboys and 'submit to the evils of the trade'. The letter had been signed by four-fifths of the entire county.[39]

Fortunately for the citizens of Abilene, the Wild West wasn't to last. The United States was industrialising at such a breakneck speed in the 19th century that many of its most iconic features and creations were quickly outdated and replaced. Indeed, one of the defining features of the West was its transience. The mountain men who trapped beavers in the Rocky Mountains were out of a job after fifteen years, when the fashion for beaver pelt became decidedly old hat. The Pony Express – the famous transcontinental mail service – didn't even survive two years before the enormous costs of maintaining its small army of riders and horses (more than $25,000 *a day* in today's money) left the owners 'pathetically insolvent'.[40] The stagecoach from St Louis to San

Francisco was in use for little more than a decade before the steam train put it out of business. The railway also drove the buffalo to near-extinction with the macabre innovation of 'hunting by rail'.[41]

The cowboy soon followed suit. The cattle ranching industry that supported their livelihood had all but vanished within 25 years of first developing in the 1860s. Partly it was a victim of its own success: overgrazing had dramatically reduced the quality of the land in Texas, while oversupply of cattle pushed down profits.[42] Technological innovations also rendered the cowboys' months-long cattle drives increasingly obsolete. In the mid-1870s farmers began using newly invented barbed wire to section off their land, squeezing out the big round-ups and trail drives.[43] This was followed a few years later by the introduction of refrigerated rail cars, which provided a far more convenient means of transportation than the arduous cattle drive. The final nail in the coffin was the terrible winter of 1886–7, described as 'hell without the heat' by one half-frozen cowboy: livelihoods were ruined when blizzards and Arctic temperatures felled as much as 90 per cent of the West's open range cattle. Many animals died standing, their feet frozen to the ground.[44] When the grim spring thaw eventually came, most ranchers sensed that the industry had been dealt a blow from which it couldn't recover. Many, including the future president Theodore Roosevelt, sold up and headed back east. They knew the Old West was over.

'Twenty years ago, half our continent was an unknown land, and the Rocky Mountains were our Pillars of Hercules,' wrote the journalist Albert Richardson in 1869. 'Five years hence, the Orient will be our neighbour. We shall hold the world's granary, the world's treasury, the world's highway. But we shall have no West.'[45]

Such eulogies may have been premature. What Richardson and others hadn't foreseen was that the West, having faded from reality, was about to return as legend. Of course, stories of the frontier had been told ever since settlers started pushing west. Among their other talents, many frontiersmen were gifted self-publicists, competing with one another to see who could boast of the diciest encounter, the boldest rescue or the narrowest escape. These tall tales found an eager audience back east, where urbanites hungrily devoured the accounts of these mountain men. There were only ever about 3,000 white trappers in the Rockies, but such was the demand for their stories that at least 300 were the subject of biographies (the many non-white trappers, in contrast, received very little attention).[46] A few pioneers, such as Daniel Boone, David Crockett and Kit Carson, even became national celebrities and lived to hear their own lives become mythologised. 'Everybody seems anxious to get a peep at me,' complained Crockett in the autobiography he wrote in order to dispel the many 'catchpenny errors' circulating about his life.[47] (The autobiography – itself no paean to modesty – failed, for Crockett the man remains buried under Crockett the myth to this day. He never called himself Davy, for instance, probably never wore a coonskin cap, and, as a Congressman for Tennessee, was more often seen in a three-piece suit than his famous buckskin.)

Even so, the West and its inhabitants weren't always the subject of such romantic veneration as they receive today. In 1819 a thoroughly unimpressed New England visitor to the Ohio Valley (which counted as the 'Southwest' back then) described the 'semi-barbarians' of the frontier as 'a meagre, sickly, spiritless and unenterprising race ... devoting the chief part of their time to hunting and drinking whiskey'.[48] Thirty years later, Mark Twain was lampooning the 'dislocated grammar and decomposed pronunciation' of the people he met out west.[49] As late as the 1870s, easterners dismissed their country's interior as the 'Great American Desert': a 'howling, hopeless, worthless, cactus-bearing waste'.[50]

It was only once the frontier had closed, and the floodgates of nostalgia opened, that the West could be truly idealised as a golden age of heroism and excitement. It became a land of superlatives: the biggest, boldest, bravest, baddest episode in American history. The Wild West served as a collective dreamtime for the country, a mythical arena where its heroes and villains could battle it out for all eternity.

The heroes, of course, were the white settlers and soldiers. Under the United States' self-serving doctrine of Manifest Destiny (yet another example of historical inevitability), they were the vanguard of civilisation, 'taming' the frontier for American expansion. The villains, it followed, were the West's indigenous inhabitants, who were portrayed as the savage foil to the civilisation of the United States. 'By just so much have we advanced; by just so much has the Indian stood still', opined an 1894 edition of *Harper's Weekly*.[51] Fictional depictions of the West reflected this mindset, often simplifying the complex relationships between settlers and Native Americans, and the systematic military campaigns against the latter, into a simplistic conflict of good versus evil.

Nowhere could this new, simplified West be seen more emphatically than in William Cody's wildly popular rodeo, *Buffalo Bill's Wild West*. As a young man Cody had actually lived and worked throughout the West, although he rarely stayed long in any one job: he had been a cowboy (for all of six months), a gold prospector, a cattle rancher, a frontier scout and a buffalo hunter before he found his true calling as a showman. Knowing that drama, danger and derring-do make for a great show, he presented a West

far removed from the world he had known on the American frontier. *Buffalo Bill's Wild West* gave its first performance in 1883,
and for the next 30 years an estimated 50 million spectators from
around the world cheered as newly-heroicised cowboys squared
off in mock shoot-outs against villainous 'Indians', who attacked
everything from settlers' cabins to wagon trains to mail coaches.
Re-enactments of Custer's Last Stand – US Lieutenant Colonel
George Custer's ill-fated battle against the Lakota, Cheyenne and
Arapaho – were particularly popular, drawing the highest praise
from none other than Libbie Custer, George Custer's widow. The
re-enactment helped transform Custer from a reckless hothead
who needlessly sacrificed his troops – an opinion held by President
Ulysses Grant, among others – into a tragic hero bravely fighting
against impossible odds. 'This is a show about the conquest of the
West, but everything that the audience sees is Indians attacking
whites', remarks the historian Richard White. 'It's conquest without the guilt. We didn't plan it; they attacked us.'[52]

Cody's brand of 'gunpowder entertainment', and the tropes
it helped popularise, proved to be enormously influential. One
hundred and sixteen copycat productions did nothing to dampen
the enormous success of his rodeo nor to satiate the growing
demand for all things Wild West. The western novel, which had
existed as a niche genre since the 1860s, exploded in popularity,
and by the 1950s publishers were churning out 35 million paper-
backs a year. The nascent film industry quickly realised that these
action-heavy, plot-light stories would translate well onto the silver
screen. During the 1920s, just two decades since the first Wild
West film, nearly a third of all Hollywood movies were westerns.
When television ownership soared in the 1950s the cowboy found
a new home, and by the end of the decade primetime viewers
in the USA could choose from 30 western shows to watch. The

Wild West remains something of a national obsession to this day, with more than 50 million US adults describing themselves as 'western enthusiasts'. Films, television shows and video games continue to be made, continue to be well-received and continue to make millions.[53]

With the notable exception of William Cody, the mania for the Old West was not a product of the frontier. The western was an eastern creation, made by eastern artists for eastern audiences. Owen Wister, widely regarded as the grandfather of cowboy literature for his 1902 novel *The Virginian*, was a wealthy, Harvard-educated Philadelphian who made only occasional junkets out west. His friend Frederic Remington, the artist whose action-packed paintings continue to colour our view of the West, left his native New York too late to witness any real cowboys riding the trails. Many more authors and artists didn't even bother to visit the old frontier; the author Richard Wheeler, for instance, was perfectly content to write dozens of western novels without ever venturing west of Illinois.[54]

But then accuracy was never the main concern of the western. New York dentist Zane Grey knew practically nothing about the West, and yet his 70-odd stories on the subject became firm favourites. (Such feats of prodigiousness were child's play to the author Prentiss Ingraham, who somehow managed to write or co-author nearly 1,000 novels and short stories in the genre.) What Grey certainly did know was that the attraction of the western genre has always been action, adventure and violence. *The Virginian* had already popularised the gunfight as a staple of the West, and Grey's books added kidnapping, fist fights, mass shoot-outs and even impalement on cacti to the mix. Violence was also central to the first western movie, *The Great Train Robbery*. Released in 1903, the film's fast pace and action sequences made it an immediate hit and helped to turn the fledgling cinema industry from a novelty act into a serious entertainment business. The film managed to squeeze two fist fights, three shoot-outs and six deaths into its twelve-minute runtime. The final scene of one of the bandits emptying his six-shooter straight at the camera was so shocking that audiences reportedly dived for cover when they first saw it.[55]

In the 117 years since *The Great Train Robbery* the Wild West has stacked up a frightening body count. Outlaws were gunned down every day on the radio, in movie theatres and on television for much of the 20th century. Things stepped up a notch in 1969 when the unremittingly bloodthirsty *The Wild Bunch* assaulted cinema-goers. 'It's not fun and games and cowboys and Indians,' explained the director, Sam Peckinpah; 'it's a terrible, ugly thing.'[56] He wasn't joking: the film's climactic battle scene sees 112 people gunned down. One of the most recent to take up the hyper-violent mantle is Quentin Tarantino, whose 2012 western, *Django Unchained*, was a predictably gore-filled gun fantasy in which more than 50 people meet a bloody end, 34 of them at the hands of the title character alone.

This fascination with the violence of the West shows no sign of fading. In 2018, for example, the highly anticipated video game *Red Dead Redemption 2* hit shelves. As the name suggests, the game is a suitably blood-soaked romp across the American frontier. Starring as the gravel-voiced antihero, Andrew Morgan, players shoot, stab, steal, dynamite and duel their way through an incredibly detailed virtual West, orchestrating jail breaks, bank robberies and stagecoach heists. In the two-minute trailer for the game Morgan kills 22 people. *Red Dead Redemption 2* has been wildly popular with fans and critics alike, earning $725 million in its opening weekend alone – a figure most Hollywood blockbusters have never come close to. One hundred and thirty-five years after *Buffalo Bill's Wild West* put on its first show, Cody's gunpowder entertainment is as popular as ever.

~

The Wild West has now been around longer as legend than it ever was as lived reality. It's hard to overemphasise the effect that books, films, television shows and games have had on our under-standing of the past. For the millions who had never known life on the frontier, William Cody's travelling circus *was* the West (Cody himself never once used the word 'show' to describe it, insisting always on its 'historical accuracy').[57] To a generation of children who grew up watching cowboys and Indians shoot each other on a daily basis, the gun-toting, self-reliant masculine hero was at the heart of the American story. Even for those who knew the frontier, images of the fictional West began to replace memories of the real West. Historians have noticed that memoirs of the Old West have a habit of recollecting events that only occurred in novels, even using similar language in some cases. Likewise, studies of oral histories in New Mexico have found that several veterans of the frontier claim to have witnessed a number of Billy the Kid's exploits that only ever appeared in fictional accounts. While some may have been deliberately spicing up their tales, it's likely that many were honestly confusing fact and fiction.[58]

The Wild West isn't unique in this regard. Jane Austen's nov-els have done more to shape our view of Regency England than any non-fiction account, for instance. The same could be said for Charles Dickens and Victorian London. And just about every-thing we think we know about pirates – from treasure maps to peg legs to pirate codes – comes from Robert Louis Stevenson's 1883 children's story *Treasure Island*. But the Wild West *is* unique in that it's become an integral part of a country's self-conception. The enormous popularity of the western, whether in books, on screen or in video games, has led many Americans to identify the genre's tropes as fundamental aspects of their country and national character.

And perhaps the most enduring of these tropes is the heroic gunman: Cody's valiant cowboys; Owen Wister's eponymous Virginian; Zane Grey's seemingly inexhaustible stock of rogues and riders. By the late 19th century the independence and self-reliance of the archetypal westerner were being praised as important American traits. Cody – Buffalo Bill himself – praised the 'rough and uncouth' cowboy for being as 'free as the air'.[59] Theodore Roosevelt, no longer ranching in the West but writing about it instead, celebrated the 'vigorous manliness' of its inhabitants as representing 'all that is best in our national life'.[60] These notions also received scholarly acceptance. Writing in the 1890s, the historian Frederick Jackson Turner famously argued that the characteristics of the American man – 'that coarseness and strength ... that practical inventive turn of mind ... that masterful grasp of material things' – were a product of taming the country's western wilderness.[61]

This concept of 'frontier masculinity', with its connotations of freedom, power and granite-jawed heroism, resonated strongly with many white American men. Advertisers were quick to appreciate its power, and during the 20th century the cowboy could be found promoting everything from laundry detergent to barbecue sauce. When, in the 1950s, the tobacco company Philip Morris wanted men to buy its Marlboro filtered cigarettes – which had originally been introduced as 'a cigarette for women' – they created the rugged cowboy known as the 'Marlboro Man' to serve as the product's new mascot. It worked: the market for Marlboros increased so quickly that Philip Morris were initially unable to produce enough cigarettes to keep up with demand, and in just two years Marlboro had become the company's best-selling cigarette brand.

Before he was peddling cigarettes or condiments, however, the cowboy was selling America guns. Firearms manufacturers had been appealing to the violent heroism and rugged individualism of the Wild West in their advertisements since the 1850s. After all, in the popular depictions of the frontier it was with a gun that a man protected his freedoms and maintained his independence, whether he was hunting animals or shooting enemies. As one revolver advertisement from the early 20th century bluntly put it: 'Between Man and Man, at the last, there is but one law – the Law of Self-Defence.'[62]

It was in this heady mix of history, masculinity, personal freedom and national pride that the gun became loaded with the symbolic power it holds for many Americans today. Since the late 20th century the prime motivation for owning firearms in the United States has switched from hunting and recreation to self-protection: both personal, against attackers and intruders, and political, against the perceived encroachments of big government and the nanny state. For a growing number of American gun owners, firearms have become conflated with the very concepts of freedom and individuality; limit gun ownership, they argue, and all other freedoms will soon follow suit.[63]

At the forefront of this shifting mentality has been – and continues to be – the National Rifle Association. Perhaps surprisingly, given its present-day political might, the NRA was founded in 1871 specifically to 'promote and encourage rifle shooting on a scientific basis'. Its founders were concerned about marksmanship and responsible gun ownership and little else. As the legal scholar

Adam Winkler recounts in his 2011 book *Gunfight*, for the next century the NRA generally enjoyed warm relations with the US government and supported restrictions on gun ownership. In the 1920s and 30s, for instance, it supported a raft of new laws requiring gun owners to have a licence to carry concealed weapons, even helping to draft the bills and lobbying state governments to adopt them. It wasn't until the 1960s and 70s that the NRA began to transform itself into the fiercely pro-gun organisation it is today. The turning point came at its 1977 convention, when a change in the NRA's leadership steered the organisation towards gun rights activism and the promotion of a politically conservative gun culture. 'We can win it on a simple concept', explained Harlon Carter, one of the architects of the NRA's change in tactics. 'No compromise. No gun legislation.'[64]

Since 1977 the NRA's forceful campaigning has produced tangible results, most notably in the widespread relaxation of laws concerning the carrying of concealed weapons. Between 1980 and 2013 a total of 38 states passed so-called 'shall issue' laws compelling state and local authorities to issue concealed weapon permits to anyone who meets the statutory criteria, regardless of whether the authority thinks the applicant has a good cause for one. In some states, such as Georgia, Iowa and South Dakota, more than one in ten adults now have such permits, and in Alabama just over one-quarter of the adult population do. Other states have gone further still: since 2010 fifteen states have introduced 'constitutional carry' laws, meaning eligible citizens don't even need to apply for a permit to carry concealed weapons.

Popular conceptions of the American West are at the heart of this transformation. 'What is ... gun culture?' asked NRA Chief Executive Wayne LaPierre in 2003. 'To millions of Americans, especially those who own firearms, the term refers to America's traditional bedrock values of self-reliance, self-defence, and self-determination.' The former marine Jeff Cooper, who joined the NRA Board of Directors in 1985, had this to say about the Colt Frontier Six-Shooter: 'Just to hold one in your hand produces a feeling of kinship with our western heritage – an appreciation of things like courage and honour and chivalry and the sanctity of a man's word.'[65] It's a message the NRA's 5 million members have taken to heart. 'The NRA and its supporters', writes the sociologist Scott Melzer, 'believe that we should rely on ourselves, not the government, for basic needs like food, shelter, love, and protection. This, they argue, is how the country was founded and what made it great.'[66]

~

Except it wasn't – at least, not in the way modern-day gun advocates describe it. As we've seen, popular conceptions of the American West owe just as much, if not more, to fictional rather than historical accounts. As a result, the reality of life on the frontier can come as a surprise to us today. 'Long-cherished notions about violence, lawlessness and justice in the Old West,' writes the historian Roger McGrath, 'are nothing more than myth.'[67]

For one thing, those heading west had little to fear from attacks by Native Americans. The average American was more likely to see a wagon raid in *Buffalo Bill's Wild West* than they were in real life. Indigenous people typically found it more profitable to operate bridge tolls and ferry crossings and sell supplies to emigrants than to murder them. When the historian John Unruh studied the history of the overland trails from 1840 to 1860, when an estimated 300,000 eastern emigrants crossed the continent, he found that Native Americans killed a grand total of 362 pioneers, and that pioneers killed 426 natives. When you factor in the tens of thousands of other fatalities suffered on those voyages, native aggression accounts for somewhere between 1 and 4 per cent of emigrant deaths. Pioneers were more likely to accidently kill themselves with their own guns.[68]

Nor was the frontier town a den of criminality. Customers at the bank, for instance, needn't worry about an impending robbery: between 1859 and 1900 there were probably no more than a dozen bank heists throughout the entire American West. Bank managers were so unaccustomed to robberies that it was common practice to leave the vault open throughout the day.[69] McGrath's detailed study of two frontier towns' records showed that mugging, theft and burglary were also rare during this time period, especially when compared to towns and cities in the eastern United States. As a testament to this, many westerners didn't lock their doors – in fact, very few shops and houses even had locks on their doors until the 20th century. As one miner recalled: 'We could sleep in our cabins with our bag of gold dust under our pillows minus locks, bolts or bars, and feel a sense of absolute security.'[70]

Even gun crime, the signature felony of the Wild West, was far less prevalent than is commonly assumed. 'This business of gunfights,' sighed the cowboy Edward Abbott in his 1939 memoir; 'so much has been made about it in fiction, and it is nearly all exaggeration.'[71] After 50 years in the West, the miner William Goulder gave a similar assessment of the frontier, admitting that he had 'never witnessed a killing or even the body of a murder victim'.[72] Most men did own a gun, and fatal shootings did occur, just as they did in the east. But even in the most homicidal towns – places like Tombstone, Deadwood and Dodge City – relatively few met their end staring down the barrel of a gun. A grand total of five murders occurred in Tombstone's most violent year; in Deadwood the record was just four. More people were killed in the first fifteen minutes of *The Wild Bunch* than in the first fifteen years of Dodge City.[73]

Very few, if any, of these gunfights were the classic quick-draw duel of the silver screen.[74] For one thing, most gun deaths took place not at high noon but late at night, usually in a saloon or gambling den, and usually when the combatants were more than a little drunk. For another, the handguns of the period were so inaccurate – being rarely able to hit a target more than 80 feet away – that speed gave you little advantage over your opponent.[75] There are records of shoot-outs in which both sides emptied their six-shooters at close range without managing to hit a single person.[76] Perhaps most significant, however, is the fact that westerners were simply nowhere near as trigger-happy as they appear in fiction.[77] 'Most men that carry guns like to get them out on slight provocation, but they loath to use them,' explained one inhabitant of the frontier. 'More than once, I have seen a whole crowd of men with their guns and not a shot fired.'[78]

This is by no means to say that the Old West was a haven of peace and tranquillity. It was, after all, populated mostly by young, unattached men, who are statistically the most violent people on Earth. Coupled with the habitual binge drinking and the prickly sense of honour common in 19th-century America, it's little wonder that brawls were 'nightly occurrences' in frontier towns. As well as fistfights and gunfights, there are accounts of people being attacked with knives, hatchets, chairs and even brooms. Outside the town limits, stagecoaches were such routine victims of highway robbery that an armed guard would often 'ride shotgun' with the driver.[79]

Even when this violence and criminality is taken into account, however, the American West was, for most people most of the time, a far more orderly, safe and sane place than the fiction it inspired. A

British visitor in the late 19th century reported, with palpable disappointment, nothing but 'the most perfect order and decorum'.[80]
Combined with the isolating vastness of the West, many found
the frontier a painfully boring and lonely place to live. 'O solitude,
solitude, how I love it,' wrote one young woman marooned on the
prairie. 'If only I had about a dozen of my acquaintances to enjoy it
with me.'[81] It was a sentiment widely shared. When not riding the
trails or irritating the citizens of Abilene, cowboys often had little
to do, especially in winter, and would while away the hours playing cards, strumming guitars or simply shooting at flies. Troops
stationed in the Black Hills of Dakota Territory in the build-up
to the Battle of Little Bighorn resorted to ant-fighting – pitching
red against black – in a desperate measure to alleviate the 'dreary
monotony'. Were it not for the occasional letters they received,
admitted one soldier, life on the plains would be 'a nullity, a void,
a hated weary burden of nothingness'.[82]

How could these people have found a place as lawless as the
West to be as uneventful as it was? The answer is that the West
was by no means lawless. Legal institutions were quickly established: a mining or cattle town out west, even if only a few months
old, could expect to have a town constable or marshal, policemen,
a county sheriff and his deputies, judges, lawyers, district attor-
neys and a county coroner all overseeing justice. There are several
reports of murderers, having settled their score, calmly laying
down their weapons and surrendering to law enforcement. When
three men managed to break out of Aurora town jail in 1864, a
fourth prisoner followed their escape route, treated himself to a
drink at the local saloon before alerting the sheriff to the three
fugitives. In one, albeit unusual, incident, the prisoners at the
Bodie town jail were so touched by the Thanksgiving meal put on
for them by the town constable they wrote to the *Bodie Standard*

to 'express our heartfelt and sincere thanks and gratitude ... for the courteous manner and bountiful feast of which we partook for Thanksgiving Dinner'.[83]

Perhaps the most surprising revelation about law and order in the Wild West is the widespread existence of gun laws. Restrictions on carrying concealed weapons in the United States had first appeared in 1813 in the now staunchly pro-gun states of Kentucky and Louisiana (both have since relaxed their restrictions). Similar laws quickly spread through the antebellum South in an effort to stamp out pistol duelling, which was far more popular in southern states than it would ever be in the West. Realising that young men, alcohol and firearms made for a combustible combination, western law enforcement quickly adopted many of the South's gun restrictions, particularly those concerning concealed weapons. In 1890 the territory of Oklahoma passed such a sweeping anti-weapons law that it prohibited carrying concealed sling-shots, sword-canes and spears. Most frontier towns went even further, enforcing outright bans on anyone carrying any weapons, concealed or otherwise. Visitors were required to leave their weapons at home or hand them in to the sheriff on arrival, who would give them a metal token as a receipt. Just like a cloakroom, visitors could then exchange their token for their weapons on the way out of town. Consequently, as Adam Winkler writes, 'frontier towns like Tombstone had some of the most restrictive gun control laws in America.'[84]

Sheriffs and marshals were serious when it came to enforcing these laws. Illegally carrying a firearm was the second most common cause for arrest after drunk and disorderly conduct. The famous O.K. Corral shoot-out in 1881, where a gunfight between the Clanton gang and the marshal's forces left three people dead, was instigated when the marshal tried to disarm members of the gang who were refusing to comply with Tombstone's strict gun laws. Law enforcement were encouraged in their actions by business owners and civic leaders, who were understandably worried that a violent reputation would be bad for business. In stark contrast to the self-defence arguments commonplace today, local newspapers and business leaders derided gun ownership as 'a senseless custom', 'a pernicious and useless habit', and a 'terribly useless' form of protection.[85] 'An honest man attending to his own business doesn't require the constant companionship of a six-shooter to make him feel easy and safe,' ran an 1878 editorial in the *Ford County Globe*; 'there is something rotten with a man's conscience if he must walk the streets with a weapon.'[86] Private businesses also adopted strict gun laws for their employees. Cattle barons frequently discouraged workers from carrying weapons, with one Texas cattle-raising association banning their cowboys from carrying six-shooters. 'Cattlemen should unite in aiding the enforcement of the law against carrying of deadly weapons,' insisted the *Texas Live Stock Journal* in 1884.[87]

It presents a striking contrast to the gun-toting tales promoted by the entertainment industry. But then the frontier has always had an escapist quality to it. Perhaps unsurprisingly, works that did strive for historical accuracy, such as Andy Adams' 1903 novel *The Log of a Cowboy* or Charles Goodnight's 1916 film *Old Texas* – which, tellingly, didn't feature a single gunfight – failed to achieve the commercial success of the much more violent shoot-'em-ups. This was particularly galling for Goodnight, who had spent much of his life herding cattle in the Old West. 'Despite all that has been said about him,' he lamented, 'the old-time cowboy is the most misunderstood man on Earth.'[88]

The reality of life in the Wild West, then, was far more complex than the simplistic images and themes promoted by the entertainment industry and modern-day gun lobbyists. This is hardly surprising: places as big and diverse and changeable as the American West can rarely be distilled into a single, simple message. In some respects the history of the frontier does support the pro-gun rhetoric of the NRA. Gun ownership was high and yet the available evidence indicates that certain crimes, such as theft and burglary, were infrequent, suggesting that the quantity of firearms may have deterred some criminals. Moreover, the numerous accounts of crowds of armed men *not* shooting each other serve as a reminder that not every gun owner has an itchy trigger finger.

However, in many other respects the West ought to make us question the NRA's claim that 'guns made America great'.[89] For one thing, certain crimes, such as highway robbery, were not only commonplace but would hardly have been possible if the perpetrators hadn't been equipped with firearms. For another, the role of armed citizens in policing in the West was limited: the US government – whether represented by sheriffs, courts or the 15,000 soldiers stationed west of the Mississippi – was a familiar presence on the frontier. Most significantly, gun laws were widespread and stringent. Today the NRA might decry firearm restrictions as 'unconstitutional, un-American and impractical', but they have been a presence in the United States for over two centuries.[90]

The opinions of the frontiersmen themselves are revealing in this regard. While a few voices in the West did argue that 'everyone should go armed' as a defence against crime, as an 1880 edition of Bodie's *Daily Free Press* suggested, many others rejected such appeals as dangerous and unnecessary. And in contrast to the deadlock that grips contemporary firearm debates in the USA, civic leaders, business owners and ordinary citizens acted quickly and decisively when threatened by gun crime. Concerned by the high levels of violence in Dodge City's early years, for example, the town's citizens swiftly formed a municipal government, passing as their first law a ban on concealed weapons. Such prohibitions were strictly upheld by law enforcement throughout the American West, who spent far more time confiscating guns than they ever did firing them.[91]

What's particularly interesting, in light of contemporary debates on gun control, is that few in the Old West considered the Second Amendment an insurmountable barrier to gun laws. A handful of legal challenges against US gun restrictions had been made in the early 19th century, but the courts usually concluded that the constitutional right to bear arms was not 'the right ... to bear them upon all occasions and in all places,' as one Alabama court explained in 1840.[92] In this, lawmakers were following a precedent set by the very framers of the constitution, who saw nothing unconstitutional about firearm proscriptions. The same Founding Fathers who wrote the Second Amendment also advocated gun restrictions so widespread – denying gun ownership on the basis of race, religion and even political beliefs – that they prohibited the majority of Americans from even buying a firearm.[93]

Ultimately, the iconic status of the self-reliant, armed frontiersman, ready to protect himself and his property with force, owes just as much to his fictional representations as to his historical reality. After all, the United States isn't the only country to have had a frontier or a history of armed men. Its northern neighbour Canada shares many of the same landscapes that define the American West, from the Rockies to the prairies to the Pacific coast, as well as a similar hunting heritage, and yet Canadians are six times less likely to die from a bullet wound than Americans.

Australia, too, has its frontier in the form of the outback, and yet the Australian government was quick to introduce strict gun laws and a buy-back scheme following the 1996 Port Arthur massacre, when a lone gunman killed 35 people and wounded 23.

In neither of these countries have firearms taken on the connotations of identity and independence that they have in the USA, where fictional accounts of the frontier continue to exercise a profound influence on the gun debate. 'Westerns are the nation's Greek chorus,' writes the historian Elliott West, 'and they won't shut up.'[94] The image of frontier freedom and justice continues to be invoked by pro-gun advocates to justify their unbending opposition to tighter gun laws in the United States, even when faced with the mounting toll from gun deaths and mass shootings. The frontier historian Robert Dykstra suggests that the mythological baggage of the frontier is having a 'pernicious' effect on present-day efforts to prevent gun crime. 'The invented tradition of an ultra-violent West,' he contends, 'spuriously legitimates America's lethal infatuation with handguns and assault rifles,' and so 'damages the nation's search for a rational gun-control policy.'[95]

The irony is that many old frontier towns have much more gun-friendly laws today than they did in the 19th century. A visitor to Dodge City in the 1880s would have been greeted with a large sign stating that 'the carrying of firearms is strictly prohibited'. No such sign exists today, even in the historical re-enactments in and around Dodge City. Acts that would have once put you in jail in Tombstone, such as carrying a gun without a licence or permit, are now perfectly legal. The hallowed frontiersman, despite all the adulation heaped upon him by generations of gun-owners, would likely be shocked by the laxity of gun laws in their towns today, and by the symbolic power that firearms hold for millions throughout the United States.

The ever-present past

The past, goes a Russian proverb, is much more unpredictable than the future. A Russian may have good reason for saying this: in the past century alone their country's official history has veered in so many directions that it can be hard to keep up. When the Soviet Union first declared itself to the world in 1922 its historians were so internationalist in outlook that the very phrase 'Russian history' was discouraged as a bourgeois concept. By the mid-1930s, however, with Stalin promoting Russian nationalism, these old Marxist views were denounced as 'contempt for the Motherland', and those caught espousing them faced a very real risk of being arrested and shot. Things changed again with the breakdown of communism in the 1980s, when Stalin himself became the subject of widespread denunciations. Now, under the tightening grip of president Vladimir Putin, Russia's 'glorious national history' seems once again to be lurching back towards the strident nationalism of the 1930s.[1]

There's always a temptation to regard history as unalterable. The fact that we can't change the past fools us into thinking that it's somehow immune from the confusion and conflict of the present. But as Russians have learned through bitter experience, history is, if anything, especially vulnerable to new ideas and ideologies, so much so that any representation of the past often says more about the time it was written than the time being written about. As the historian Frederick Jackson Turner diagnosed back in 1891:

'Each age writes the history of the past anew with reference to the conditions uppermost in its own time.'[2]

This is something we've seen at work throughout this book. It was the 19th-century belief in the superiority of light skin that convinced European art historians of the whiteness of classical statues and led archaeologists to frame the history of civilisation as a steady progression from dark-skinned savagery to light-skinned enlightenment. Eurocentric biases like these have also come to define our understanding of the Middle Ages as a time of ignorance and superstition, with early Renaissance scholars like Petrarch failing to consider the notion that enlightened civilisations might have existed beyond Europe. And don't forget that the barbarians, the people traditionally blamed for causing the Dark Ages in the first place, were the victims of a strident pro-Roman bias in the writings of late antiquity. The classical world also witnessed the transformation of Pythagoras from bean-obsessed cult leader to unrivalled mathematical genius as his followers sought to create a pagan rival to the increasingly popular Jesus of Nazareth. An equally unlikely makeover would take place in the newly independent USA, when the need to find a non-English national hero turned Christopher Columbus from despotic crank into noble adventurer. Elsewhere, similar desires for grand, inspiring national histories have bequeathed the world a legacy of dubious history, from non-existent Finnish Vikings to the Styrofoam columns festooning the North Macedonian capital of Skopje. Each age, it seems, has given its own unique twist on our view of the past: the 18th-century fashion for 'natural' families encouraged historians to ignore the long history of working women; the 20th-century growth of the movie industry convinced many that the Wild West was won by violent, independent gunmen; the ongoing proliferation of pseudoscience, meanwhile, is duping people into rejecting the very foundations of history and archaeology.

This book itself is by no means immune to contemporary agendas. Many of the perspectives explored here first arose outside the study of the past, as broader critiques of society, before going on to influence history and archaeology. It was largely thanks to the advent of feminism, for example, that the near-total absence of women from the historical record began to look suspicious to the male-dominated world of academia. And it was due to 20th-century independence movements in European colonies like India and Algeria, and the subsequent dismantling of Western empires, that Western historians and archaeologists began to seriously question the validity of Eurocentric world histories.

This flexibility of history – its ability to be written and rewritten – is a double-edged sword. On the one hand, it allows us to revise earlier interpretations in the light of new evidence. On the other hand, it leaves the past open to deliberate manipulation by those looking to justify and support contemporary agendas. Few of George Orwell's observations are truer than his famous summary of the politics of the past that appears in *Nineteen Eighty-Four*: 'Who controls the past controls the future: who controls the present controls the past.' The shifting sands of official Russian history offer a prime example of this dictum in action, but by no means the only one. In Maoist China, for instance, state archaeologists were ordered to 'make the past serve the present', marshalling events in such a way as to make communism look like the inevitable – and thus incontestable – end-point of Chinese history. When Nazi archaeologists discovered a 3rd-century urn near the Polish city of Łódź they were delighted to find a swastika-like symbol among its decorations – surely this was proof that Poland rightly belonged to Hitler's *Lebensraum*? The urn was considered such a valuable piece of propaganda that it was even incorporated into Łódź's coat of arms while the city was under Nazi occupation.[3]

You don't need to look as far as Mao's China or Hitler's Germany, however, to find the past being used to serve contemporary ideologies. From the Hindu nationalists renaming Indian cities to erase colonial and Muslim history to the Identity Evropa leaflets and their depictions of white classical sculpture that are still littering US universities, history remains a worldwide battleground for competing beliefs. On the right, many see the past as a golden age from which modern society has strayed – just think of the enthusiasm generated by nostalgic slogans like Donald Trump's 'Make America Great Again' and Brexit's 'Take Back Control'. On the left, history has all too often been reduced to an exercise in hand-wringing remorse, and it's become common practice to demand apologies from modern-day politicians for historic crimes.

This desire of people to have history on their side – even if they have to mangle it beyond recognition – is a testament to its importance. History matters. It tells us who we are, where we've come from and where we might be heading. Whether we regard it as a venerable tradition to protect and pass on or an outdated embarrassment to reject and rebel against, we use it to make sense of the world we find ourselves in: to justify it; to praise or condemn it; to measure its successes and failures.

And this is the other half of our relationship with history: not only do contemporary issues shape our perception of the past, but those contemporary issues are themselves shaped by our perception of the past. Whether it's the celebration of questionable national histories, the continued endorsement of housebound motherhood as the 'innate' desire and role of all women, or the lingering shadow of the Law of Progress, history refuses to take its hand off the steering wheel of modern society. History, whether we like it or not, has an annoying habit of being relevant.

~

Looking at the past like this can be a little disheartening. If history is so susceptible to our own prejudices, so readily bent from one shape to another, can it ever really be trusted? Is it forever destined to be buffeted from one ideology to another? Is it anything more than a mirror to our own biases, showing us only what we want to see?

The answer, thankfully, is no. As we saw in the exploration of pseudoarchaeology, historians and archaeologists are able to minimise interference from personal bias when investigating the past by following the scientific principles of gathering evidence, forming hypotheses and then testing those hypotheses. When they find a piece of evidence, whether that's an undiscovered shard of pottery in the ground or an overlooked passage in a book, they study it to see what it can tell us about the past. Perhaps the pottery came from a decorated Maya cacao vessel, indicating that its owner was a member of the wealthy Maya elite. Maybe the passage is written in a script known as Willis shorthand, suggesting it was penned somewhere in 17th-century England. Before any conclusions can be drawn, however, these inferences must be tested against what's already known from other evidence. If the pottery was unearthed in China, for instance, or if the book was printed in the 20th century, then the investigator must reconsider their find.

On paper this all looks straightforward enough. In reality, however, it's hard work, requiring constant vigilance against presumption and prejudice and a willingness to change our minds in light of new evidence. Nevertheless, it can open up the past to us in a way no ideology ever could, for it can show us the world as it really was and not simply as how we would like it to have been. It can tell us that prehistoric hunter-gatherers were capable of building complex stone temples, for example, or that many medieval women were working in highly demanding jobs, in defiance of ideologies which have denied the possibility of such things. Conversely, whenever we abandon an evidence-based approach to history our understanding of the past is liable to become skewed. All the mistakes explored in this book were made in the absence of evidence in one form or another. Sometimes, as with the initial academic endorsement of crystal skulls as genuine artefacts, it was because not enough evidence had yet been uncovered; other times, as with the refusal to accept colourful classical statues, it owed more to a wilful rejection of available evidence that conflicted with preconceived ideas.

The process is by no means perfect. Mistakes will still be made. Future generations will still find many things to correct. But the great strength of history and archaeology, like all intellectual endeavours, is that they allow us to recognise our mistakes, to learn from them, and to avoid making them all over again. Just occasionally we even get it right.

Endnotes

Introduction

1. Anonymous (2017). 'Gods in Color: Painted sculptures of antiquity'. *Liebieghaus Skulpturen Sammlung* (online): http://buntegoetter. liebieghaus.de/en (accessed 27/08/18)

2. Kiilerich, B. (2016). 'Towards a "polychrome history" of Greek and Roman sculpture'. *Journal of Art Historiography* 15: 1–18
   Kopczynski, N., de Viguerie, L., Neri, E., Nasr, N., Walter, P., Bejaoui, F. and Baratte, F. (2017). 'Polychromy in Africa Proconsularis: Investigating Roman statues using X-ray fluorescence spectroscopy'. *Antiquity* 91(355): 139–54

3. Boone, E. (ed.) (1985). *Painted Architecture and Polychromatic Monumental Sculpture in Mesoamerica*. Washington, DC: Dumbarton Oaks, Harvard University. p. 1
   Brazil, R. (2017). 'Colouring in the past'. *Chemistry World* (online): https://www.chemistryworld.com/features/raiders-of-the-lost-pigments/3007237.article (accessed 30/11/18)

4. Rudolph, C. (1988). 'Bernard of Clairvaux's Apologia as a description of Cluny, and the controversy over monastic art'. *Gesta* 27(1/2): 125–32

5. Skelton, H. (2004). 'A history of pigment use in western art: Part 1'. *Paint & Coatings Industry* 20(1): 32

6. Talbot, M. (2018). 'The Myth of Whiteness in Classical Sculpture'. *The New Yorker* (online): https://www.newyorker.com/magazine/2018/10/29/the-myth-of-whiteness-in-classical-sculpture (accessed 01/12/18)
   Spivey, N. (2006). 'Art and archaeology'. *Greece and Rome* 52(2): 272–5. p. 272

7. Evans, S. (2015). 'Save Chartres Cathedral'. *Change.org* (online): https://www.change.org/p/save-chartres-cathedral (accessed 29/11/18)

8. Anonymous (2017)
   Talbot (2018)

9. Ibid.

10. Somervill, B. (2005). *Michelangelo: Sculptor and Painter*. Minneapolis: Compass Point Books. p. 80

11. Neuenfeld, N. (2015). 'The Colouring of Ancient Sculptures: The Driving Force of Expression?' pp. 67–75 in: Klose, C., Bossert, L., and Leveritt, W. (eds.): *Fresh Perspectives on Graeco-Roman Visual Culture. Proceedings of an International Conference at Humboldt-Universität, Berlin, 2nd–3rd September 2013*.

    Bond, S. (2017). 'Why We Need to Start Seeing the Classical World in Color'. *Hyperallergic* (online): https://hyperallergic.com/383776/why-we-need-to-start-seeing-the-classical-world-in-color/ (accessed 27/08/18)

12. Oddy, A. (2002). 'The conservation of marble sculptures in the British Museum before 1975'. *Studies in Conservation* 47(3): 145–54

13. Kennedy, M. (1999). 'Mutual attacks mar Elgin Marbles debate'. *The Guardian* (online): https://www.theguardian.com/uk/1999/dec/01/maevkennedy (accessed 01/12/18)

14. Anonymous (2018). 'Identity Evropa'. *Southern Poverty Law Center* (online): https://www.splcenter.org/fighting-hate/extremist-files/group/identity-evropa (accessed 17/08/18)

    Jaschik, S. (2017). '"Unprecedented" White Supremacist Activity'. *Inside Higher Ed* (online): https://www.insidehighered.com/news/2017/03/07/report-documents-white-supremacist-activity-campuses (accessed 27/08/18)

15. Morse, H. (2018). 'Classics and the Alt-Right: Historicizing Visual Rhetorics of White Supremacy'. *University of Michigan LearnSpeakAct* (online): https://sites.lsa.umich.edu/learn-speak-act/2018/02/15/classics-and-the-alt-right/ (accessed 27/08/18)

16. Anonymous (2018)

17. Harloe, K. (2007). 'Allusion and ekphrasis in Winckelmann's Paris description of the Apollo Belvedere'. *The Cambridge Classical Journal*, 53, 229–52. pp. 230–31

18. Morse (2018)

19. Chapoutot, J. and Nybakken, R. (trans.) (2016). *Greeks, Romans, Germans: How the Nazis Usurpers Europe's Classical Past*. Oakland: University of California Press. p. 175–6

20. Gori, G. (1999). 'Model of masculinity: Mussolini, the 'new Italian' of the Fascist era'. *The International Journal of the History of Sport* 16(4): 27–61. pp. 49

21. Morse (2018)

    Panzanelli, R. (ed.) (2008). *The Color of Life: Polychromy in Sculpture from Antiquity to the Present*. Los Angeles: The J. Paul Getty Museum and the Getty Research Institute.

Bradley, M. (2009). 'The importance of colour on ancient marble sculpture'. *Art History* 32: 427–57

22. Platnauer, M. (1921). 'Greek colour-perception'. *The Classical Quarterly*, 15(3–4), 153–62

    Whitmarsh, T. (2018). 'Black Achilles'. *Aeon* (online): https://aeon. co/essays/when-homer-envisioned-achilles-did-he-see-a-black-man (accessed 06/12/18)

Chapter 1

1. Trigger, B. (2006). *A History of Archaeological Thought, Second Edition.* Cambridge: Cambridge University Press. p. 85

2. Goodrum, M. (2008). 'Questioning thunderstones and arrowheads: The problem of recognizing and interpreting stone artifacts in the seventeenth century'. *Early Science and Medicine* 13(5): 482–508. pp. 482, 495

    Hodgen, M. (1964). *Early Anthropology in the Sixteenth and Seventeenth Centuries.* Philadelphia: University of Pennsylvania Press. p. 466

    Woolf, D. (2011). *A Global History of History.* Cambridge: Cambridge University Press. pp. 301–2

3. Kehoe, A. (1998). *The Land of Prehistory: A Critical History of American Archaeology.* New York: Routledge. p. xiii

4. Hobbes, T. (1985). *Leviathan.* London: Penguin Books. p. 186

5. Kehoe (1998), p. 2

6. Hunter, M. (1971). 'The Royal Society and the origins of British archaeology: I'. *Antiquity* 45(178): 113–21. p. 114

    Trigger (2006), pp. 90, 119, 124, 127

7. Numbers, R. (2000). '"The most important biblical discovery of our time": William Henry Green and the demise of Ussher's chronology'. *Church History* 69(2): 257–76. p. 257

8. Goodrum (2008), p. 456

    Trigger (2006), pp. 95, 119, 137

    Dean, D. (1981). 'The age of the earth controversy: Beginnings to Hutton'. *Annals of Science* 38(4): 435–56. p. 454

9. Fagan, B. (2018). *A Little History of Archaeology.* New Haven: Yale University Press. p. 53

    Woolf (2011), pp. 352–3, 380–82

    Lubbock, J. (1913). *Prehistoric Times.* London: Williams and Norgate. pp. 491–2

10. Cavanaugh, J. (2001). 'The Causes of the Morant Bay Rebellion'. *Emancipation: The Caribbean Experience* (online): https://scholar.library. miami.edu/emancipation/jamaica4.htm (accessed 13/08/19)

Szreter, S. (2004). 'Industrialization and health'. *British Medical Bulletin* 69(1): 75–86. p. 80

11. Fagan (2018), p. 53
    Marett, R. (1919). 'Progress in Prehistoric Times'. pp. 27–47, in: Marvin, F. (ed.). *Progress and History*. Oxford: Oxford University Press. p. 45

12. Kehoe (1998), p. 23

13. Riede, F. (2006). 'The Scandinavian connection: The roots of Darwinian archaeology in 19th-century Scandinavian archaeology'. *Bulletin of the History of Archaeology* 16(1): 4–19. p. 7
    Morgan, L. (1877). *Ancient Society: Or Researches in the Lines of Human Progress from Savagery through Barbarism to Civilization*. Chicago: Charles H. Kerr & Company. p. 506

14. Kehoe (1998), p. 33

15. Ibid., p. 12

16. Morgan (1877), p. 3
    Wilson, D. (1862). *Prehistoric Man: Researches into the Origin of Civilisation in the Old and the New World, Volume I*. Cambridge: Macmillan And Co. p. 304

17. Trigger (2006), pp. 101–2
    Fagan (2018), p. 53

18. Russell, B. (1945). *The History of Western Philosophy*. New York: Simon and Schuster, Inc. p. 738

19. Morgan (1877), p. 19
    Trigger (2006), p. 202
    Palmer (2017), p. 321

20. Kehoe (1998), p. 128

21. Trigger, B. (1995). 'Romanticism, Nationalism, and Archaeology'. pp. 263–79, in: Kohl, P. and Fawcett, C. (eds.). *Nationalism, Politics, and the Practice of Archaeology*. Cambridge: Cambridge University Press. p. 268
    Buchan, B. and Heath, M. (2006). 'Savagery and civilization: From Terra Nullius to the "Tide of History"'. *Ethnicities* 6(1): 5–26
    Owen, J. (2006). 'Collecting artefacts, acquiring empire: Exploring the relationship between Enlightenment and Darwinist collecting and late-nineteenth-century British imperialism'. *Journal of the History of Collections* 18(1): 9–25. pp. 21, 24
    Trigger (2006), p. 169

22. Wilson, J. (1843). *The Noctes Ambrosianae of 'Blackwood'*. Philadelphia: Carey and Hart. p. 408

23. Kehoe (1998), p. 52

24. Schmidt, K. (2007). *Göbekli Tepe: A Stone Age Sanctuary in South-Eastern Anatolia*. Munich: C. H. Beck. p. 15

25. Ibid., pp. 17–18, 23

    Curry, A. (2008). 'Gobekli Tepe: The World's First Temple? *Smithsonian* (online): https://www.smithsonianmag.com/history/gobekli-tepe-the-worlds-first-temple-83613665/ (accessed 27/06/19)

    Symes, P. (2010). 'Turkey: Archeological Dig Reshaping Human History'. *Newsweek* (online): https://www.newsweek.com/turkey-archeological-dig-reshaping-human-history-75101 (accessed 27/06/19)

    Schmidt (2007), pp. 17–18, 23

26. Schmidt (2007), p. 15

27. Ibid., p. 17

    Curry (2008)

28. Schmidt (2007), pp. 18, 89–92, 143, 151

29. Watkins, T. (2010). 'New light on Neolithic revolution in south-west Asia'. *Antiquity* 84(325): 621–34. p. 626

    Dietrich, O. and Notroff, J. (2015). 'A Sanctuary, or So Fair a House? In Defense of an Archaeology of Cult at Pre-Pottery Neolithic Göbekli Tepe'. pp. 75–89 in: Laneri, N. (ed.). *Defining the Sacred: Approaches to the Archaeology of Religion in the Near East.* Oxford: Oxbow Books. p. 86

    Watkins, T. (2018). 'From Mobile Foreigners to Complex Societies in Southwest Asia'. pp. 198–229, in: Scarre, C. (ed.) *The Human Past: World Prehistory and the Development of Human Societies.* London: Thames & Hudson. p. 216

    Graeber, D. and Wengrow, D. (2018). 'How to change the course of human history'. *Eurozine* (online): https://www.eurozine.com/change-course-human-history/ (accessed 04/07/19)

30. Watkins (2018), p. 216

    Schmidt (2007), pp. 10, 93, 216

    Symes (2010)

    Gresky, J., Haelm, J., and Clare, L. (2017). 'Modified human crania from Göbekli Tepe provide evidence for a new form of Neolithic skull cult'. *Science Advances* 3(6): e1700564

31. Schmidt (2007), pp. 17, 85, 121

    Watkins (2018), p. 216

32. Schmidt (2007), p. 98

    Symes (2010)

33. Dietrich and Notroff (2015), p. 83

34. Symes (2010)

35. Trigger (2006), p. 155

36. Barkai, R., and Liran, R. (2008). 'Midsummer sunset at Neolithic Jericho'. *Time and Mind* 1(3): 273–83. p. 277

    Schmidt (2007), pp. 29–30, 65–9, 72–3, 76, 78

37. McBrearty, S., and Brooks, A. (2000). 'The revolution that wasn't: A new interpretation of the origin of modern human behavior'. *Journal of Human Evolution* 39(5): 453–563. pp. 513, 515

Hodder, I. and Meskell, L. (2011). 'A "curious and sometimes a trifle macabre artistry": Some aspects of symbolism in neolithic Turkey'. *Current Anthropology* 52(2): 235–63. p. 259

Mayer, D., Gümüş, B. and İslamoğlu, Y. (2010). 'Fossil hunting in the Neolithic: Shells from the Taurus Mountains at Çatalhöyük, Turkey'. *Geoarchaeology* 25(3): 375–92

Watkins, T. (2019). Personal communication

38. Just, P. (1980). 'Time and leisure in the elaboration of culture'. *Journal of Anthropological Research* 36(1): 105–15. p. 108

Laskow, S. (2015). 'Cavemen Inherited Their Clubs From 16th Century European Wildmen'. *Atlas Obscura* (online): https://www.atlasobscura.com/articles/cavemen-inherited-their-clubs-from-16th-century-european-wildmen (accessed 08/08/19)

Isabella, J. (2013). 'The Caveman's Home Was Not a Cave'. *Nautilus* (online): http://nautil.us/issue/8/home/the-cavemans-home-was-not-a-cave (accessed 08/08/19)

39. Morgan (1877), p. 25

40. Starling, A. and Stock, J. (2007). 'Dental indicators of Nubian agriculturists: A difficult transition and gradual recovery'. *American Journal of Physical Anthropology* 134: 520–28. p. 520

Eshed, V., Gopher, A. Pinhasi, R. and Hershkovitz, I. (2010). 'Palaeopathology and the origin of agriculture in the Levant'. *American Journal of Physical Anthropology* 143: 121–33. p. 122, 129

Larsen, C. (2006). 'The agricultural revolution as environmental catastrophe: Implications for health and lifestyle in the Holocene'. *Quaternary International* 150(1): 12–20. pp. 12–14

Weisdorf, J. (2005). 'From foraging to farming: Explaining the Neolithic Revolution'. *Journal of Economic Surveys* 19(4): 561–86. p. 567

Hershkovitz, I. and Gopher, A. (2008). 'Demographic, Biological, and Cultural Aspects of the Neolithic Revolution: A View from the Southern Levant'. pp. 441–79, in: Bocquet-Appel, J. and Bar-Yosef, O. (eds.) *The Neolithic Demographic Transition and Its Consequences*. Berlin: Springer. p. 455

41. Slingenbergh, J., Gilbert, M., Balogh, K. et al. (2004). 'Ecological sources of zoonotic diseases'. *Revue Scientifique et Technique-Office International des Épizooties* 23(2): 467–84. p. 471

Hershkovitz, I., Donoghue, H., Minnikin, D. et al. (2015). 'Tuberculosis origin: The Neolithic scenario'. *Tuberculosis* 95: S122–S126. p. 453

Watkins, T. (2008). 'Supra-regional networks in the Neolithic of Southwest Asia'. *Journal of World Prehistory* 21(2): 139–71. p. 163

Trueba, T. (2014). 'The Origin of Human Infectious Diseases'. pp. 3–11, in: Yamada, A. (ed.). *Confronting Emerging Zoonoses*. Tokyo: Springer. p. 7

Larsen (2006), p. 14

42. Hershkovitz and Gopher (2008), pp. 441, 454–5

    Eshed et al. (2010), pp. 122, 130

43. Childe, V. (1971). *Progress and Archaeology*. Westport: Greenwood Press. p. 112

44. Weisdorf (2005), p. 561

45. Ibid, p. 562–5

    Watkins (2010), p. 632

    Watkins (2018), p. 204

    Starling and Stock (2007), p. 520

46. Wilson (1862), pp. 444–5

    Weisdorf (2005), p. 562

    Schoop, U. (2019). Personal communication

    Williams, S. (1991). *Fantastic Archaeology: The Wild Side of North American Prehistory*. Philadelphia: The University of Pennsylvania Press. p. 315

    Watkins (2018), pp. 214, 224

47. Watkins, T. (2019). Personal communication

    Graeber and Wengrow (2018)

    Trigger (2006), p. 533

    Watkins (2018), p. 224

48. Shea, J. (2019). 'Refuting a Myth About Human Origins'. *American Scientist* (online): https://www.americanscientist.org/article/refuting-a-myth-about-human-origins (accessed 01/08/19)

    Nalawade-Chavan, S., McCullagh, J., and Hedges, R. (2014). 'New hydroxyproline radiocarbon dates from Sungir, Russia, confirm early Mid Upper Palaeolithic burials in Eurasia'. *PloS one* 9(1): e76896

    Watkins (2010), pp. 624–5

49. Kehoe (1998), p. 219

    Trigger (2006), p. 533

    Harris, M. (2001). *The Rise of Anthropological Theory: A History of Theories of Culture*. Walnut Creek: AltaMira Press. p. 627

    Kradin, N. (2002). 'Nomadism, evolution and world-systems: Pastoral societies in theories of historical development'. *Journal of World-Systems Research* 8(3): 368–88. p. 368

50. Palmer (2017), p. 323

51. Ibid., p. iv

52. Popper, K. (1961). *The Poverty of Historicism*. London: Routledge & Kegan Paul Ltd. pp. 108–9

53. Fisher, H. (1916). *A History of Europe*. London: Edward Arnold. p. v

54. Owen, J. (2006). 'Collecting artefacts, acquiring empire: Exploring the relationship between Enlightenment and Darwinist collecting and late-nineteenth-century British imperialism'. *Journal of the History of Collections* 18(1): 9–25. p. 9

55. McCann, W. (1990). '"Volk und Germanentum": The Presentation of the Past in Nazi Germany'. pp. 74–88, in: Gathercole, P. and Lowenthal, D. (eds.). *The Politics of the Past*. London: Unwin Hyman Ltd. p. 75

56. Krozewski, G. (2008). 'Contextualising violence in colonial Africa – European national development, empire and lineages of conflict'. *Development Dialogue* 50: 53–74. p. 58

57. Berlin, I. (1954). *Historical Inevitability*. Oxford: Oxford University Press. pp. 34, 42

58. Maij, D., van Schie, H., and van Elk, M. (2019). 'The boundary conditions of the hypersensitive agency detection device: An empirical investigation of agency detection in threatening situations'. *Religion, Brain & Behavior* 9(1): 23–51. p. 23

59. Popper, K. (1957). *The Open Society and its Enemies, Volume 2*. London: Routledge & Kegan Paul Ltd. p. 280
    Popper, K. (1952). *The Open Society and its Enemies, Volume 1*. London: Routledge & Kegan Paul Ltd. p. 4

60. Schmidt (2007), p. 43

Chapter 2

1. Rowett, C. (2014). 'The Pythagorean Society and Politics'. pp. 112–30, in: Huffman, C. (ed.). *A History of Pythagoreanism*. Cambridge: Cambridge University Press. p. 114

2. Kahn, C. (2001). *Pythagoras and the Pythagoreans: A brief history*. Indianapolis/Cambridge: Hackett Publishing Company, Inc. pp. 6–7
   Russell, B. (1945). *The History of Western Philosophy*. New York: Simon & Schuster, Inc. p. 30

3. Joost-Gaugier, C. (2006). *Measuring Heaven: Pythagoras and His Influence on Thought and Art in Antiquity and the Middle Ages*. Ithaca: Cornell University Press. p. 27

4. Hopper, V. (2000). *Medieval Number Symbolism: Its Sources, Meaning, and Influence on Thought and Expression*. Mineola: Dover Publications. pp. 33–4
   Joost-Gaugier (2006), p. 17
   Ferguson, K. (2010). *Pythagoras: His Lives and the Legacy of a Rational Universe*. London: Icon Books Ltd. p. 4.

Huffman, C. (2018). 'Pythagoras'. *Stanford Encyclopedia of Philosophy* (online): https://plato.stanford.edu/entries/pythagoras/ (accessed 22/09/19)

5. Kahn, C. (2001). *Pythagoras and the Pythagoreans: A Brief History.* Indianapolis/Cambridge: Hackett Publishing Company, Inc. p. 12

    Cornelli, G. (2013). *In Search of Pythagoreanism: Pythagoreaism as an Historiographical Category.* Berlin/Boston: Walter de Gruyter. pp. 95–6

    Laks, A. (2014). 'Diogenes Laertius' *Life of Pythagoras'.* pp. 360–80, in: Huffman, C. (ed.). *A History of Pythagoreanism.* Cambridge: Cambridge University Press. p. 378

    Zhmud, L. (2012). *Pythagoras and the Early Pythagoreans.* Oxford: Oxford University Press. p. 217

    Ferguson (2010), p. 4.

    Ibid., p. 152

    Joost-Gaugier (2006), p. 13

    Kahn (2001), p. 12

6. Lloyd, G. (2014). 'Pythagoras'. pp. 24–45, in: Huffman, C. (ed.). *A History of Pythagoreanism.* Cambridge: Cambridge University Press. p. 32

    Huffman (2018)

    Croxall, S. (1741). *The Antiquity, Dignity and Advantages of Music.* London: J. Watts. p. 8

7. Kahn (2001), p. 3

    Ferguson (2010), p. 66

    Kim, H. (2001). 'Archaic Coinage as Evidence for the Use of Money'. pp. 7-23, in: Meadows, A. and Shipton, K. (eds.). *Money and Its Uses in the Ancient Greek World.* Oxford: Oxford University Press. pp. 9–10

    Kak, S. (1996). 'The knowledge of the planets in the third millennium BC'. *Quarterly Journal of the Royal Astronomical Society* 37: 709–15. p. 710

    Ratner, B. (2009). 'Pythagoras: Everyone knows his famous theorem, but not who discovered it 1000 years before him'. *Journal of Targeting, Measurement and Analysis for Marketing* 17(3): 229–42. p. 233

8. Kahn (2001), p. 32

    Joost-Gaugier (2006), p. 29

    Hopper (2000), p. 36

    Fowler, D. and Robson, E. (1998). 'Square root approximations in Old Babylonian mathematics: YBC 7289 in context'. *Historia Mathematica* 25(4): 366–78. pp. 366–7

    Lloyd (2014), p. 35

9. Kahn (2001), p. 49

10. Cornelli (2013), p. 64

    Kahn (2001), pp. 8–9

    Zhmud (2012), p. 149

Navon, R. (1986). *The Pythagorean Writings: Hellenistic Texts from the 1st Cent. B.C.–3rd Cent. A.D.* Kew Gardens, New York: Selene Books. p. 81

11. Navon (1986), pp. 61, 63, 70–71
12. Marciano, M. (2014). 'The Pythagorean Way of Life and Pythagorean Ethics'. pp. 131–48, in: Huffman, C. (ed.). *A History of Pythagoreanism.* Cambridge: Cambridge University Press. pp. 138, 140
13. Philip, J. (1966). *Pythagoras and the Pythagoreans.* Toronto: University of Toronto Press. p. 135
    Gray, H. F. (1940). 'Sewerage in ancient and mediaeval times'. *Sewage Works Journal,* pp. 939–46.
14. Kahn (2001), pp. 9, 83
    Navon (1986), p. 170
    Russell (1945), pp. 30, 56–7
15. Kahn (2001), pp. 31–3, 64
    Lloyd, G. (2014). 'Pythagoras'. pp. 24–45, in: Huffman, C. (ed.). *A History of Pythagoreanism.* Cambridge: Cambridge University Press. p. 33
    Dudley, U. (1997). *Numerology: Or, What Pythagoras Wrought.* Washington, DC: The Mathematical Association of America. pp. 33–4
    Huffman (2016)
16. Choike, J. (1980). 'The pentagram and the discovery of an irrational number'. *The Two-Year College Mathematics Journal* 11(5): 312–16. p. 312
    Von Fritz, K. (1945). 'The discovery of incommensurability by Hippasus of Metapontum'. *Annals of Mathematics* 46(2): 242–64. pp. 244–5
    Huffman, C. (2016). 'Archytas'. *Stanford Encyclopedia of Philosophy* (online): https://seop.illc.uva.nl/entries/archytas/ (accessed 25/09/19)
17. Huffman (2016)
    Hopper, V. (2000). *Medieval Number Symbolism: Its Sources, Meaning, and Influence on Thought and Expression.* Mineola: Dover Publications. p. 34
18. Navon (1986), pp. 102–3, 164
    Hopper (2000), p. 34
    Huffman, C. (2016). 'Philolaus'. *Stanford Encyclopedia of Philosophy* (online): https://plato.stanford.edu/entries/philolaus/ (accessed 25/09/19)
19. Cartledge, P. (2002). *The Cambridge Illustrated History of Ancient Greece.* Cambridge: Cambridge University Press. p. 156
    Littman, R. (1974). *The Greek Experiment: Imperialism and Social Conflict 800–400 BC.* London: Thames And Hudson. pp. 31, 33–4
20. Littman (1974), pp. 9–10, 12–13, 15, 18
21. Cartledge, P. (2002)'. 'Power and the State'. pp. 139–165, in: Cartledge, P. (ed.). *The Cambridge Illustrated History of Ancient Greece.* Cambridge: Cambridge University Press. p. 155

Littman (1974), pp. 89–90

Crane, G. (2003). 'Money and the corrosion of power in Thucydides: The Sicilian expedition and its aftermath, and: Thucydides and internal war'. *American Journal of Philology* 124(1): 150–53. p. 151

22. Valdez, D. (2014). *German Philhellenism: The Pathos of the Historical Imagination from Winckelmann to Goethe.* New York: Palgrave Macmillan. p. 2

23. Temple, W. (1814). *The Works of Sir William Temple, Volume III.* London: S. Hamilton. p. 460

24. Van Steen, G. (2001). 'Playing by the censors' rules? Classical drama revived under the Greek junta'. *Journal of the Greek Diaspora* 27(1&2): 133–94. p. 135

25. Lintott, A. (1982). *Violence, Civil Strife and Revolution in the Classical City, 750–330 BC.* London: Croom Helm Ltd. pp. 9, 24

    Katz, M. (2002). 'Women, Children and Men'. pp. 100–138, in: Cartledge, P. (ed.). *The Cambridge Illustrated History of Ancient Greece.* Cambridge: Cambridge University Press. p. 110

    Sternberg, R. (2006). *Tragedy Offstage: Suffering and Sympathy in Ancient Athens.* Austin: University of Texas Press. p. 159

26. Cartledge (2002), pp. 149, 151, 153

27. Glassman, R. (2017). *The Origins of Democracy in Tribes, City-States and Nation-States.* New York: Springer. p. 1056

28. Fisher, N. (2002). 'Rich and Poor'. pp. 76–99, in: Cartledge, P. (ed.). *The Cambridge Illustrated History of Ancient Greece.* Cambridge: Cambridge University Press. pp. 88–9, 92

    Katz (2002), pp. 110, 113

29. Jones, A. (1956). 'Slavery in the ancient world'. *The Economic History Review* 9(2): 185–99. pp. 185–6

    Fisher (2002), pp. 98–9

    Katz (2002), p. 110

30. Ibid., pp. 100, 114, 117

    Cartledge (2002), p. 139

    Littman (1974), pp. 19, 36

31. Littman (1974), pp. 36, 91, 142

    Cartledge (2002), p. 160

    Lintott, A. (1982). *Violence, Civil Strife and Revolution in the Classical City, 750–330 BC.* London: Croom Helm Ltd. p. 250

    Jordović, I. (2008). 'Critias and Democracy'. *Balcanica* XXXIX: 33–46. p. 34

32. Littman, R. (1974). *The Greek Experiment: Imperialism and Social Conflict 800–400 BC.* London: Thames and Hudson. p. 113

33. Crane, G. (2019). 'Thucydides, *The Peloponnesian War*'. *Perseus Digital Library* (online): https://www.perseus.tufts.edu/hopper/ (accessed 02/01/19)

34. Laale, H. (2011). *Ephesus (Ephesos): An Abbreviated History from Androclus to Constantine XI.* Bloomington: WestBow Press. p. 30
    Graham, D. (2019). 'Heraclitus'. *Stanford Encylopedia of Philosophy* (online): https://plato.stanford.edu/entries/heraclitus/ (accessed 03/10/19)

35. Navon, R. (1986). *The Pythagorean Writings: Hellenistic Texts from the 1st Cent. B.C. – 3rd Cent. A.D.* Kew Gardens, New York: Selene Books. pp. 87, 94–5

36. Littman (1974), p. 138
    Dillon, J. (2008). 'Dion and Brutus: Philosopher Kings Adrift in a Hostile World'. pp. 351–64, in: Nikolaides, A. (ed.). *The Unity of Plutarch's Work: 'Moralia' Themes in the 'Lives', Features of the 'Lives' in the 'Moralia'.* Berlin: Walter de Gruyter. p. 351
    Popper, K. (1952). *The Open Society and Its Enemies, Volume I.* London: Routledge & Kegan Paul Ltd. p. 248

37. Ibid., pp. 102–3
    Russell, B. (1945). *The History of Western Philosophy.* New York: Simon and Schuster. pp. 108–10, 112

38. Popper (1952), pp. 136–7
    Dean-Jones, L. (2002). 'Philosophy and Science'. pp. 288–319, in: Cartledge, P. (ed.). *The Cambridge Illustrated History of Ancient Greece.* Cambridge: Cambridge University Press. p. 305

39. Theophrastus, Bennett, C. and Hammond, W. (trans.) (1902). *The Characters of Theophrastus.* London: Longmans, Green, and Co. p. 31

40. Godwin, W. (1834). *Lives of the Necromancers.* London: Frederick J. Mason. pp. 75, 95, 98–9
    Lucian, Fowler, H. and Fowler, F. (trans.) (1905). *The Works of Lucian of Samosata.* Oxford: The Clarendon Press. p. 219
    Kahn (2001), pp. 145–6

41. Lucian and Costa, C. (2005). *Lucian: Selected Dialogues.* Oxford: Oxford University Press. p. 136

42. Laertius, D., Mensch, P. (trans.) and Miller, J. (ed.) (2018). *Lives of the Eminent Philosophers.* Oxford: Oxford University Press. p. xiii
    Philip, J. (1966). *Pythagoras and the Pythagoreans.* Toronto: University of Toronto Press. p. 186

43. Lehman, B. (1928). *Carlyle's Theory of the Hero: Its Sources, Development, History, and Influence on Carlyle's Work.* Durham, North Carolina: Duke University Press. p. 60

44. Carlyle, T. and Gray, H. (ed.) (1904). *On Heroes, Hero-Worship and the Heroic in History.* New York: Longmans, Green & Co. pp. 13–4, 44, 73

Wallace, M. (2012). 'Towards a Wise Despotism: Traces of Thomas Carlyle in the BBC North and South (2004)'. *Between*, 2(4): 1–16. p. 3

Lehman (1928), p. 85

45. Ridley, J. (2019). 'Is There Still Value in "Great Man" History?' *History Today* (online): https://www.historytoday.com/archive/head-head/ there-still-value-%E2%80%98great-man%E2%80%99-history (accessed 13/10/19)

46. Atkinson, J. (2010). *Victorian Biography Reconsidered: A Study of Nineteenth Century 'Hidden' Lives*. Oxford: Oxford University Press. p. 4

47. Goldberg, M. (1989). '"Demigods and philistines": Macaulay and Carlyle – a study in contrasts'. *Studies in Scottish Literature* 24(1): 116–28. p. 118

Goldberg, M. (1993). 'Introduction'. pp. xxi-lxxxi, in: *Thomas Carlyle: On Heroes, Hero Worship, & The Heroic In History*. Berkerley, California: University of California Press. p. lxiii

48. Kahn, A. and Onion, R. (2016). 'Is History Written About Men, by Men?' *Slate* (online): http://www.slate.com/articles/news_and_politics/ history/2016/01/popular_history_why_are_so_many_history_books_ about_men_by_men.html?via=gdpr-consent (accessed 10/10/19)

49. Lovell, C. (2014). 'That's What He Said: Quoting Mark Twain'. *HuffPost* (online): https://www.huffpost.com/entry/thats-what-he-said- quotin_b_4282800 (accessed 05/10/19)

50. Dunning, B. (2013). 'The Cult of Nikola Tesla'. *Skeptoid* (online): https:// skeptoid.com/episodes/4345 (accessed 20/09/19)

51. Chua, D. (2007). 'Rioting with Stravinsky: A particular analysis of The Rite of Spring'. *Music Analysis* 26(1–2): 59–109. p. 60

Levitz, T. (2017). 'Racism at *The Rite*'. unpag., in: Neff, S., Carr, M. and Horlacher, G. (eds.). *The Rite of Spring at 100*. Bloomington: Indiana University Press. Unpaginated.

Shaver-Gleason, L. (2018). 'Did Stravinsky's The Rite of Spring incite a riot at its premiere?' *Not Another Music History Cliché!* (online): https:// notanothermusichistorycliche.blogspot.com/2018/06/did-stravinskys- rite-of-spring-incite.html#more (accessed 20/09/19)

52. Marshall, J. (1804). *The Life of George Washington*. Philadelphia: C. P. Wayne. p. 12

Mayo, B. (2010). *Myths and Men: Patrick Henry, George Washington, Thomas Jefferson*. Athens: University of Georgia Press. p. 33

Chapter 3

1. Burgess, R. (1988). *Hydatius: A Late Roman Chronicler in Post-Roman Spain*. University of Oxford: PhD thesis. Volume I. p. 157, 168

Burgess, R. (1988). *Hydatius: A Late Roman Chronicler in Post-Roman Spain*. University of Oxford: PhD thesis. Volume II. pp. 1, 119

Burgess, R. (1992). 'From *Gallia Romana* to *Gallia Gothica* the View from Spain'. pp. 19-27, in: Drinkwater, J. and Elton, H. (eds.). *Fifth Century Gaul: A Crisis of Identity?* Cambridge: Cambridge University Press. p. 22

2. Díaz, P. and Menendez, L. (2005). 'The Cantabrian Basin in the Fourth and Fifth Centuries: From Imperial Province to Periphery'. In: Bowes, K. and Kulikowski, M. (eds.). *Hispania in Late Antiquity: Current Perspectives*. Leiden: Brill. pp.265–97.

   James, E. (2009). *Europe's Barbarians, AD 200–600*. Harlow: Pearson Education Limited. pp. 60, 191

   Burgess (1998ii), p. 108

3. Fielding, I. (2014). 'Physical ruin and spiritual perfection in fifth-century Gaul: Orientius and his contemporaries on the "landscape of the soul"'. *Journal of Early Christian Studies* 22(4): 569–85. p. 573

   Ammianus, M. and Rolfe, J. (trans.) (1935). *Ammianus Marcellinus, with and English translation by John C. Rolfe*. London: W. Heinemann. p. 531

   Frend, W. (1989). 'Augustine and Orosius: On the end of the ancient world'. *Augustinian Studies* 20(1): 1–38. p. 2

   James (2009), p. 59

   Burgess (1988i), p. 157

4. Gildas and Giles, J. A. (trans.) (1999). 'Liber Querulus De Excidio Britanniae. English'. *Project Gutenberg* (online): http://www.gutenberg.org/cache/epub/1949/pg1949-images.html (accessed 06/02/19)

5. Roberts, M. (1992). 'Barbarians in Gaul: The Response of the Poets'. pp. 97–106, in: Drinkwater, J. and Elton, H. (eds.). *Fifth Century Gaul: A Crisis of Identity?* Cambridge: Cambridge University Press. pp. 31, 99–100

6. Goffart, W. (1981). 'Rome, Constantinople, and the barbarians'. *The American Historical Review* 86(2): 275–306. p. 227

   Gillett, A. (2009). 'The Mirror of Jordanes: Concepts of the Barbarian, Then and Now'. pp. 392–408, in: Rousseau, P. and Raithel, J. (eds.): *A Companion to Late Antiquity*. Chichester: Wiley-Blackwell. p. 396

   Ward-Perkins, B. (2005). *The Fall of Rome and the End of Civilisation*. Oxford: Oxford University Press. pp. 5, 50

7. James (2009), pp. 216–17, 244

8. Ibid., pp. 1–2

9. Ibid., p. 99

10. Curta, F. (2006). *Southeastern Europe in the Middle Ages, 500–1250*. Cambridge: Cambridge University Press. p. 63

11. Ward-Perkins (2005), p. 25

Curta (2006), p. 62

James (2009), pp. 24, 45–6, 96–7, 200

12. Ward-Perkins (2005), p. 27

13. Gibbon, E. (1978). 'Safety from Barbarian Attack'. pp. 175–179, in: Kagan, D. (ed.). *The End of the Roman Empire: Decline or Transformation?* Lexington: D.C. Heath and Company. p. 175

Goffart (1981), p. 275

14. Curta (2006), p. 62

James (2009), p. 94

Pohl, W. (1998). 'Telling the Difference: Signs of Ethnic Identity'. pp. 17–70, in: Pohl, W. and Reimitz, H. (eds.). *Strategies of Distinction: The Construction of Ethnic Communities, 300–800.* Leiden: Brill. p. 57

15. Merrills, A. and Miles, R. (2010). *The Vandals.* Chichester: John Wiley & Sons. p. 5

16. James (2009), p. 143

Vinding, N. and Moyer-Vinding, B. (trans.) (2005). *The Viking Discovery of America, 985–1008: The Greenland Norse and Their Voyages to Newfoundland.* New York: The Edwin Mellen Press.

17. Ward-Perkins (2005), pp. 30, 118

James (2009), pp. 23, 27, 131, 150, 155, 249, 251

Merrills and Miles (2010), p. 222

Theuws, F. and Alkemade, M. (2000). 'A Kind of Mirror for Men: Sword Depositions in Late Antique Northern Gaul'. pp. 401–476, in: Theuws, F. and Nelson, J. (eds.). *Rituals of Power from Late Antiquity to the Early Middle Ages'.* Leiden: Brill. p. 401

18. Ibid., p. 276

19. Brogan, O. (1936). 'Trade between the Roman Empire and the free Germans'. *The Journal of Roman Studies* 26(2): 195–222. pp. 208–18, 219–20

20. Boak, A. (1978). 'Manpower Shortage and the Fall of Rome'. pp. 38–51, in: Kagan, D. (ed.). *The End of the Roman Empire: Decline or Transformation?* Lexington: D.C. Heath and Company. p. 42

James (2009), pp. 44, 161, 164

Ward-Perkins (2005), pp. 38–9

21. Kagan, D. (ed.) (1978). *The End of the Roman Empire: Decline or Transformation?* Lexington: D.C. Heath and Company. p. xii

James (2009), pp. 169–71

22. Ward-Perkins (2005), pp. 42–3

23. Hekster, O. (1974). *Commodus: An Emperor at the Crossroads.* Lieden: Gieben. pp. 147, 154

McKeown, J. (2010). *A Cabinet of Roman Curiosities: Strange Tales and Surprising Facts from the World's Greatest Empire*. Oxford: Oxford University Press. p. 130

White, M. (2014). 'Body Count of the Roman Empire'. *Necrometrics* (online): http://necrometrics.com/romestat.htm (accessed 31/01/19)

24. Hekster, (1974), pp. 137–8
25. Cornell, T. (1993). 'The End of Roman Imperial Expansion'. pp. 139–70, in: Rich, J. and Shipley, G. (eds.). *War and Society in the Roman World*. London: Routledge. pp. 139–40

Woolfe, G. (1993). 'Roman Peace'. pp. 171–94, in: Rich, J. and Shipley, G. (eds.). *War and Society in the Roman World*. London: Routledge. pp. 171–2

26. Ward-Perkins (2005), p. 25
27. Tacitus and Townshend, R. (trans.) (1894). *The Agricola and Germania of Tacitus*. London: Methuen & Co. pp. 32–4
28. Frazer, J. (1890). 'Some popular superstitions of the ancients'. *Folklore* 1(2): 145–71. pp. 162, 167

Ogilvie, R. (2011). *The Romans and their Gods*. London: Vintage Books.

29. Walbank, F. (1978). 'Trends in the Empire of the Second Century A.D'. pp. 23–37, in: Kagan, D. (ed.). *The End of the Roman Empire: Decline or Transformation?* Lexington: D.C. Heath and Company. p. 24
30. Pölönen, J. (2004). 'Plebeians and repression of crime in the Roman Empire: From torture of convicts to torture of suspects'. *RIDA* 51: 217–257. pp. 217–18

James (2009), p. 256

Dowling, M. (2006). *Clemency and Cruelty in the Roman World*. Ann Arbor: The University of Michigan Press. p. 225

31. Charlesworth, M. (1933). 'The tradition about Caligula'. *Cambridge Historical Journal* 4(2): 105–19. pp. 105, 111, 118
32. Tacitus and Ramsey, G. (1909). *The Annals of Tacitus: Books XI–XVI*. London: John Murray. p. 275

Gyles, M. (1947). 'Nero fiddled while Rome burned'. *The Classical Journal* 42(4): 211–17.

33. Mikkelson, D. (1997). 'Was Catherine the Great killed by a Horse?' *Snopes* (online): https://www.snopes.com/fact-check/unbridled-lust/ (accessed 17/02/19)
34. Lugli, A., Kopp Lugli, A., and Horcic, M. (2005). 'Napoleon's autopsy: New perspectives'. *Human Pathology* 36(4): 320–24

Hopper, T. (2016). 'Greatest cartooning coup of all time: The Brit who convinced everyone Napoleon was short'. *National Post* (online): https://nationalpost.com/news/world/greatest-cartooning-coup-of-all-time-the-brit-who-convinced-everyone-napoleon-was-short (accessed 19/02/19)

35. Anonymous (2015). 'Hitler really did have only one testicle, German researcher claims'. *The Guardian* (online): https://www.theguardian.com/world/2015/dec/19/hitler-really-did-have-only-one-testicle-german-researcher-claims (accessed 17/02/19)

36. Pearson, G. (1983). *Hooligan: A History of Respectable Fears*. London: The Macmillan Press Ltd. pp. 74–5

37. Hughes, G. (2006). *An Encyclopedia of Swearing: The Social History of Oaths, Profanity, Foul Language, and Ethnic Slurs in the English language*. Armonk: M.E. Sharpe. p. 18

38. Acheraïou, A. (2008). *Rethinking Postcolonialism: Colonialist Discourse in Modern Literatures and the Legacy of Classical Writers*. London: Springer Nature. p. 63
    Acheraïou, A. (2011). *Questioning Hybridity, Postcolonialism and Globalization*. Basingstoke: Palgrave Macmillan. p. 42

39. Acheraïou (2011), p. 33

40. Pagden, A. (1993). *European Encounters with the New World*. New Haven: Yale University Press. p. 120
    Goodwin, K. (2009). 'Travelogue writers in the age of inquiry: Law, orientalism, and enlightenment ideology in Southeast Asia'. *The Forum: Journal of History* 1(1): 2–17. pp. 2, 11

41. Carlos, J. (1997). 'From savages and barbarians to primitives: Africa, social typologies, and history in eighteenth-century French philosophy'. *History and Theory* 36(2): 190–215. pp. 199–200, 203
    James (2009), p. 5

42. Acheraïou (2008), p. 25
    Francis, M. (1998). 'The "civilizing" of indigenous people in nineteenth-century Canada'. *Journal of World History* 9(1): 51–87. p. 56
    Berger, S. (ed.) (2007). *Writing the Nation: A Global Perspective*. London: Palgrave Macmillan. p. 23–4
    Thioub, I. (2007). 'Writing National and Transnational History in Africa: the Examples of the "Dakar School"'. pp. 197–212, in: Berger, S. (ed.) *Writing the Nation: A Global Perspective*. London: Palgrave Macmillan. p. 200

43. Acheraïou (2008), pp. 57–8

44. Becker, S. (1986). 'The Muslim east in nineteenth-century Russian popular historiography'. *Central Asian Survey* 5(3–4): 25–47. pp. 33, 37, 42–3

45. Acheraïou (2008), p. 71

46. Yusof, S. Hassan, F., Hassan, M. and Osman, M. (2013). 'The framing of international media on Islam and terrorism'. *European Scientific Journal* 9(8): 104–21. p. 109

Brown, M. (2006). 'Comparative analysis of mainstream discourses, media narratives and representations of Islam in Britain and France prior to 9/11'. *Journal of Muslim Minority Affairs* 26(3): 297–312

Kabir, N. (2006) 'Representation of Islam and Muslims in the Australian media, 2001–2005'. *Journal of Muslim Minority Affairs* 26(3): 313–28

Saeed, A. (2007). 'Media, Racism and Islamophobia: The representation of Islam and Muslims in the media'. *Sociology Compass* 1: 1–20. pp. 11, 260

Powell, K. (2011). 'Framing Islam: An analysis of U.S. media coverage of terrorism since 9/11'. *Communication Studies* 62(1): 90–112. p. 102

47. Ferguson, N. (2015). 'Paris and the Fall of Rome'. *The Boston Globe* (online): https://www.bostonglobe.com/opinion/2015/11/16/paris-and-fall-rome/ErlRjkQMGXhvDarTIxXpdK/story.html (accessed 24/03/19)

48. Ward-Perkins (2005), pp. 1, 37–8

    James (2009), pp. 51–2

    Goffart (1981), p. 284

    Halsall, G. (2007). *Barbarian Migrations and the Roman World, 376–568.* Cambridge: Cambridge University Press. p. 177

49. Bury, J. (1978). 'Decline and Calamities of the Empire'. pp. 15–19, in: Kagan, D. (ed.). *The End of the Roman Empire: Decline or Transformation?* Lexington: D.C. Heath and Company. p. 16

    Jones, A. (1964). *The Later Roman Empire, 284–602: A Social, Economic and Administrative Survey.* Oxford: Basil Blackwell. p. 680

    Ward-Perkins (2005), p. 41

50. Boak (1978), p. 44

    Heitland, W. (1978). 'The Roman Fate'. pp. 79–91, in: Kagan, D. (ed.). The End of the Roman Empire: Decline or Transformation? Lexington: D.C. Heath and Company. p. 81

51. Goffart (1981), p. 282

    Ward-Perkins (2005), pp. 41, 44

52. James (2009), pp. 33, 59

53. Thompson, E. (1980). 'Barbarian invaders and Roman collaborators'. Florilegium 2: 71–88. pp. 77–8

54. Ibid., p. 82

55. James (2009), p. 202

56. Thompson (1980), pp. 76, 79, 83

57. Jones, A. (1978). 'East and West'. pp. 9-12, in: Kagan, D. (ed.). The End of the Roman Empire: Decline or Transformation? Lexington: D.C. Heath and Company. p. 9

58. Ward-Perkins (2005), pp. 27, 46

    James (2009), p. 56

Thompson (1980), p. 81

59. Ward-Perkins (2005), p. 28
    James (2009), p. 55

60. Grant, M. (1978). 'The Other World against This World'. pp. 102–14, in: Kagan, D. (ed.). *The End of the Roman Empire: Decline or Transformation?* Lexington: D.C. Heath and Company. pp. 107–8
    James (2009), p. 57
    Frend (1989), pp. 3, 20, 34–5 n. 122

61. Johnson, M. (1988). 'Toward a History of Theoderic's Building Program'. Dumbarton Oaks Papers 42: 73–96. pp. 76, 94

62. Merrills and Miles (2010), pp. 59, 196–7, 222–3

63. Ward-Perkins (2005), pp. 74–5

64. James (2009), p. 76

65. Ward-Perkins (2005), pp. 104, 108, 110, 138–9

66. Ibid., p. 123

Chapter 4

1. Logan, J. (1972). 'The French philosophes and their enlightening medieval past'. *Rice Institute Pamphlet-Rice University Studies* 58(4). pp. 83–4

2. Ibid., pp. 83–4

3. Consenza, M. (1910). *Petrarch's Letters to Classical Authors*. Chicago: University of Chicago Press. pp. 58, 67, 84
   Mazzotta, G. (1993). *The Worlds of Petrarch*. Durham: Duke University Press. p. 17

4. Murphy, J. (1974). *Rhetoric in the Middle Ages: A History of Rhetorical Theory from St. Augustine to the Renaissance*. Berkeley: University of California Press. p. 49

5. Polkowski, M. (2014). 'Reconstructing the Middle Ages: Dirck van Bleyswijck's Beschryvinge der stadt Delft and its uneasy relationship with the past'. *De Zeventiende Eeuw* 29(2): 247–64. p. 252

6. Frassetto, M. (2008). 'Medieval Attitudes Toward Muslims and Jews'. pp. 76–82, in: Harris, S. and Grigsby, B. (eds.). *Misconceptions About the Middle Ages*. New York: Routledge. p. 76
   Mommsen, T. (1942). 'Petrarch's Conception of the "Dark Ages"'. *Speculum* 17(2): 226–42. p. 228

7. Ward-Perkins, B. (2005). *The Fall of Rome and the End of Civilisation*. Oxford: Oxford University Press. p. 12

8. El Cheikh, N. (2004). *Byzantium Viewed by the Arabs*. Cambridge: Harvard University Press. p. 106

9. Littlewood, A. (2005). 'Literature'. pp. 133–46, in: Harris, J. (ed.). *Byzantine History*. Basingstoke: Palgrave Macmillan. p. 137

308   Notes to pages 103–114

10. Runciman, S. (1970). *The Last Byzantine Renaissance*. Cambridge: Cambridge University Press. p. 94
11. Ibid., p. 46
    Chrysostomos (2016). *The Sculptor and His Stone: Selected Readings on Hellenistic and Christian Learning and Thought in the Early Greek Fathers*. Eugene: Pickwick Publications. p. 75
12. Halsall, P. (2019). 'Medieval Sourcebook: Procopius of Caesarea: The Secret History'. *Fordham University* (online): https://sourcebooks.fordham.edu/basis/procop-anec.asp (accessed 07/06/19)
13. Ruthven, M. (1997). *Islam: A Very Short Introduction*. Oxford: Oxford University Press. pp. 33, 35
14. Peters, F. (1991). 'The quest of the historical Muhammad'. *International Journal of Middle East Studies* 23(3): 291–315. p. 292
15. Ruthven (1997), pp. 24, 33, 3–8
    Peters (1991), pp. 296, 301
    Cook, M. (2000). *The Koran: A Very Short Introduction*. Oxford; Oxford University Press. pp. 130–32
    Yunus, M., & Syed, A. (2015). 'Muhammad and the prophetic mission'. *New Age Islam* (online): http://www.newageislam.com/ (accessed 10/06/19)
16. Masood, E. (2009). *Science and Islam: A History*. London: Icon Books Ltd. pp. 18, 24
    Tougher, S. (2005). 'Political History (602–1025)'. pp. 24–38, in: Harris, J. (ed.). *Byzantine History*. Basingstoke: Palgrave Macmillan. p. 30
17. Foltz, R. (2010). *Religions of the Silk Road: Premodern Patterns of Globalisation*. New York: Palgrave Macmillan. p. 228
    Masood (2009), p. 30
18. Hussey, J. (1967). *The Byzantine World*. London: Hutchinson & Co Ltd. p. 153
19. Masood (2009), p. 44
20. Shamma, T. (2009). 'Translating into the Empire: The Arabic Version of *Kalila wa Dimna*'. *The Translator* 15(1): 65–86. p. 70
    Sonn, T. (2004). *A Brief History of Islam*. Malden: Blackwell Publishing. p. 48
21. Masood (2009), p. 39
22. Adamson, P. (2016). 'Arabic translators did far more than just preserve Greek philosophy'. *Aeon* (online): https://aeon.co/ideas/arabic-translators-did-far-more-than-just-preserve-greek-philosophy (accessed 25/02/19)
23. Masood (2009), pp. 4–5, 139–41

Arndt, A. (1983). 'Al-Khwarizmi'. *Mathematics Teacher* 76(9): 668–70. p. 669

24. Guessoum, N. (2008). 'Copernicus and Ibn Al-Shatir: Does the Copernican revolution have Islamic roots?' *The Observatory* 128: 231–9. p. 233

25. Masood (2009), p. 126
Rufus, W. (1939). 'The influence of Islamic astronomy in Europe and the Far East'. *Popular Astronomy* 47: 233–8. p. 235

26. Shoja, M. and Tubbs, R. (2007). 'The history of anatomy in Persia'. *Journal of Anatomy* 210(4): 359–78. p. 364
Syed, I. (2002). 'Islamic Medicine: 1000 years ahead of its times'. *Jishim*, 2: 2–9. p. 7
Savage-Smith, E. (2000). 'The practice of surgery in Islamic lands: Myth and reality'. *Social History of Medicine* 13(2): 307–21. p. 309

27. El-Daly, O. (2016). *Egyptology: The Missing Millennium: Ancient Egypt in Medieval Arabic Writings*. London: Routledge. pp. 71–2
Masood, E. (2009). *Science and Islam: A History*. London: Icon Books Ltd. pp. 104–5
Malik, A., Ziermann, J. and Diogo, R. (2018). 'An untold story in biology: The historical continuity of evolutionary ideas of Muslim scholars from the 8th century to Darwin's time'. *Journal of Biological Education* 52(1): 3–17. pp. 4–6
Overbye, D. (2001). 'How Islam Won, and Lost, the Lead in Science'. *New York Times* (online): https://www.nytimes.com/2001/10/30/science/how-islam-won-and-lost-the-lead-in-science.html (accessed 19/06/19)

28. Masood, E. (2009). *Science and Islam: A History*. London: Icon Books Ltd. p. 169

29. Ibid., p. 49

30. Burnett, C. (2001). 'The coherence of the Arabic-Latin translation program in Toledo in the twelfth century'. *Science in Context* 14(1–2): 249–88. pp. 251, 253–4

31. Mommsen, T. (1942). 'Petrarch's Conception of the "Dark Ages"'. *Speculum* 17(2): 226–42. p. 240
Musa, M. (1996). *Petrarch: Canzoniere*. Bloomington: Indiana University Press. p. xvi

32. Stanley, E. (1997). 'The Early Middle Ages = The Dark Ages = The Heroic Age of England and in English'. pp. 43–78, in: Alamichel, M. and Brewer, D. (eds.). *The Middle Ages After the Middle Ages*. Cambridge: D. S. Brewer. p. 56
Parker, M. (2005). 'Organisational gothic'. *Culture and Organization* 11(3): 153–66. p. 155

Kidd, C. (2004). 'Subscription, the Scottish Enlightenment and the moderate interpretation of history'. *The Journal of Ecclesiastical History* 55(3): 502–19. pp. 502–3

Winckelmann, J. and Irwin, D. (ed.) (1972). *Winckelmann: Writings on Art*. London: Phaidon. p. 24

33. Hussey, J. (1967). *The Byzantine World*. London: Hutchinson & Co Ltd. p. 9

Masood (2009), pp. 8

Orser, C. (2012). 'An archaeology of Eurocentrism'. *American Antiquity* 77(4): 737–75. p. 738

34. Connell, W. (2012). 'Italian Renaissance Historical Narrative'. pp. 347–63, in: Radasa, J., Sato, M. Tortarolo, E. and Woolf, D. (eds.). *The Oxford History of Historical Writing. Volume 3: 1400–1800*. Oxford: Oxford University Press. p. 350

35. Goffman, D. (2002). *The Ottoman Empire and Early Modern Europe*. Cambridge: Cambridge University Press. p. 13

Masood, E. (2009). *Science and Islam: A History*. London: Icon Books Ltd. p. 180

36. Ibid., p. 180

37. Goody, J. (2006). *The Theft of History*. Cambridge: Cambridge University Press.

Berger, S. (ed.) (2007). *Writing the Nation: A Global Perspective*. London: Palgrave Macmillan. p. 8

Ruoff, H. (ed.) (1916). *The Circle of Knowledge*. Boston: Standard Publishing Co. p. 277

Scarre, C. (1990). 'The Western World View in Archaeological Atlases'. pp. 11–18, in: Gathercole, P. and Lowenthal, D. (eds.). *The Politics of the Past*. London: Unwin Hyman Ltd. p. 17

38. Maitland, S. (1853). *The Dark Ages: A Series of Essays Intended to Illustrate the State of Religion and Literature in the Ninth, Tenth, Eleventh and Twelfth Centuries. Third Edition*. London: Gilbert and Rivington. p. 2

39. Briggs, C. (2000). 'Literacy, reading, and writing in the medieval West'. *Journal of Medieval History* 26(4): 397–420. pp. 407, 413–4

Connell, W. (2012). 'Italian Renaissance Historical Narrative'. pp. 347–63, in: Radasa, J., Sato, M. Tortarolo, E. and Woolf, D. (eds.). *The Oxford History of Historical Writing. Volume 3: 1400–1800*. Oxford: Oxford University Press. p. 348

Harris, W. (1991). *Ancient Literacy*. Cambridge: Harvard University Press. p. 259

40. Bishop, L. (2008). 'The Myth of the Flat Earth'. pp. 97–101, in: Harris, S. and Grigsby, B. (eds.). *Misconceptions About the Middle Ages*. New York: Routledge. pp. 97–8

Dendle, P. (2008). 'The Middle Ages Were a Superstitious Time'. pp. 117–23, in: Harris, S. and Grigsby, B. (eds.). *Misconceptions About the Middle Ages*. New York: Routledge. pp. 120–21

41. Anonymous (2019). 'Mystical & Psychic Services Market Valued at $2B'. *Socialnomics* (online): https://socialnomics.net/2019/03/22/mystical-psychic-services-market-valued-at-2b/ (accessed 31/05/19)

    Field, C. (2014). 'Supernatural, Superstitious, and Other News'. *British Religion in Numbers* (online): http://www.brin.ac.uk/supernatural-superstition-and-other-news/ (accessed 31/05/19)

Chapter 5

1. Koning, H. (1991). *Columbus: His Enterprise: Exploding the Myth*. New York: Monthly Review Press. pp. 43, 51, 53

   Phillips, W. and Phillips, C. (1992). *The Worlds of Christopher Columbus*. Cambridge: Cambridge University Press. p. 85

   Pelta, K. (1991). *Discovering Christopher Columbus: How History Is Invented*. Minneapolis: Lerner Publications Company. p. 26

2. Fernández-Armesto, F. (1996). *Columbus*. London: Duckworth. pp. 1, 16, 18–19, 43

   Phillips and Phillips (1992), pp. 87, 93–4

   Rickey, V. (1992). 'How Columbus encountered America'. *Mathematics Magazine* 65(4): 219–25. p. 219

3. Beazley, C. (1905). 'The French conquest of the Canaries in 1402–6, and the authority for the same'. *The Geographical Journal* 25(1): 77–81. p. 78

   Arnold, D. (2002). *The Age of Discovery, 1400–1600*. London: Routledge. p. xiii

   Randles, W. (1988). *Bartolomeu Dias and the Discovery of the South-East Passage Linking the Atlantic to the Indian Ocean*. Coimbra: University of Coimbra Press. p. 25.

4. Wintle, M. (1999). 'Renaissance maps and the construction of the idea of Europe'. *Journal of Historical Geography* 25(2): 137–65. p. 141.

5. Brooke-Hitching, E. (2016). *The Phantom Atlas: The Greatest Myths, Lies and Blunders on Maps*. London: Simon & Schuster. pp. 84–5, 124, 175–81, 201, 216, 220, 238

   Kline, N. (2001). *Maps of Medieval Thought: The Hereford Paradigm*. Woodbridge: The Boydell Press. pp. 95–7

   Mancall, P. (2006). *Travel Narratives from the Age of Discovery: An Anthology*. Oxford: Oxford University Press. p. 69

6. Arnold (2002), p. 11.

7. Brooke-Hitching (2016), p. 98

Nightingale, P. (2013). 'A crisis of credit in the fifteenth century or of historical interpretation?' *British Numismatic Journal* 83: 149–63. pp. 149, 152.

8. Fernández-Armesto (1996), pp. 20, 24, 69
    Delaney, C. (2011). *Columbus and the Quest for Jerusalem*. New York: Free Press. p. 237
9. Fernández-Armesto (1996), p. 43
10. Ibid., p. 20
    Ruddock, A. (1966). 'John Day of Bristol and the English voyages across the Atlantic before 1497'. *The Geographical Journal* 132(2): 225–33. pp. 229–30.
11. Parry, J. (1981). *The Discovery of the Sea*. Berkeley: University of California Press. p. 162
12. Edgerton, S. (1974). 'Florentine interest in Ptolemaic cartography as background for Renaissance painting, architecture, and the discovery of America'. *Journal of the Society of Architectural Historians* 33(4): 275–92. p. 275
    Fernández-Armesto (1996), pp. 30–31.
13. Ibid., pp. 130–31
14. Freedman, R. (2007). 'Coming to America: Who was First?' *NPR* (online): https://www.npr.org/templates/story/story.php?storyId=15040888 (accessed 17/01/19)
    Arnold (2002), p. 16
15. Fernández-Armesto (1996), pp. 69, 72
    Freedman (2007)
16. Koning, pp. 41, 44
17. Ibid., p. 48.
18. Fernández-Armesto (1996), pp. 49, 76, 79, 129
    Mancall (2006), p. 30
19. Koning (1991), p. 51.
20. Freedman (2007)
21. Ibid.
    Dunn, O. and Kelley, J. (1988). *The Diario of Christopher Columbus's First Voyage to America, 1492–1493*. Norman: The University of Oklahoma Press. p. 75
    Parry (1981), p. 162
    Koning (1991), pp. 51–3
22. Freedman (2007)
23. Dunn and Kelley (1988), p. 153
    Fernández-Armesto (1996), p. 89
24. Ibid., p. 86.

25. Ibid., p. 92.
26. Traboulay, D. (1994). *Columbus and Las Casas: The Conquest and Christianization of America, 1492–1566*. Lanham: University Press of America. pp. 25–6

    Fernández-Armesto (1996), pp. 106–7, 112–3

    Sued-Badillo, J. (1992). 'Christopher Columbus and the enslavement of the Amerindians in the Caribbean'. *Monthly Review* 44(3): p. 71
27. Ibid.

    MacGuill, D. (2018). 'Did Christopher Columbus Seize, Sell, and Export Sex Slaves?' *Snopes* (online): https://www.snopes.com/fact-check/columbus-sex-slaves/ (accessed 29/10/19).
28. Fernández-Armesto (1996), p. 139.
29. Searle, C. (1992). Unlearning Columbus: A review article. *Race & Class* 33(3): 67–77. p. 69

    Poole, R. (2011). 'What Became of the Taíno?' *Smithsonian* (online): https://www.smithsonianmag.com/travel/what-became-of-the-taino-73824867/ (accessed 29/10/19)

    Keen, B. (1969). 'The Black legend revisited: Assumptions and realities'. *The Hispanic American Historic Review* 49(4): 703–19. p. 709

    Szászdi, I. (2012). 'Castilian justice and Columbian injustice: The end of the government of Christopher Columbus in Hispaniola'. *Journal on European History of Law* (2): 53–8. p. 54
30. Mancall (2006), p. 32

    Bergreen, L. (2011). *Columbus: The Four Voyages, 1492–1504*. New York: Penguin.

    Lindskog, P. (1998). 'From Saint Domingue to Haiti: Some consequences of European colonisation on the physical environment of Hispaniola'. *Caribbean Geography* 9(2): 71–86. p. 72
31. Dunn and Kelley (1988), p. 75.
32. Fernández-Armesto (1996), p. 137.
33. Soule, E. (2018). 'From Africa to the Ocean Sea: Atlantic slavery in the origins of the Spanish Empire'. *Atlantic Studies* 15(1): 16–39. p. 21

    Fernández-Armesto (1996), p. 111
34. Sued-Badillo (1992)

    Soule (2018) p. 31.
35. Szászdi (2012)
36. Searle (1992), p. 69

    Weinberg, P. (1992). 'Columbus 500 years later: An environmental perspective'. *Journal of Civil Rights and Economic Development* 7(2): 587–90. p. 588

    Fernández-Armesto (1996), p. 105–07.

37. Sued-Badillo (1992)
38. Fernández-Armesto (1996), pp. viii, 39, 92, 115–16, 168
    Phillips and Phillips (1992), p. 212
39. Fernández-Armesto (1996), pp. 109–10.
40. Ibid., pp. 162–75
41. Handwerk, B. (2015). 'Why Christopher Columbus was the Perfect Icon for a New Nation Looking for a Hero'. *Smithsonian.com* (online): https://www.smithsonianmag.com/history/why-christopher-columbus-was-perfect-icon-new-nation-looking-hero-180956887/ (accessed 03/11/19)
    Weddle, G. (1994). 'National Portraits: The Columbian Celebrations of 1792, 1892–3 and 1992 as Cultural Moments'. pp. 111–26, in: Browne, R. and Marsden, M. (eds.). *The Cultures of Celebrations*. Bowling Green: Bowling Green State University Popular Press. p. 111.
42. Schuman, H., Schwartz, B., and d'Arcy, H. (2005). 'Elite revisionists and popular beliefs: Christopher Columbus, hero or villain?' *Public Opinion Quarterly* 69(1): 2–29. p. 6.
43. Larner, J. (1993). 'North American hero? Christopher Columbus 1702–2002. *Proceedings of the American Philosophical Society* 137(1): 46–63. p. 50.
44. Irving, W. (1901). *The Life and Times of Christopher Columbus*. London: T. Nelson and Sons. pp. 286–7.
45. Carle, R. (2019). 'Remembering Columbus: Blinded by politics'. *Academic Questions* 32(1): 105–13. p. 105.
46. Irving (1901), p. 287
    Hazlett, J. (1983). 'Literary nationalism and ambivalence in Washington Irving's *The Life and Voyages of Christopher Columbus*'. *American Literature*: 55(4): 560–75. p. 563.
47. Schuman et al. (2005), p. 6.
48. Ibid., p. 27.
49. Goodrich, A. (1874). *A History of the Character and Achievements of the So-Called Christopher Columbus*. New York: D. Appleton and Company. pp. v–vi.
50. Winsor, J. (1891). *Christopher Columbus and How He Received and Imparted the Spirit of Discovery*. Boston: Houghton, Mifflin and Company. p. 512.
51. Kubal, T. (2008). *Cultural Monuments and Collective Memory: Christopher Columbus and the Rewriting of the National Origin Myth*. New York: Palgrave Macmillan. p. 50.
52. Vinding, N. and Moyer-Vinding, B. (trans.) (2005). *The Viking Discovery of America, 985–1008: The Greenland Norse and Their Voyages to Newfoundland*. New York: The Edwin Mellen Press. pp. 43–5.

53. Brown, M. (1887). *The Icelandic Discoverers of America; Or, Honour to Whom Honour is Due*. London: Trubner & Co. p. 70.

54. Anderson, R. (1891). *An Historical Sketch of the Discovery of America by the Norsemen in the Tenth Century*. Chicago: S. C. Griggs and Company. p. 8

   Bowen, B. (1876). *America Discovered By The Welsh in 1170 A.D.* Philadelphia: J. B. Lippincott & Co

   Goudsward, D. (2010). *The Westford Knight and Henry Sinclair: Evidence of a 14th Century Scottish Voyage to North America*. Jefferson: McFarland & Co., Inc. p. 73–4

55. Morgan, D. (1996). 'Marco Polo in China — or not'. *Journal of the Royal Asiatic Society* 6(2): 221–5. p. 222.

56. Associated Press (2014). 'Muslims discovered America says Turkish president'. *The Guardian* (online): https://www.theguardian.com/world/2014/nov/16/muslims-discovered-america-erdogan-christopher-columbus (accessed 17/01/19).

57. Kurlansky, M. (1997). 'The Race to Codlandia'. *The New York Times* (online): https://archive.nytimes.com/www.nytimes.com/books/first/k/kurlansky-cod.html (accessed 09/11/19).

58. Fox, A. (2018). 'Sweet Potato migrated to Polynesia thousands of years before people did'. *Natures* (online): https://www.nature.com/articles/d41586-018-04488-4 (accessed 02/11/19)

   Smith, R. (2014). 'Chicken DNA Challenges Theory That Polynesians Beat Europeans to Americas'. *National Geographic* (online): https://news.nationalgeographic.com/news/2014/03/140318-polynesian-chickens-pacific-migration-america-science/ (accessed 13/01/19).

59. Vinding and Moyer-Vinding (2005), p. 61

   Boissoneault, L. (2015). 'L'Anse aux Meadows and the Viking Discovery of North America'. *Jstor Daily* (online): https://daily.jstor.org/anse-aux-meadows-and-the-viking-discovery-of-north-america/ (accessed 16/11/19).

60. Anonymous (1963). 'Viking ruins found'. *Science Newsletter* 84: 306

   Boissoneault (2015)

61. Forsyth, M. (2011). *The Etymologicon*. London: Icon Books Ltd. p. 197

62. Whitehead, N. (1984). 'Carib cannibalism. The historical evidence'. *Journal de la Société des Américanistes* 70: 69–87. p. 70.

63. Koch, A., Brierley, C., Maslin, M. and Lewis, S. (2019). 'European colonisation of the Americas killed 10 percent of the world population and caused global cooling'. *PRI* (online): https://www.pri.org/stories/2019-01-31/european-colonization-americas-killed-10-percent-world-population-and-caused (accessed 13/11/19).

64. Robertson, D. (2013). *Navigating Indigenous Identity*. University of Massachusetts Amherst: PhD thesis. p. 59.

65. Hendrix, S. (2017). 'The Columbus Day holiday is under attack, and so are the statues honouring the famed explorer'. *Washington Post* (online): https://www.washingtonpost.com/news/retropolis/wp/2017/10/09/the-columbus-day-holiday-is-under-attack-and-so-are-statues-honoring-the-famed-explorer/ (accessed 12/11/19)

    Fry, H. (2019). 'Christopher Columbus statue doused in red paint ahead of federal holiday'. *Los Angeles Times* (online): https://www.latimes.com/california/story/2019-10-14/christopher-columbus-statue-san-francisco-red-paint-federal-holiday (accessed 13/11/19)

    Banda, P. (2000). 'Denver Meets on Columbus Day Parade'. *Washington Post* (online): https://www.washingtonpost.com/wp-srv/aponline/20001006/aponline210044_000.htm? (accessed 12/11/19)

    Taylor, K. (2017). 'Christopher Columbus Statue Spray Painted in NYC's Central Park'. *NBC News* (online): https://www.nbcnews.com/news/us-news/christopher-columbus-statue-spray-painted-nyc-s-central-park-n800726 (accessed 12/11/19)

66. Schaeffer, B. (2010). 'In Defense of Christopher Columbus'. *Breitbart* (online): https://www.breitbart.com/national-security/2010/10/11/in-defense-of-christopher-columbus/ (accessed 14/11/19)

Chapter 6

1. Bessières, Y. and Niedzwiecki, P. (1991). *Women in the French Revolution*. Brussels: Commission of the European Communities (online): http://aei.pitt.edu/34003/1/A480.pdf (accessed 08/02/20). p. 13.

2. Bell, S. and Offen, K. (1983). *Women, the Family, and Freedom: The Debate in Documents. Volume One: 1750–1880*. Stanford: Stanford University Press. pp. 106–7

3. d'Aelders, E. (2020). 'Etta Palm d'Aelders, "Discourse on the Injustice of the Laws in Favour of Men, at the Expense of Women". (30 December 1790)'. *Liberté, Egalité, Fraterinté: Exploring the French Revolution* (online): http://chnm.gmu.edu/revolution/d/476 (accessed 14/02/20)

4. Phillips, R. (1976). 'Women and family breakdown in eighteenth-century France: Rouen 1780–1800'. *Social History* 1(2): 197–218, p. 203

5. Landes, J. (2013). 'Public and Private: Public and Private Lives in Eighteenth-Century France'. pp. 121–41, in: Pollak, E. (ed.). *A Cultural History of Women in the Age of Enlightenment*. London: Bloomsbury Academic. p. 140

    Bessières and Niedzwiecki (1991)

6. Godineau, D. and Streip, K. (trans.) (1998). *The Women of Paris and Their French Revolution*. Berkeley: University of California Press. pp. 168–9
7. Bessières and Niedzwiecki (1991), p. 8
8. Miles, R. (1988). *The Women's History of the World*. London: Penguin. p. 122
    Shahar, S. (2003). *The Fourth Estate: A History of Women in the Middle Ages*. London: Routledge. pp. 230–31, 239–41
    Opitz, C. (1992). 'Life in the Late Middle Ages'. pp. 267–317, in: Duby, G. and Perrot, M. (eds.). *A History of Women in the West. Volume II: Silence of the Middle Ages*. Cambridge: The Belknap Press. pp. 294–5
9. Shahar (2003), p. 204
10. Ibid., pp. 180, 187–90, 203–4
    Landes (2013), p. 127
11. Shahar (2003), pp. 190–94, 244
    Optiz (1992), pp. 270, 283, 300–301
    Miles (1988), p. 131
12. Shahar (2003), p. 194
    Opitz (1992). p. 296
    Brown, M. and McBride, K. (2013). 'Education and Work'. pp. 143–62, in: Raber, K. (ed.). *A Cultural History of Women in the Renaissance*. London: Bloomsbury Academic. p. 148
13. Shahar (2003), p. 198
14. Ibid., p. 241
    Opitz (1992), pp. 300–301
15. Ibid., pp. 298–9
16. Miles (1988), p. 133
17. Fleming, P. (2016). 'Women in Bristol, 1373–1660'. pp. 15–44, in: Dresser, M. (ed.). *Women and the City: Bristol, 1373–2000*. Bristol: Redcliffe Press. p. 27
    Miles (1988), p. 132
    Walters, P. (2019). *The Little History of Coventry*. Cheltenham: The History Press.
    Shahar (2003), p. 195
18. Landes (2013), p. 128
    Shahar (2003), pp. 193, 240–41
    L'Hermite-Leclercq, P. (1992). 'The Feudal Order'. pp. 202–49, in: Duby, G. and Perrot, M. (eds.). *A History of Women in the West. Volume II: Silence of the Middle Ages*. Cambridge: The Belknap Press. p. 231
19. Shahar (2003), pp. 195, 199–200
20. Ibid., pp. 200, 242
    Landes (2013), p. 128
    L'Hermite-Leclercq (1992), p. 231

21. Jordan, W. (2010). 'The Great Famine: 1315–1322 Revisited'. pp. 44–61, in: Bruce, S. (ed.). *Ecologies and Economies in Medieval and Early Modern Europe*. Leiden: Brill. pp. 49–50

Slavin, P. (2014). 'Market failure during the Great Famine in England and Wales (1315–1317)'. *Past and Present* 222(1): 9–49. p. 12

22. Gottfried, R. (1983). *The Black Death: Natural and Human Disaster in Medieval Europe*. New York: The Free Press. p. 35

Bovey, A. (2015). 'Peasants and their role in rural life'. *British Library* (online): https://www.bl.uk/the-middle-ages/articles/peasants-and-their-role-in-rural-life (accessed 26/01/20)

Pamuk, Ş. (2007). 'The Black Death and the origins of the "Great Divergence" across Europe, 1300–1600'. *European Review of Economic History* 11(3): 289–317. p. 293

Wrigley, E. and Schofield, R. (1989). *The Population History of England 1541–1871: A Reconstruction*. Cambridge: Cambridge University Press. p. 210

23. Ibeki, M. (2011). 'Black Death'. *BBC History* (online): http://www.bbc.co.uk/history/british/middle_ages/black_01.shtml (accessed 06/02/20)

24. Bardsley, S. (2001). 'Women's work reconsidered: Gender and wage differentiation in late medieval England: Reply'. *Past & Present* (173): 199–202. p. 199

25. Shahar (2003), p. 178, 200–201

Opitz (1992), p. 302

26. Ward, J. (2016). *Women in Medieval Europe: 1200–1500*. Abingdon: Routledge. p. 100

Opitz (1992), pp. 302–3

27. Cody, L. (2013). 'Medicine and Disease: Women, Practice, and Print in the Enlightenment Medical Marketplace'. pp. 99–120, in: Pollak, E. (ed.). *A Cultural History of Women in the Age of Enlightenment*. London: Bloomsbury Academic. pp. 101, 105

28. Gabbatiss, J. (2017). 'Prehistoric women were stronger than modern rowers, say Cambridge scientists'. *The Independent* (online): https://www.independent.co.uk/news/science/prehistoric-women-strength-muscles-men-rowers-upper-body-university-cambridge-a8082591.html (accessed 25/01/20)

Macintosh, A., Pinhasi, R., and Stock, J. (2017). 'Prehistoric women's manual labor exceeded that of athletes through the first 5500 years of farming in Central Europe'. *Science Advances* 3(11): eaao3893.

29. McKeon, M. (1995). 'Historicizing patriarchy: The emergence of gender difference in England, 1660–1760'. *Eighteenth-Century Studies* 28(3): 295–322. p. 299

30. Earle, P. (1989). *The Making of the English Middle Class: Business, Society and Family Life in London 1660–1730*. Berkeley: University of California Press. pp. 163–5

31. Brown, K. (2013). 'The Life Cycle: Motherhood during the Enlightenment'. pp. 29–43, in: Pollak, E. (ed.). *A Cultural History of Women in the Age of Enlightenment*. London: Bloomsbury Academic. pp. 30, 34

32. Trouille, M. (1994). 'Sexual/textual politics in the Enlightenment: Diderot and D'Epinay respond to Thomas's essay on women'. *Romanic Review* 85(2): 191
    Cody (2013), pp. 113–14
    Pollak, E. (2013). 'Introduction: Women daring to know in the age of Enlightenment'. pp. 1–28, in: Pollak, E. (ed.). *A Cultural History of Women in the Age of Enlightenment*. London: Bloomsbury Academic. p. 9

33. Duncan, C. (1973). 'Happy mothers and other new ideas in French art'. *The Art Bulletin* 55(4): 570–83. p. 570
    Kord, S. (2013). 'Work and Education: The case of laboring women poets in England, Scotland, and Germany'. pp. 143–166, in: Pollak, E. (ed.). *A Cultural History of Women in the Age of Enlightenment*. London: Bloomsbury Academic. pp. 145–6
    Pollak (2013), pp. 9–10
    Brown (2013), p. 41

34. Duncan (1973), p. 582
    Rousseau, J. (2018) 'Emile'. *Project Gutenberg* (online): http://www.gutenberg.org/files/5427/5427-h/5427-h.htm (accessed 21/02/20)
    Brown (2013), p. 39

35. Pollak (2013), pp. 13–14
    Montagu, M. (1812). *The Works of the Right Honourable Lady Mary Wortley Montagu, Vol. I*. London: Longman, Hurst, Rees, Orme and Brown. p. 64

36. Berg, M. (1991). 'Women's work and the Industrial Revolution'. *ReFresh* 12: 1–4. p. 2
    Wrigley, E. (1966). Family limitation in pre-industrial England. *The Economic History Review* 19(1): 82–109. pp. 86–7
    Lanser, S. (2013). 'Bodies and Sexuality: Sex, Gender, and the Limits of Enlightenment'. pp. 45–70, in: Pollak, E. (ed.). *A Cultural History of Women in the Age of Enlightenment*. London: Bloomsbury Academic. p. 55

37. Duncan (1973), p. 574
    Brown (2013), pp. 40–41
    Pollak (2013), p. 7
    d'Aelders (2020)

38. Rousseau (2018)
    Landes (2013), p. 138
    Abray, J. (1975). 'Feminism in the French Revolution'. *The American Historical Review* 80(1): 43–62. p. 62
    Godineau and Streip (1998), pp. 168–9
    Bessières and Niedzwiecki (1991), p. 16
39. Miles (1988), p. 148
    Anonymous (2020). 'The Trial of Olympe de Gouges'. *Liberté, Egalité, Fraterinté: Exploring the French Revolution* (online): http://chnm.gmu. edu/revolution/d/488 (accessed 10/02/20)
40. Anonymous (2020). 'Woman and the Revolution'. *Liberté, Egalité, Fraternité: Exploring the French Revolution* (online): http://chnm.gmu. edu/revolution/exhibits/show/liberty--equality--fraternity/women-and-the-revolution (accessed 10/02/20).
41. Miles (1988), p. 188
42. Ibid., p. 189
    Lewis, H. (1980). 'The legal status of women in nineteenth-century France'. *Journal of European Studies* 10(39): 178–88. pp. 181–3
43. Opitz (1992), pp. 292–3
44. Parkman, F. (1910). *The Oregon Trail*. Boston: Ginn And Company. p. 83
    New, C. (1873). *Life, Wanderings, and Labours in Eastern Africa*. London: Hodder And Stoughton. p. 197
    Brown (2013), p. 30
45. Thane, P. (2013). 'The Life Cycle: Women and the Life Cycle, ca. 1800–1920'. pp. 21–46, in: Mangum, T. (ed.) *A Cultural History of Women in the Age of Empire*. London: Bloomsbury Academic. pp. 27–8
    Abrams, L. (2001). 'Ideals of Womanhood in Victorian Britain'. *BBC History* (online): http://www.bbc.co.uk/history/trail/victorian_britain/ women_home/ideals_womanhood_04.shtml (accessed 11/02/20)
    Kord (2013), pp. 144–5
46. Cody (2013), p. 106
47. Burnette, J. (2008). 'Women Workers in the British Industrial Revolution'. *Economic History Association* (online): http://www.eh.net/?s=women+ workers+and+the+industrial+revolution (accessed 11/02/20)
48. Greenlees, J. (2016). Workplace health and gender among cotton workers in America and Britain, c. 1880s–1940s. *International Review of Social History* 61(3): 459–585
49. Pike, E. (1966). *Human Documents of the Industrial Revolution*. London: Routledge. pp. 249–50
    Miles (1988), p. 153
50. Burnette (2008)

Hopkins, E. (1982). 'Working hours and conditions during the Industrial Revolution: A re-appraisal'. *The Economic History Review* 35(1): 52–66. p. 53

Nicholas, S. and Oxley, D. (1993). 'The living standards of women during the Industrial Revolution, 1795–1820'. *The Economic History Review* 46(4): 723–49. pp. 726, 739

Galbi, D. (1994). 'Economic Change and Sex Discrimination in the Early English Cotton Factories'. *Galbi Think* (online): https://www.galbithink. org/womwork.htm (accessed 11/02/20)

51. Pető, A. (2009). 'From Visibility to Analysis'. In: Salvaterra, C. and Waaldijk, B. (eds.). *Paths to Gender: European Historical Perspectives on Women and Men*. Pisa: Pisa University Press.

    Berger, S. (2007). 'The Power of National Pasts: Writing National History in Nineteenth- and Twentieth-Century Europe'. pp. 30–62, in: Berger, S. (ed.) *Writing the Nation: A Global Perspective*. London: Palgrave Macmillan. pp. 35–36.

52. Austin, J. (1903). *Northanger Abbey*. Boston: Little, Brown and Company. p. 129.

53. Gilchrist, R. (1999). *Gender and Archaeology: Contesting the Past*. London: Routledge. pp. 18, 32

    Conkey, M. and Tringham, R. (1995). 'Archaeology and the Goddess: Exploring the Contours of Feminist Archaeology'. pp. 199–245, in: (Stanton, D. and Stewarts, A. (eds.). *Feminism in the Academy*. Ann Arbor: The University of Michigan Press. p. 201

    Jones, S. and Pay, S. (1990). 'The Legacy of Eve'. pp. 160–71, in: Gathercole, P. and Lowenthal, D. (eds.). *The Politics of the Past*. London: Unwin Hyman Ltd. p. 165

    Nelson, S. (1997). *Gender in Archaeology: Analyzing Power and Prestige*. London: Sage Publications, Ltd. pp. 19–20, 133

54. Price, N., Hedenstierna-Jonson, C., Zachrisson, T. et al. (2019). 'Viking warrior women? Reassessing Birka chamber grave Bj.581'. *Antiquity* 93(367): 181–98. p. 194.

55. Miles (1988), p. 114.

Chapter 7

1. Rousseau, J. and Cranston, M. (trans.) (2004). *The Social Contract*. London: Penguin Group.

2. Bryce, J. (1918). *The Holy Roman Empire*. Altenmünster: Jazzybee Verlag Jürgen Beck. pp. 79, 127

3. Hunt, L. (2010). 'The French Revolution in Global Context'. pp. 20–36, in: Armitage, D. and Subrahmanyam, S. (eds.). *The Age of Revolutions*

in Global Context, c. 1760–1840. Basingstoke: Palgrave Macmillan. p. 21–2

Schor, K. (2001). 'The Crisis of French Universalism'. *Yale French Studies* 100: 43–64. p. 47

Dubois, L. and Garrigus, J. (trans.) (2019). 'The Haitian Declaration of Independence'. *Duke Today* (online): https://today.duke.edu/showcase/haitideclaration/declarationstext.html (accessed 03/05/19)

4. Mazzini, J. (1850). *Royalty and Republicanism in Italy; Or, Notes and Documents Relating to the Lombard Insurrection, and to the Royal War of 1848*. London: Charles Gilpin. p. 12

5. Bruter, M. (2003). 'Winning hearts and minds for Europe: The impact of news and symbols on civic and cultural European identity'. *Comparative Political Studies* 36(10): 1148–1179. pp. 1148–9

6. Connor, W. (1990). 'When is a Nation?' *Ethnic and Racial Studies* 13(1): 92-103. pp. 93–4

    Kohl, P. and Fawcett, C. (1995). 'Archaeology in the service of the state: theoretical considerations'. pp. 3–20, in: Kohl, P. and Fawcett, C. (eds.). *Nationalism, Politics, and the Practice of Archaeology*. Cambridge: Cambridge University Press. p. 12

7. Stiles, A. (2001). *The Unification of Italy: 1815–1870*. London: Hodder & Stoughton.

8. Boym, S. (2001). *The Future of Nostalgia*. New York: Basic Books. p. 14

9. Trumpener, K. (2000). 'Béla Bartók and the Rise of Comparative Ethnomusicology: Nationalism, Race Purity, and the Legacy of the Austro-Hungarian Empire. pp. 403–58, in: Radano, R. and Bohlman, P. (eds.). *Music and the Racial Imagination*. Chicago: The University of Chicago Press. pp. 401–11

10. Macha-Bizoumi, N. (2012). 'Amalia Dress: The invention of a new costume tradition in the service of Greek national identity'. *Catwalk: The Journal of Fashion, Beauty and Style* 1(1): 65–90. pp. 67–8

    Stevens, C. (2004). 'Welsh costume: The survival of tradition or national icon?' *Folk Life* 43(1): 56–70. pp. 64–6

    Gailey, A. (1989). 'The nature of tradition'. *Folklore* 100(2): 143–61. p. 156

    Crang, M. (1999). 'Nation, region and homeland: History and tradition in Dalarna, Sweden'. *Ecumene* 6(4): 447–70. p. 485

    Anonymous (2018). 'Blue and yellow: the Swedish national costume'. *Nordstjernan* (online): http://www.nordstjernan.com/news/traditions/8476/ (accessed 30/04/19)

11. Sweet, R. (2007). 'A rattleskull genius: The many faces of Iolo Morganwg'. *The English Historical Review* 122(496): 557–8. p. 557

12. Chhabra, D., Healy, R., and Sills, E. (2003). 'Staged authenticity and heritage tourism'. *Annals of Tourism Research* 30(3): 702–19. p. 706

13. Trevor-Roper, H. (1983). 'The Highland tradition of Scotland'. pp. 15–43, in: Hobsbawm, E. and Ranger, T. (eds.). *The Invention of Tradition*. Cambridge: Cambridge University Press.
Warren, J. (1998). *The Past and Its Presenters: An introduction to issues in historiography*. Abingdon: Hodder and Stoughton. pp. 169–70

14. Roud, S. (2008). *The English Year*. London: Penguin. pp. 510–12
Bloomfield, A. (2001). 'The quickening of the national spirit: Cecil Sharp and the pioneers of the folk-dance revival in English state schools (1900–26)'. *History of Education* 30(1): 59–75

15. Guttmann, A. and Thompson, L. (2001). *Japanese Sports: A History*. Honolulu: University of Hawaii Press. pp. 141–3
Shun, I. (1998). 'The Invention of Martial Arts'. pp. 163–73, in: Vlastos, S. (ed.). *Mirror of Modernity: Invented Tradition in Modern Japan*. Berkeley, California: University of California Press.
Wang, Q. (2007). 'Between Myth and History: the Construction of a National Past in Modern East Asia'. pp. 126–54, in: Berger, S. (ed.) *Writing the Nation: A Global Perspective*. London: Palgrave Macmillan. p. 137
Adams, L. (1999). 'Invention, institutionalization and renewal in Uzbekistan's national culture'. *European Journal of Cultural Studies* 2(3), 355–73. pp. 356, 364–6
Gellner, E. (1983). *Nations and Nationalism*. Ithaca: Cornell University Press. p. 64

16. Marciano, M. (2014). 'The Pythagorean Way of Life and Pythagorean Ethics'. pp. 131–48, in: Huffman, C. (ed.). *A History of Pythagoreanism*. Cambridge: Cambridge University Press. pp. 138, 140

17. Lillios, K. (1995). 'Nationalism and Copper Age Research in Portugal During the Salazar Regime (1932–1974)'. pp. 57–69, in: Kohl, P. and Fawcett, C. (eds.). *Nationalism, Politics, and the Practice of Archaeology*. Cambridge: Cambridge University Press. p. 57

18. Palacký, F. (1948). 'Letter sent by František Palacký to Frankfurt'. *The Slavonic and East European Review* 26(67): 303–8. p. 304

19. Baár, M. (2010). *Historians and Nationalism: East-Central Europe in the Nineteenth Century*. Oxford: Oxford University Press. pp. 23–5, 43, 46

20. Hewitson, M. (2010). *Nationalism in Germany, 1848–1866: Revolutionary Nation*. Basingstoke: Palgrave Macmillan. pp. 29–30

21. Mazzini, G. (1862). *The Duties of Man*. London: Chapman & Hall. pp. 70, 72, 89

22. Harsin, J. (2002). *Barricades: The War of the Streets in Revolutionary Paris, 1830–1848*. Basingstoke: Palgrave Macmillan. p. 258

23. Yanov, A. (2014). 'Nicholas I and the Revolutions of 1848'. *Institute of Modern Russia* (online): https://imrussia.org/en/nation/647-nicholas-i-and-1848 (accessed 06/05/19)

24. Mackay, C. (1877). *Forty Years' Recollections of Life, Literature, and Public Affairs from 1830 to 1870, Vol. II*. London: Chapman & Hall. p. 49

25. Donson, A. (2003). 'Fatherlands: State-building and nationalism in nineteenth-century Germany (review)'. *Journal of Social History* 37(2): 521–3. p. 521

    Cannadine, D. (1983). 'The Context, Performance and Meaning of Ritual: The British Monarchy and the "Invention of Tradition", c. 1820–1977'. pp. 101–63, in: Hobsbawm, E. and Ranger, T. (eds.). *The Invention of Tradition*. Cambridge: Cambridge University Press. p. 108

26. Trigger, B. (1995). 'Romanticism, nationalism, and archaeology'. pp. 263–79, in: Kohl, P. and Fawcett, C. (eds.). *Nationalism, Politics, and the Practice of Archaeology*. Cambridge: Cambridge University Press.

    Soysal, Y. and Strang, D. (1989). 'Construction of the first mass education systems in nineteenth-century Europe'. *Sociology of Education* 62(4): 277–88. p. 277

    Broers, M. (1996). *Europe After Napoleon: Revolution, Reaction, and Romanticism, 1814–1848*. Manchester: Manchester University Press. pp. 98, 119

27. Zhimin, C. (2005). 'Nationalism, internationalism and Chinese foreign policy'. *Journal of Contemporary China* 14(42): 35–53. pp. 38–9

28. Kohl and Fawcett (1995), pp. 8, 12–13
    Trigger (1995), p. 268

29. Voudouri, D. (2010). 'Law and the politics of the past: Legal protection of cultural heritage in Greece'. *International Journal of Cultural Property* 17(3): 547–68. p. 547

30. Woolf, D. (2011). *A Global History of History*. Cambridge: Cambridge University Press. p. 359

    Berger, S. (2007). 'The Power of National Pasts: Writing National History in Nineteenth- and Twentieth-Century Europe'. pp. 30–62, in: Berger, S. (ed.) *Writing the Nation: A Global Perspective*. London: Palgrave Macmillan. pp. 40, 46

31. Liakos, A. (2012). 'Greece: A Land Caught Between Ancient Glories and the Modern World'. p. 52, in: Furtado, P. (ed.). *Histories of Nations*. London: Thames & Hudson. pp. 52, 102

    Woolf (2011), p. 359

    Gathercole, P. and Lowenthal, D. (1990). *The Politics of the Past*. London: Unwin Hyman Ltd. p. 308

Just, R. (1989). 'Triumph of the Ethnos'. *History and Ethnicity*, 71–88. p. 74

32. Aronsson, P. (2012). 'Sweden: From Viking Community to Welfare State'. p. 188–97, in: Furtado, P. (ed.). *Histories of Nations*. London: Thames & Hudson. p. 192

   Seifter, P. (2012). 'The Czech Republic: National History and the Search for Identity'. p. 126–7 In: Furtado, P. (ed.). *Histories of Nations*. London: Thames & Hudson. pp. 126–7

   Johnstone, I. (2016). 'Ossian, the "Homer of the North", and the truth behind the world's greatest literary hoax'. *Independent* (online): https://www.independent.co.uk/arts-entertainment/books/news/ossian-literary-hoax-james-macpherson-fingal-mathematics-social-network-study-a7371806.html (accessed 25/05/19)

33. Siviloglu, M. (2012). 'Turkey: The Land with a Lost Empire'. pp. 154–61, in: Furtado, P. (ed.). *Histories of Nations*. London: Thames & Hudson.

   Anderson, B. (2006). *Imagined Communities*. London: Verso. p. 11

   Isaacs, H. (1975). *Idols of the Tribe*. New York: Harper & Row. pp. 123–4

34. Danforth, L. (1993). 'Claims to Macedonian identity: The Macedonian question and the breakup of Yugoslavia'. *Anthropology Today* 9(4): 3–10. p. 4

   Prelec, T. (2014). 'The 'Skopje 2014' project: Rebranding a city along ethnic lines'. *LSEE* (online): https://blogs.lse.ac.uk/lsee/2014/12/15/brand-old-skopje/ (accessed 25/05/19)

   Bloodworth, A. (2018). 'Statues & Styrofoam: Why is Macedonia Faking Its Own Past?' *Amuse* (online): https://amuse.vice.com/en_us/article/438adw/macedonia-faking-own-past (accessed 25/05/19)

35. Bassir, H. (2012). 'Egypt: Pharaohs, Kings and Presidents'. pp. 19–25, in: Furtado, P. (ed.). *Histories of Nations*. London: Thames & Hudson. p. 19

36. Taylor, D. (2004). 'Boudica, mythic warrior queen or feminist role model?' *Independent* (online): https://www.independent.co.uk/voices/commentators/d-j-taylor-boudicca-mythic-warrior-queen-or-feminist-role-model-5544572.html (accessed 27/04/19)

37. Kewes, P. (2011). 'Henry Savile's Tacitus and the politics of Roman history in late Elizabethan England'. *Huntington library quarterly* 74(4): 515–51. p. 515

   Boase, T. (1954). 'The decoration of the new Palace of Westminster, 1841–1863'. *Journal of the Warburg and Courtauld Institutes* 17(3/4): 319–58. p. 342

38. Bueno, C. (2016). *The Pursuit of Ruins: Archaeology, History, and the Making of Modern Mexico*. Albuquerque: University of New Mexico Press. p. 6

39. McCabe, D. (2002). 'Patriotic Gore, Again'. In: Primoratz, I. (ed.). *Patriotism.* Amherst, New York: Humanity Books. p. 125

40. Berger (2007), p. 24
    Kohl Fawcett (1995), p. 13

41. Barber, T. (2016). 'Sarkozy seeks to seduce the French with tales of Gaul'. *Financial Times* (online): https://www.ft.com/content/fbd2316a-83c5-11e6 -a29c-6e7d9515ad15 (accessed 10/05/19)

42. Anonymous (2017). 'France election: Far-right's Le Pen rails against globalisation'. *BBC* (online): http://www.bbc.co.uk/news/world-europe-38872335 (accessed 06/02/17)

43. Tzilivakis, K. (2013). '"Greek race" debate enters the army, police'. *Enet English* (online): http://www.enetenglish.gr/?i=news.en.article&id=112 (accessed 10/05/19)
    Cole, M. (2019). 'How the Far Right Perverts History – And Why It Matters'. *Daily Beast* (online): https://www.thedailybeast.com/how-the-far-right-perverts-ancient-historyand-why-it-matters (accessed 10/05/19)

44. Walker, S. (2018). 'Hungarian leader says Europe is now "under invasion" by migrants'. *Guardian* (online): https://www.theguardian.com/ world/2018/mar/15/hungarian-leader-says-europe-is-now-under-invasion-by-migrants (accessed 11/05/19)
    Balogh, E. (2015). 'Viktor Orbán's claims of historical antecedents'. *Hungarian Spectrum* (online): http://hungarianspectrum.org/2015/09/27/ viktor-orbans-claims-of-historical-antecedents/ (accessed 11/05/19)

45. Ratnagar, S. (2004). 'Archaeology at the heart of a political confrontation: The case of Ayodhya'. *Current Anthropology* 45(2): 239–259. pp. 239–40, 242–3
    Kazmin, A. (2019). 'How Hindu nationalism went mainstream in Modi's India'. *Financial Times* (online): https://www.ft.com/content/4b68c89 c-711c-11e9-bf5c-6eeb837566c5 (accessed 10/05/19)

46. Kaiser, T. (1995). 'Archaeology and Ideology in Southeast Europe'. pp. 99–119, in: Kohl, P. and Fawcett, C. (eds.). *Nationalism, Politics, and the Practice of Archaeology.* Cambridge: Cambridge University Press. p. 119 n.2
    Warren (1998), pp. 163–4

47. Kaiser (1995), pp. 99, 116
    Chapman, J. (1994). 'Destruction of a common heritage: The archaeology of war in Croatia, Bosnia and Hercegovina'. *Antiquity* 68(258): 120–26

48. Carr, E. (1945). *Nationalism and After.* London: Macmillan & Co. Ltd. pp. 31, 33–4, 66–7, 73–4

49. Thompson, A. and Fevre, R. (2001). 'The national question: Sociological reflections on nation and nationalism'. *Nations and Nationalism* 7(3): 297–315

50. Nairn, T. (1997). *Faces of Nationalism: Janus Revisited*. London: Verso. p. 47

51. Ibid., p. 47–8

52. Mazzini, M. (2018). 'Poland's right-wing government is rewriting history – with itself as the hero'. *Washington Post* (online): https://www. washingtonpost.com/news/monkey-cage/wp/2018/02/27/polands-right-wing-government-is-rewriting-history-with-itself-as-hero/?utm_term=. d3e727f05359 (accessed 11/05/19)

53. Vij-Aurora, B. (2018). 'Allahabad to Prayagraj: The Politics Of Name Change'. *Outlook* (online): https://www.outlookindia.com/magazine/story/allahabad-to-prayagraj-the-politics-of-name-change/300886 (accessed 24/01/19)

54. Reuters (2017). 'China changes start date of war with Japan, says will bolster patriotic education'. *Business Insider* (online): http://static1.businessinsider.com/r-china-changes-start-date-of-war-with-japan-says-will-bolster-patriotic-education-2017-1 (accessed 02/05/19)
    Anonymous (2019). 'Brazil textbook 'to be revised to deny 1964 coup'. *BBC News* (online): https://www.bbc.co.uk/news/world-latin-america-47813480 (accessed 04/04/19)
    Brandes, H. (2015). 'Oklahoma lawmaker to rewrite bill on state's AP U.S. history funding'. *Reuters* (online): http://www.reuters.com/article/us-usa-oklahoma-education-idUSKBN0LN20C20150219 (accessed 17/01/17)
    Rockmore, E. (2015). 'How Texas Teaches History'. *New York Times* (online): https://www.nytimes.com/2015/10/22/opinion/how-texas-teaches-history.html (accessed 02/05/19)

Chapter 8

1. Anonymous (2018). 'Mystery of the Crystal Skulls: The Stare of Death'. *The Unredacted* (online): https://theunredacted.com/mystery-of-the-crystal-skulls-the-stare-of-death/ (accessed 29/11/19)
   Laycock, J. (2015). 'The controversial history of the crystal skulls: A case study in interpretive drift'. *Material Religion* 11(2): 164–88. pp. 176–7. p. 176

2. Crystal, E. (2019). 'Crystal Skulls'. *Crystalinks* (online): https://www. crystalinks.com/crystalskulls.html (accessed 29/11/19)

3. Anonymous (2018). '13 Crystal Skulls: Legend and Prophecy'. *Crystal Skulls* (online): https://crystalskulls.com/13-crystal-skulls.html (accessed 29/11/19)

4. Walsh, J. (2008). 'Legend of the Crystal Skulls: The truth behind Indiana Jones's latest quest'. *Archaeology* (online): https://archive.archaeology.org/0805/etc/indy.html (accessed 26/11/19)
5. Ibid.
    Sax, M., Walsh, J., Freestone, I., Rankin, I. and Meeks, N. (2008). 'The origins of two purportedly pre-Columbian Mexican crystal skulls'. *Journal of Archaeological Science* 35: 2751–60. p. 2751
    Walsh, J. and Topping, B. (2019). *The Man Who Invented Aztec Crystal Skulls: The Adventures of Eugène Boban.* New York: Berghahn Books. p. 12.
6. Laycock (2015), pp. 164, 171
    Digby, A. (1936). 'Comments on the morphological comparison of two crystal skulls'. *Man* 36: 107–9. pp. 108–9
7. Laycock (2015), p. 173
    Walsh, J. (2010). 'The Skull of Doom'. *Archaeology* (online): https://archive.archaeology.org/online/features/mitchell_hedges/ (accessed 21/12/19)
8. Barthel, M. (producer), Reinl, H. and Romine, C. (directors) (1976). *Mysteries of the Gods* [motion picture]. New York: Hemisphere Pictures.
9. Ibid.
10. Laycock (2015), p. 174–5
    Anonymous (2018). 'Mystery of the Crystal Skulls: The Stare of Death'. *The Unredacted* (online): https://theunredacted.com/mystery-of-the-crystal-skulls-the-stare-of-death/ (accessed 29/11/19)
11. Galde, P. (1998). *The Truth About Crystal Healing.* St Paul: Llewellyn Press.
12. Walsh and Topping (2019), pp. 1, 4
    Sax, M., Walsh, J., Freestone, I. Rankin, A. and Meeks, N. (2017). 'Study of two large crystal skulls in the collection of the British Museum and the Smithsonian Institution'. *The British Museum* (online): https://research.britishmuseum.org/research/news/studying_the_crystal_skull.aspx (accessed 29/11/19)
    Sax et al. (2008)
    Laycock (2015), p. 180
    Walsh (2008)
13. Sax et al. (2008), pp. 2751, 2758–9
14. Ibid.
15. Walsh (2008)
    Laycock (2015), p. 181
    Walsh and Topping (2019), pp. 62–3
    Walsh (2010)
16. Laycock (2015), p. 181.

17. Walsh (2008)
18. Walsh and Topping (2019), pp. 12–13.
19. Weindling, D. and Colloms, M. (2017). 'Indiana Jones and the West Hampstead Conman'. *West Hampstead Life* (online): http://westhampstead life.com/2017/03/10/indiana-jones-and-the-west-hampstead-conman/ 19302 (accessed 26/05/20)
    Laycock (2015), p. 172
    Walsh (2010)
20. Ibid.
21. Nickel, J. and Fischer, J. (1988). *Secrets of the Supernatural: Investigating the World's Occult Mysteries*. Prometheus Books. p. 39
22. Walsh (2010)
23. Colavito, J. (2013). 'Review of Ancient Aliens S06E02 "The Crystal Skulls"'. *Jason Colavito* (online): http://www.jasoncolavito.com/blog/ review-of-ancient-aliens-s06e02-the-crystal-skulls (accessed 29/11/19)
24. Laycock (2015), pp. 171–3, 176
    Walsh (2010)
25. Lovett, R. and Hoffman, S. (2019). 'Crystal Skulls'. *National Geographic* (online): https://www.nationalgeographic.com/history/archaeology/ crystal-skulls/ (accessed 29/11/19)
    Walsh and Topping (2019), p. 4
26. Bond, S. (2018). 'Pseudoarchaeology and the Racism Behind Ancient Aliens'. *Hyperallergic* (online): https://hyperallergic.com/470795/ pseudoarchaeology-and-the-racism-behind-ancient-aliens/ (accessed 23/11/19)
27. Holloway, A. (2013). 'Could this Finding Dwarf the Pyramids of Giza? Long-Lost Pyramids Confirmed in Egyptian Desert'. *Ancient Origins* (online): https://www.ancient-origins.net/news-history-archaeology/ could-finding-dwarf-pyramids-giza-long-lost-pyramids-confirmed- egypt-00660 (accessed 07/12/19)
    Edwards, A. (2019). 'Did the discovery of Gobekli Tepe change everything we thought we knew about human history?' *Mysterious Unexplained History* (online): https://mysteriousunexplainedhistory.com/did-the- discovery-of-gobekli-tepe-change-everything-we-thought-we-knew- about-human history/ (accessed 07/12/19)
28. Dunning, B. (2009). 'The Bosnian Pyramids'. *Skeptoid* (online): https:// skeptoid.com/episodes/4140 (accessed 28/11/19)
    Woodward, C. (2009). 'The Mystery of Bosnia's Ancient Pyramids'. *Smithsonian Magazine* (online): https://www.smithsonianmag.com/ history/the-mystery-of-bosnias-ancient-pyramids-148990462/ (accessed 31/12/19)

29. Doubleday, J. (2018). 'Jock Doubleday: Mystery of the Bosnian Pyramids'. *Podbay* (online): https://podbay.fm/podcast/843060147/e/1544853008 (accessed 23/05/20)

30. Joseph, F. (2005). *The Atlantis Encyclopedia*. Franklin Lakes: New Page Books. p. 49
Reece, K. (2006). 'Memoirs of a true believer'. pp. 96–106, in: Fagan, G. (ed.). *Archaeological Fantasies: How Pseudoarchaeology Misrepresents the Past and Misleads the Public*. Abingdon: Routledge. pp. 96–7.

31. Feder, K. (2006). 'Skeptics, fence sitters, and true believers: Student acceptance of an improbable prehistory'. pp. 71–95, in: Fagan, G. (ed.). *Archaeological Fantasies: How pseudoarchaeology misrepresents the past and misleads the public*. Abingdon: Routledge. p. 95
Wade, L. (2019). 'Belief in aliens, Atlantis are on the rise'. *Science* 6436:110-111.364

32. Robinson, A. (2017). *The Story of Writing: Alphabets, Hieroglyphs & Pictograms*. London: Thames & Hudson. pp. 146–8

33. Basu, T. (2013). 'Have We Found the Lost Colony of Roanoke Island?' *National Geographic* (online): https://www.nationalgeographic.com/news/2013/12/131208-roanoke-lost-colony-discovery-history-raleigh/ (accessed 01/01/20)
Lawler, A. (2015). 'We Finally Have Clues to How the Lost Roanoke Colony Vanished'. *National Geographic* (online): https://www.national geographic.com/news/2015/08/150807-lost-colony-roanoke-hatteras-outer-banks-archaeology/ (accessed 23/05/20)

34. Robinson (2017), pp. 145–55

35. Baynes, C. (2017). 'Archaeologists decipher 3,200-year-old stone telling of invasion of mysterious sea people'. *Independent* (online): https://www.independent.co.uk/news/world/europe/archaeologists-decipher-ancient-stone-turkey-invasion-mysterious-sea-people-luwain-hieroglyphic-a7992141.html (accessed 23/05/20)

36. Williams, S. (1991). *Fantastic Archaeology: The Wild Side of North American Prehistory*. Philadelphia: The University of Pennsylvania Press. p. 13.

37. Killgrove, K. (2015). 'What Archaeologists Really Think About Ancient Aliens, Lost Colonies, And Fingerprints Of The Gods'. *Forbes* (online): https://www.forbes.com/sites/kristinakillgrove/2015/09/03/what-archaeologists-really-think-about-ancient-aliens-lost-colonies-and-fingerprints-of-the-gods/#2f4313117ab0 (accessed 23/11/19)

38. Moore, R. (1972). 'Spiritualism and science: Reflections on the first decade of the spirit rappings'. *American Quarterly* 24(4): 474–500. pp. 476–7, 499

39. Capron, E. (1855). *Modern Spiritualism: Its Facts And Fanaticisms, Its Consistencies And Contradictions, With An Appendix*. Boston: Bela Marsh. p. 12.

40. Stoehr, T. (1987). 'Robert H. Collyer's Technology of the Soul'. pp. 21–45, in: Wrobel, A. (ed.). *Pseudoscience and Society in Nineteenth-Century America*. Lexington: University Press of Kentucky. p. 27.

41. Williams (1991), pp. 286–9
    Anonymous (2008). 'Discover Glastonbury Abbey – the psychic way'. *BBC Somerset* (online): http://www.bbc.co.uk/somerset/content/articles/2008/06/04/glastonbury_abbey_archeology_feature.shtml (accessed 05/12/19)

42. Williams (1991), pp. 132, 136–8
    Donnelly, I. (1882). *Atlantis: The Antediluvian World*. New York: Harper & Brothers. pp. 1–2, 309, 328
    DeMeules, D. (1961). 'Ignatius Donnelly: A Don Quixote in the world of science'. *Minnesota History* 37(6): 229–34. p. 229

43. Clarke, H. (1886). 'Examination of the legend of Atlantis in reference to protohistoric communication with America'. *Transactions of the Royal Historical Society* 3(1): 1–46. p. 16.

44. Thrussell, D. (2015). 'Magicians of the Gods: An Interview with Graham Hancock'. *New Dawn* (online): https://www.newdawnmagazine.com/articles/magicians-of-the-gods-an-interview-with-graham-hancock (accessed 20/12/19)

45. Fleming, N. (2006). 'The Attraction of Non-rational Archaeological Hypotheses: The Individual and Sociological Factors'. pp. 47–70, in: Fagan, G. (ed.). *Archaeological Fantasies: How Pseudoarchaeology Misrepresents the Past and Misleads the Public*. Abingdon: Routledge. p. 63.

46. Shenefield, T. (2019). 'Combatting Pseudoarchaeology in the Internet Age'. *Real Archaeology* (online): https://pages.vassar.edu/realarchaeology/2019/12/08/combatting-pseudoarchaeology-in-the-internet-age/ (accessed 11/12/19)
    Wade (2019)

47. Liverani, M. (1999). 'Ancient near eastern history: From eurocentrism to an open world'. *Isimu* 2: 3–9. p. 9.

48. Heaney, C. (2017). 'The Racism Behind Alien Mummy Hoaxes'. *The Atlantic* (online): https://www.theatlantic.com/science/archive/2017/08/how-to-fake-an-alien-mummy/535251/ (accessed 23/11/19)
    Bond (2018)

49. Gansemer (2018), pp. 19–20

50. Seidel, J. (2014). 'Why did two German 'hobbyists' deface a cartouche of Khufu inside the Great Pyramid and what does it have to do with

Atlantis?' *News.com* (online): https://www.news.com.au/why-did-two-german-hobbyists-deface-a-cartouche-of-khufu-inside-the-great-pyramid-and-what-does-it-have-to-do-with-atlantis/news-story/7db71b6e1e74976cdbe7736c0e5af4c4 (accessed 23/11/19)

51. Dunning (2009)
Moshenska, G. (2017). 'Alternative Archaeologies'. pp. 122–37, in: Moshenska, G. (ed.). *Key Concepts in Public Archaeology*. London: UCL Press. pp. 133–4

52. Jarus, O. (2018). 'These "Alien" Mummies Appear to Be a Mix of Looted Body Parts'. *LiveScience* (online): https://www.livescience.com/62045-alien-mummies-explained.html (accessed 31/12/19)

53. Hancock, G. (2019). 'The latest shots fired in the ongoing ideological war waged by orthodox scholars to maintain their elite monopoly over the right to interpret our collective past'. *Twitter* (online): https://twitter.com/Graham__Hancock (accessed 07/12/19)

54. Adams, M. (2009). 'Free Energy Technology Could Destroy the Natural World (But It Doesn't Have To)'. *Natural News* (online): https://www.naturalnews.com/026116_energy_free_population.html (accessed 25/05/20)

55. Palermo, E. (2015). 'Does Magnetic Therapy Work?' *LiveScience* (online): https://www.livescience.com/40174-magnetic-therapy.html (accessed 01/01/20)

56. Sokal, A. (2006). 'Pseudoscience and Postmodernism: Antagonists or Fellow Travellers?' pp. 286–361, in: Fagan, G. (ed.). *Archaeological Fantasies: How Pseudoarchaeology Misrepresents the Past and Misleads the Public*. Abingdon: Routledge. p. 339.

57. Colavito, J. (2019). 'Helena Blavatsky on Ancient Astronauts'. *Jason Colavito* (online): http://www.jasoncolavito.com/blavatsky-on-ancient-astronauts.html (accessed 05/12/19)

Chapter 9

1. Watling, E. (2018). 'America's gun violence epidemic: mass shootings getting deadlier'. *Newsweek* (online): https://www.newsweek.com/americas-gun-violence-epidemic-mass-shootings-getting-deadlier-1146879 (accessed 25/11/18)

2. Anonymous (2018). 'Past Summary Ledgers'. *Gun Violence Archive* (online): https://www.gunviolencearchive.org/past-tolls (accessed 25/11/18)
Schaeffer, C. (2018). 'US citizens own 40% of all guns in the world – more than the next 25 top-ranked countries combined, study suggests'. *Independent* (online): https://www.independent.co.uk/news/world/

americas/gun-ownership-country-us-legal-firearm-citizens-statistics-a8406941.html (accessed 04/11/18)

IBIS World (2020). 'Guns & Ammunition Manufacturing Industry in the US – Market Research Report'. *IBIS World* (online): https://www.ibis world.com/united-states/market-research-reports/guns-ammunition-manufacturing-industry/ (accessed 15/05/20)

3. Fox, K. (2019). 'How US gun culture compares with the world'. *CNN* (online): https://edition.cnn.com/2017/10/03/americas/us-gun-statistics/index.html (accessed 18/05/20)

    Palmer, B. (2010). 'Have Gun, Want To Travel'. *Slate* (online): https://slate.com/news-and-politics/2010/12/do-other-countries-have-a-constitutional-right-to-bear-arms.html (accessed 30/03/19)

    Kirby, E. (2013). 'Switzerland guns: Living with firearms the Swiss way'. *BBC News* (online): https://www.bbc.co.uk/news/magazine-21379912 (accessed 01/04/19)

    Alpers, P., Wilson, M. (2019). 'Switzerland – Gun Facts, Figures and the Law'. *Sydney School of Public Health, The University of Sydney* (online): https://www.gunpolicy.org/firearms/region/switzerland (accessed 01/04/19)

4. Parker, K. et al. (2017). 'Guns and daily life: Identity, experiences, activities and involvement'. *Pew Research Center* (online): https://www.pew socialtrends.org/2017/06/22/guns-and-daily-life-identity-experiences-activities-and-involvement/ (accessed 20/05/20)

    Mencken F. and Froese, P. (2019). 'Gun culture in action'. *Social Problems* 66(1): 1–25. p. 1

5. Melzer, S. (2009). *Gun Crusaders: The NRA's Culture War*. New York: New York University Press. p. 81

6. De Vaca, C. (2007). *The Shipwrecked Men*. London: Penguin. pp. 0–1, 12–14, 18, 28, 33, 58–63, 124

7. Weddle, R. (1972). 'La Salle's survivors'. *The Southwestern Historical Quarterly* 75(4): 413–33. pp. 413–6

    Wood, P. (1984). 'La Salle: Discovery of a lost explorer'. *The American Historical Review* 89(2): 294–323. pp. 297–9, 323

8. Aguilar, J. (2013). 'Researching the Pueblo Revolt of 1680'. *Expedition* 55(3): 34–5. p. 34

    Roberts, D. (2004). *The Pueblo Revolt: The Secret Rebellion that Drove the Spaniards Out of the Southwest*. New York: Simon & Schuster. pp. 24, 27, 176–7

    Burns, K. and Ives, S. (2001). 'Episode One: The People'. *PBS* (online): http://www.pbs.org/weta/thewest/program/episodes/one/ (accessed 03/04/19)

9. Kastor, P. (2004). *The Nation's Crucible: The Louisiana Purchase and the Creation of America (Western Americana Series)*. New Haven: Yale University Press. pp. 19, 39–41

Elman, C. (2004). 'Extending offensive realism: The Louisiana purchase and America's rise to regional hegemony'. *The American Political Science Review* 98(4): 563–76

Brown, E. (1956). 'Law and Government in the Louisiana Purchase: 1803–1804'. *Wayne Law Review* 2(3): p. 169–89.

10. Parezo, N. and Fowler, D. (2007). *Anthropology Goes to the Fair: The 1904 Louisiana Purchase Exposition*. Lincoln: University of Nebraska Press. p. 1

Anonymous (1904). *Territorial and Commercial Expansion of the United States, 1800–1903*. Washington: Government Printing Office. p. 4303

11. Bryson, B. (1994). 'How the West wasn't won'. *The Independent* (online): https://www.independent.co.uk/life-style/how-the-west-wasnt-won-wagon-trains-gunfights-grizzled-white-cowboys-the-stuff-of-western-legend-but-5432584.html (accessed 13/10/18)

12. Parkman, F. (1905). *The California and Oregon Trail*. New York: Thomas Y. Crowell & Co. p. 179

13. Minto, J. (1901). 'Reminiscences of experiences on the Oregon Trail in 1844 – II'. *The Quarterly of the Oregon Historical Society* 2(3): 209–54. p. 219

14. Frantz, J. and Choate, J. (1955). *The American Cowboy: The Myth and The Reality*. Norman: University of Oklahoma Press. p. 131–2

Bryson, (1994)

Burns, K. and Ives, S. (2001). 'Episode Two: Empire Upon The Trails'. *PBS* (online): http://www.pbs.org/weta/thewest/program/episodes/two/ (accessed 03/04/19)

Young, F. (1900). 'The Oregon Trail'. *The Quarterly of the Oregon Historical Society* 1(4): 339–70. p. 363

15. Unruh, J. (1993). *The Plains Across: The Overland Emigrants and the Trans-Mississippi West*. Urbana: University of Illinois Press. pp. 119–20

16. Bryson (1994)

Unruh (1993), pp. 29, 45

17. McGrath, R. (1984). *Gunfighters, Highwaymen & Vigilantes Violence on the Frontier*. Berkeley, California: University of California Press. pp. 11–12

18. Burns, K. and Ives, S. (2001). 'Episode Eight: One Sky Above Us'. *PBS* (online): http://www.pbs.org/weta/thewest/program/episodes/eight/ (accessed 03/04/19)

Metcalfe, J. (2017). 'When Lager Reigned'. *CityLab* (online): https://www.citylab.com/life/2017/02/when-lager-reigned/517230/ (accessed 17/05/20)

19. McGrath (1984), pp. 11–13, 57–8, 107, 114–7

20. Limerick, P., Milner, C. and Rankin, C. (1991). *Trails: Toward a New Western History*. Lawrence: University of Kansas. Picture panel 3, between pp. 144–5

21. Anonymous (2006). 'Population of Chinese in the United States 1860–1940'. *The Chinese Experience in 19th Century America* (online): http://teachingresources.atlas.illinois.edu/chinese_exp/resources/resource_2_9.pdf (accessed 09/11/18)

    Burns, K. and Ives, S. (2001). 'Episode Eight: One Sky Above Us'. *PBS* (online): http://www.pbs.org/weta/thewest/program/episodes/eight/ (accessed 03/04/19)

22. McGrath (1984), pp. 135–6

23. Taylor, A. (2001). *American Colonies: The Settling of North America*. New York: Penguin Group. p. 40

    Anonymous (1951). *Statistical Abstract of the United States, 1951*. (Online): https://www2.census.gov/prod2/statcomp/documents/1951-02.pdf (accessed 19/11/18). p. 14

    Anonymous (2001). 'Aboriginal Peoples of Canada'. *Statistics Canada* (online): http://www12.statcan.ca/english/census01/Products/Analytic/companion/abor/canada.cfm (accessed 19/11/18)

24. Cook, N. (1998). *Born to Die: Disease and New World Conquest, 1492–1650*. Cambridge: Cambridge University Press. pp. 213–14

25. Michno, G. (2003). *Encyclopedia of Indian Wars: Western Battles and Skirmishes, 1850–1890*. Missoula: Mountain Press Publishing Company. p. 535

    Roberts, G. (1984). *Sand Creek: Tragedy and Symbol*. Norman: University of Oklahoma.

26. Del Papa, E. (1975). 'The Royal proclamation of 1763: Its effect upon Virginia land companies'. *The Virginia Magazine of History and Biography* 83(4): 406–11. p. 406

    Burns, K. and Ives, S. (2001). 'Episode Eight: One Sky Above Us'. *PBS* (online): http://www.pbs.org/weta/thewest/program/episodes/eight/ (accessed 03/04/19)

27. Weaver, J. (1997). 'Indian presence with no Indians present: NAGPRA and its discontents'. *Wicazo Sa Review* 12(2): 13–30. p. 13

28. Burns, K. and Ives, S. (2001). 'Episode Three: Speck Of The Future'. *PBS* (online): http://www.pbs.org/weta/thewest/program/episodes/three/ (accessed 03/04/19)

Sederquist, B. (2018). 'Gold Rush Women'. *Sierra Foothill Magazine* (online): http://www.sierrafoothillmagazine.com/women.html (accessed 14/11/18)

29. Walsh, M. (1995). 'Women's place on the American frontier'. *Journal of American Studies* 29(2): 241–55.

30. McGrath (1984), p. 157

31. Bird, I. (2007). *Adventures in the Rocky Mountains.* London: Penguin. pp. 7, 15–16

32. McGrath (1984), p. 151
    Walsh (1995), p. 254
    Various (2015). 'Women and the Myth of the American West'. *Time* (online): https://time.com/3662361/women-american-west/ (accessed 19/05/20)
    Hirata, L. (1979). 'Free, indentured, enslaved: Chinese prostitutes in nineteenth-century America'. *Signs* 5(1): 3–29. pp. 8–10

33. Burns, K. and Ives, S. (2001). 'Episode Three: Speck Of The Future'. *PBS* (online): http://www.pbs.org/weta/thewest/program/episodes/three/ (accessed 03/04/19)

34. McGrath (1984), p. 251

35. Manzoor, S. (2013). 'American's forgotten black cowboys'. *BBC News* (online): https://www.bbc.co.uk/news/magazine-21768669 (accessed 09/11/18)
    Nodjimbaden, K. (2017). 'The Lesser-Known History of African American Cowboys'. *Smithsonian.com* (online): https://www.smithsonianmag.com/history/lesser-known-history-african-american-cowboys-180962144/ (accessed 14/11/18)

36. Frantz and Choate (1955), p. 46

37. Ibid., pp. 27–31
    Sherow, J. (2018). *The Chisholm Trail: Joseph McCoy's Great Gamble.* Norman: University of Oklahoma Press. p. 33
    Bryson (1994)

38. Savage, W. (1979). *The Cowboy Hero: His Image in American History and Culture.* Norman: University of Oklahoma Press. pp. 109–10

39. Frantz and Choate (1955), pp. 91–2
    Cushman, G. (1940). 'Abilene, first of the Kansas cow towns'. *Kansas Historical Quarterly* 9(3): 240–58

40. Jackson, W. (1966). 'A new look at Wells Fargo, stage-coaches and the Pony Express'. *California Historical Society Quarterly* 45(4): 291–324. p. 311

41. King, G. (2012). 'Where the Buffalo No Longer Roamed'. *Smithsonian* (online): https://www.smithsonianmag.com/history/where-the-buffalo-no-longer-roamed-3067904/ (accessed 10/11/18)

42. Frantz and Choate (1955), p. 67

43. Krell, A. (2002). *The Devil's Rope: A Cultural History of Barbed Wire*. London: Reaktion Books.

44. Clark, L. (2015). 'The 1887 Blizzard That Changed the American Frontier Forever'. *Smithsonian.com* (online): https://www.smithsonian mag.com/smart-news/1887-blizzard-changed-american-frontier-forever-1-180953852/ (accessed 10/11/18)

    Burns, K. and Ives, S. (2001). 'Episode Seven: The Geography of Hope'. *PBS* (online): http://www.pbs.org/weta/thewest/program/episodes/seven/ (accessed 03/04/19)

45. White, R. (1994). 'Frederick Jackson Turner and Buffalo Bill'. *The Frontier in American Culture* pp. 7–65

46. Swagerty, W. (1980). 'Marriage and settlement patterns of Rocky Mountain trappers and traders'. *The Western Historical Quarterly* 11(2): 159–80. p. 159

    Carter, H. and Spencer, M. (1975). 'Stereotypes of the mountain man'. *The Western Historical Quarterly* 6(1): 17–32. p. 22

47. Crockett, D. (1834). *Narrative of the Life of David Crockett of the State of Tennessee*. Philadelphia: E. L. Carey and A. Hart. pp. 3, 7

48. Wright, J. (1966). *Letters from the West; or a caution to emigrants*. Ann Arbor: University Microfilms, Inc. pp. vi, 21, 29

49. Twain, M. (1985). *Roughing It*. New York: Penguin Books.

50. Frantz and Choate (1955), pp. 16–17

51. White, K. (2006) '"Through their eyes": Buffalo Bill's Wild West as a drawing table for American identity'. *Constructing the Past* 7(1): 35–50. p. 39

52. Courtwright, D. (1999). 'The Cowboy Subculture'. In: Dizard, J. Muth, R. and Andrews, S. (eds.). *Guns in America: A Reader*. New York: New York University Press. pp. 97–8

    Burns, K. and Ives, S. (2001). 'Episode Seven: The Geography of Hope'. *PBS* (online): http://www.pbs.org/weta/thewest/program/episodes/seven/ (accessed 03/04/19)

53. Courtwright (1999), pp. 98–9

    Udall, S. et al. (2000). 'How the West got wild: American media and frontier violence: a roundtable'. *The Western Historical Quarterly* 31(3): 277–95. p. 279

    Bryson (1994)

    West, E. (1995). *The Way to the West: Essays on the Central Plains*. Albuquerque: University of New Mexico Press.

54. Frantz and Choate (1955), pp. 146, 148, 156, 174

    Limerick et al. (1991), pp. 113–14

    Bryson (1994)

55. Hopkins, T. (ed.) (2007). *The Rough Guide to Film*. London: Rough Guides Ltd. pp. 429–30

56. Udall et al. (2000), p. 287

57. Burns, K. and Ives, S. (2001). 'Episode Seven: The Geography of Hope'. *PBS* (online): http://www.pbs.org/weta/thewest/program/episodes/seven/ (accessed 03/04/19)

58. Bellesiles, M. (2000). 'Guns don't kill, movies kill: The media's promotion of frontier violence'. *The Western Historical Quarterly* 31(3): 277–95. p. 289

59. White (2006), p. 38

60. Watts, S. (2003). *Rough Rider in the White House: Theodore Roosevelt and the Politics of Desire*. Chicago: The University of Chicago Press. pp. 156–7

61. Walsh (1995), pp. 241–2

62. Witkowski, T. (2011). 'Early Brand Development in the US Firearms Industry'. *CHARM Proceedings 2011*: 194–209. p. 200

63. Mencken F., Froese, P. (2019). 'Gun culture in action'. *Social Problems* 66(1): 1–25. p. 2
    Yamane, D. (2017). 'The sociology of US gun culture'. *Sociology Compass* 11(7): e12497. p. 5

64. Achenbach, J., Higham, S. and Horwitz, S. (2013). 'How NRA's true believers converted a marksmanship group into a might gun lobby'. *Washington Post* (online): https://www.washingtonpost.com/politics/how-nras-true-believers-converted-a-marksmanship-group-into-a-mighty-gun-lobby/2013/01/12/51c62288-59b9-11e2-88d0-c4cf65c3ad15_story.html (accessed 19/05/20)

65. Melzer (2009), p. 29

66. Ibid., p. 2

67. McGrath (1984), pp. 259–60

68. Burns, K. and Ives, S. (2001). 'Episode Three: Speck Of The Future'. *PBS* (online): http://www.pbs.org/weta/thewest/program/episodes/three/ (accessed 03/04/19)
    Unruh (1993), pp. 119–20, 185
    Meldahl, K. (2007). *Hard Road West: History and Geology Along the Gold Rush Trail*. Chicago: University of Chicago Press.

69. Hill, P. (2005). 'Old West violence mostly myth'. *PERC* (online): https://www.perc.org/2005/07/17/old-west-violence-mostly-myth/ (accessed 05/10/18)
    Schweikart, L. (2001). 'The Non-Existent Frontier Bank Robbery'. *Foundation for Economic Education* (online): https://fee.org/articles/the-non-existent-frontier-bank-robbery/ (accessed 16/11/18)

70. McGrath (1984), pp. xvi, 176–8, 263

Winkler, A. (2013). *Gunfight: The Battle over the Right to Bear Arms in America*. New York: W. W. Norton & Company. p. 164

Ibid., pp. 266–7

71. Frantz and Choate (1955), pp. 77–8

72. Udall et al. (2000), p. 292

73. Winkler (2013), p. 163–4

Roth, R. (2017). 'Criminologists and Historians of Crime: A Partnership Well Worth Pursuing'. *Crime, History and Societies* 21(2): 389–401.

74. Fernández-Armesto (1996), p. 20

Ruddock, A. (1966). 'John Day of Bristol and the English Voyages across the Atlantic before 1497'. *The Geographical Journal* 132(2): 225–33. pp. 229–30.

75. Parry, J. (1981). *The Discovery of the Sea*. Berkeley: University of California Press. p. 162

76. Edgerton, S. (1974). 'Florentine interest in Ptolemaic cartography as background for renaissance painting, architecture, and the discovery of America'. *Journal of the Society of Architectural Historians* 33(4): 275–92. p. 275

Fernández-Armesto (1996), pp. 30–31.

77. Winkler, A. (2011). 'Did the Wild West Have More Gun Control Than We Do Today?' *Huffington Post* (online): https://www.huffingtonpost.com/adam-winkler/did-the-wild-west-have-mo_b_956035.html?guccounter=2 (accessed 19/11/18)

McGrath (1984), pp. 259–60

78. Frantz and Choate (1955), p. 85–6

79. McGrath (1984), pp. 157–9, 253

Winkler (2013), p. 164

80. Ibid., pp. 163–4

81. West (1995), p. 136

82. Burns, K. and Ives, S. (2001). 'Episode Six: Fight No More Forever'. *PBS* (online): http://www.pbs.org/weta/thewest/program/episodes/six/ (accessed 03/04/19)

83. McGrath (1984), pp. 14, 83, 119

84. Jancer, M. (2018). 'Gun Control Is as Old as the Old West'. *Smithsonian.com* (online): https://www.smithsonianmag.com/history/gun-control-old-west-180968013/ (accessed 13/10/18)

Winkler (2013), pp. 13, 163–9

85. Courtwright (1999), p. 96

86. Vandenack,T. (2006). 'Proponents: "Old West" Concerns Not Valid'. *Hutchinson News* (online): https://www.gunpolicy.org/firearms/citation/quotes/11281 (accessed 20/11/18)

87. Collins, R. (1999). 'Gun Control and the Old West'. *History News Service* (online): https://www.ndsu.edu/pubweb/~rcollins/scholarship/guns.html (accessed 16/08/18)
88. Frantz and Choate (1955), p. 198
89. Anonymous (2018). 'Guns Made America Great'. *America's 1st Freedom* (online): https://www.americas1stfreedom.org/articles/2018/10/22/guns-made-america-great/ (accessed 19/05/20)
90. Miniter, F. (2019). 'A National Gun Register Is Now on the Ballot for 2020'. *America's 1st Freedom* (online): https://www.americas1stfreedom.org/articles/2019/5/10/a-national-gun-registry-is-now-on-the-ballot-for-2020/ (accessed 20/05/20)
91. McGrath (1984), pp. xvi, 178–82, 277
92. Winkler (2013), p. 168
    Cramer, C. (1999). *Concealed Weapon Laws of the Early Republic: Duelling, Southern Violence, and Moral Reform*. Westport: Praeger. pp. 81–2
93. Winkler (2013), pp. xvii–xviii, 12, 115–16
94. West (1995), p. 164
95. Dykstra, R. and McKenna, C. (2003). 'Body Counts and murder rates: The contested statistics of Western violence'. *Reviews in American History* 31(4): 554–63. p. 555

Conclusion

1. Shnirelman, V. (1995). 'From Internationalism to Nationalism: Forgotten Pages of Soviet Archaeology in the 1930s and 1940s'. pp. 120–38, in: Kohl, P. and Fawcett, C. (eds.). *Nationalism, Politics, and the Practice of Archaeology*. Cambridge: Cambridge University Press. p. 125, 130
    Khapaeva, D. (2013). 'Russia: Fractures in the Fabric of Culture'. pp. 108–19, in: Furtado, P. (ed.). *Histories of Nations: How their Identities were Forged*. London: Thames & Hudson. pp. 117–19.
2. Cronon, W. (1987). 'Revisiting the vanishing frontier: The legacy of Frederick Jackson Turner'. *The Western Historical Quarterly* 18(2): 157–76. p. 161.
3. Tong, E. (1995). 'Thirty Years of Chinese Archaeology (1949–1979)'. pp. 177–97, in: Kohl, P. and Fawcett, C. (eds.). *Nationalism, Politics, and the Practice of Archaeology*. Cambridge: Cambridge University Press. p. 178, 181
    Wang, Q. (2007). 'Between Myth and History: the Construction of a National Past in Modern East Asia'. pp. 126–54, in: Berger, S. (ed.) *Writing the Nation: A Global Perspective*. London: Palgrave Macmillan. p. 149

Mikołajczyk, A. (1990). 'Didactic Presentations of the Past: Some Retrospective Considerations in Relation to the Archaeological and Ethnographical Museum, Łódź, Poland. pp. 247–56, in: Gathercole, P. and Lowenthal, D. (eds.). *The Politics of the Past*. London: Unwin Hyman Ltd. p. 250.

Acknowledgements

My thanks to the following people who helped me research and write this book: Amar Acheraïou, David Courtwright, Brian Dunning, Nicky Garland, David Hemming, Richard Hingely, Tim Holmes, Gëzim Krasniqi, Maïwenn Le Mouée, James Mountain, Steve Mountain, Bronwen Needham, Cindy Needham, Greg Nobles, Jens Notroff, Abbie Rumsey, Ulf-Dietrich Schoop, Trevor Watkins, Abby Wise and Adam Winkler.

Thanks also to the team at Icon, including Hanna Milner, Hamza Jahanzeb, Ruth Killick, Andrew Furlow and Lydia Wilson, and to Julian Humphries for helping to make this book. Special thanks must go to Tom Webber, for giving me the opportunity to write it and for showing me the some of the best ice cream in London, and to Kiera Jamison, for picking up many mistakes of my own. I'm especially grateful to Emily Sweet for her support and encouragement.

Special thanks also to Adina Mahuta for first helping me realise how ever-present the past really is. And, as always, my love and thanks to Karima for her endless support and humour.